CALI-BAJA CUISINE

MICHAEL A. GARDINER

PHOTOGRAPHY BY CINTIA SOTO

CALI-BAJA CUISINE

TIJUANA TACOS, ENSENADA AGUACHILES, SAN DIEGO CALI BURRITOS + MORE

RIZZOLI
NEW YORK

New York · Paris · London · Milan

This book is dedicated to my parents, Edwin and Wita Gardiner, who first took me across the border to Tijuana in 1969. That day my world became larger, and in doing so, my parents planted the seeds that grew into this book.

CONTENTS

CALI-BAJA CUISINE
The Cuisine of the Baja Borderlands

There's a line between Northern Baja and Southern California.
From the northern side it's called *the border*. From the southern side some call it *la línea* or *la frontera*. But fish don't care about that line, neither does the climate, and the soil doesn't suddenly change. Nature knows no such borders and, it seems, neither does food.

People aren't always overly bothered with the political border, either. Contrary to popular mythology, many of the border crossings from Mexico to the United States are entirely legal. Indeed, more than one hundred thousand people cross the San Diego–Tijuana border every day to go to school, to work, to see a doctor, or to go shopping. After all, the land port of entry between San Diego and Tijuana is the world's busiest land border crossing, with more than ninety thousand crossings a day. Estimates from the San Diego–Tijuana Smart Border Coalition put that higher: fifty million per year. It has been that way every year since 2015. In 2018 and 2019 the coalition put the value of cross-border trade at more than $50 trillion annually.

The Baja border both separates and connects two of North America's biggest cities: the seventh largest in the United States and the fifth biggest in Mexico. Together they have nearly 5 million in population. That would put the combined municipality at fourth largest in Mexico and third in the United States.

But while that border is often seen as separating San Diego and Tijuana—Southern California and Baja California—it can also be seen as connecting them. Indeed, while the term *la línea* is used to describe the border itself, it can also be used to refer to the line at the San Ysidro border crossing. That, quite literally, is what connects Baja California to its northern neighbor and the people on either side of the border. It is what, for many, makes the San Diego–Tijuana area—the Southern California–Baja California area—a single region.

It was perhaps Fernando Perez Castro, founder and winemaker of La Lomita Winery in the Valle de Guadalupe, who put it best. Speaking to a friend of mine, he said that in his view, his wine—the wine of the Valle—belongs not only to Baja and its people but also to Southern California and *its* people. "Forget about the fence that is dividing us,"

he said. "This is our local wine—so it is also your local wine. The wine speaks to your land, your weather, your lifestyle, and the food you eat. This is your wine region too, so embrace it!"

But just as Southern California is a lot more than San Diego and Los Angeles, Baja California is a lot more than Tijuana. The terrain of Baja is both varied and spectacular. There are the long beaches that start at the border wall and continue south, the rocky coastline between Rosarito and Ensenada with cliffs plunging dramatically hundreds of feet from the toll road down into the Pacific Ocean, and the lush vineyards of Mexico's wine country in the Valle de Guadalupe. There's the mysterious moonscape where the Gulf of California Rift Zone transitions into the San Andreas Fault, a surficial expression and powerful reminder of the earth's sheer muscle. And there are the stark peaks just to the west of the Sierra de Juarez mountains and the Sierra de San Pedro Mártir just south of those. The terrain of Baja is a southern reflection of the terrain of Southern California north of the border.

Portions of Tijuana display great wealth and others crushing poverty. Go south of Tijuana to the stretch of coastline between Rosarito Beach and Ensenada and it might feel something like an expat American colony. Meanwhile, the Valle de Guadalupe wine region has been called Mexico's Napa Valley. It is, perhaps, an exaggeration that denies the Valle credit for its own character. But it is not all wrong.

And the story is similar with Baja's food: both varied and spectacular. Baja's food culture has long influenced Southern California, and vice versa. Some say the fish taco is San Diego's signature dish, but it comes from Baja. The Caesar salad does too. The streets of Tijuana, a city famous for its street food, sport nearly as many takes on the hot dog as on the taco. And Baja has a serious love affair with pizza. Then, of course, there's the "high end." The same ideas that are the most enduring features of California cuisine are at the core of much of the new Baja cuisine.

Food and culinary culture crossed the membrane that is the border in more ways, too, hitchhiking with the people who have crossed that border (legally and, no doubt, in some cases less so). Some of the greatest chefs cooking Baja cuisine own or have run restaurants on both sides of the border, such as Javier Plascencia (Misión 19, Finca Altozano, Animalón, and more), whose family and family restaurants are in Tijuana, and who went to school in the United States and has lived and owned restaurants on both sides of the border. As I write these words, Roberto Alcocer runs restaurants in both Oceanside, California, and the Valle de Guadalupe.

While the food of Baja has been remarkable for a long time, it began to come into serious popular focus around the time Anthony Bourdain

featured it on his Travel Channel program *No Reservations* in 2012. By turning his cameras on Javier Plascencia and Misión 19, Diego Hernandez and Corazón de Tierra, and the street food of both Tijuana and Ensenada, Bourdain shined a spotlight on Baja's culinary culture. That light has not gone away or even dimmed. If anything, it's grown brighter.

And yet, Baja's culinary culture likely would not be what it is today without the rise of the Valle de Guadalupe, Baja's—indeed, Mexico's—premier wine region and the one likely recognized by wine connoisseurs around the world. It was the Valle's ascendency that provided fertile soul for world-class restaurants like Jair Téllez's Laja and Corazón de Tierra, helmed by Diego Hernandez (who is now cooking his Cali-Baja food at Venice Beach restaurant Dudley Market). It was ultimately the synergy between the food and the wine that put the Valle over the top as a destination and attracted still more world-class restaurants and wineries. Today, the Valle has moved beyond the status of a niche tourist attraction for foodies and wine people to draw younger, hipper crowds. Those changes have not been devoid of controversy (and hardly without good reason), but even the most ardent opponents of the drop in the average age of Valle tourists recognize the significance of the changes.

Cali-Baja cuisine is not, ultimately, just chef-driven restaurant food. It's a cuisine built on the natural bounty of the region (on both sides of the border) and the flavors loved by the people who live there. It's the fish of Popotla and San Diego's sea urchins. It's the wine of the Valle de Guadalupe and perhaps the greatest craft beer scene anywhere just across the border and increasingly in Baja itself. It is Los Angeles pocho cuisine and Tijuana street food. It's the asparagus of Mexicali, California artichokes, and the ubiquitous avocados on both sides of the border. It's the multicultural and cross-cultural palate of all who live there, influenced by everywhere they may have come from.

A BRIEF HISTORY OF BAJA AND ALTA CALIFORNIA

Prior to the arrival of the Spaniards, the Baja California peninsula—the land of today's Mexican states of Baja California and Baja California Sur—was inhabited by three major ethnic groups: the Cochimí in the north, the Guaycura in the central section, and the Pericú on the southern cape. Archaeological artifacts suggest that these tribes inhabited the peninsula as early as ten thousand years ago. All three tribes were hunters and gatherers, though an isolated group of Cochimí living on Cedros Island developed a fairly complex agricultural system. Today, the modern-day descendants of the Guaycura and Pericú still live on the northernmost part of the peninsula.

In 1532, after the Spanish had conquered the Mexican mainland, Spanish conquistador Hernán Cortés led an expedition westward to search for a fabled island of gold. When he landed near La Paz, Cortés found black pearls but no gold. Less than a decade later, Spanish captain Francisco de Ulloa explored the entire length of the Sea of Cortez and made the discovery that Baja was, in reality, a peninsula, not an island. Apparently uninterested in a peninsula with black pearls instead of an island of gold, the Spanish did not return to Baja for another century.

It was not until 1695 that a Jesuit priest named Juan María Salvatierra established the region's first permanent Spanish settlement. The Misión Nuestra Señora de Loreto Conchó quickly became the peninsula's religious and administrative capital. Over the course of the next century the Jesuits, followed by the Franciscans and then the Dominicans, built a network of missions stretching the full length of the peninsula and up into what is today California.

When the United States won the Mexican-American War (1846–1848), Baja California was originally slated to be ceded to the victor along with Alta California, Nevada, Utah, Colorado, Arizona, New Mexico, and Wyoming. By the time the treaty was finalized, though, the Baja peninsula was omitted from the deal due to its proximity to the Mexican state of Sonora.

Despite playing a significant role in the Mexican Revolution (1910–1920), it was not until December 31, 1952, that Baja California officially

became Mexico's twenty-ninth state. It would be another twenty-two years before Baja California Sur achieved statehood. Tijuana's population around the time of statehood was just over 60,000. Today, its population is over 2,221,000; an approximately 3,500 percent increase! When I first visited Tijuana in 1969, its population was 273,647. Tijuana has grown by 712 percent since then. This extraordinary population growth—and growth rate—has vastly changed both Tijuana and Baja. It could hardly have been otherwise.

One of the primary sources of Baja's massive population growth is internal immigration in Mexico. Over 45 percent of Baja California's population was born in another Mexican state. In Tijuana, immigrants from other parts of the country account for over half the city's population. Within Mexico, Baja California is the second greatest internal immigration magnet, surpassed only by Mexico City.

Surely one of the sources of Baja's attraction as an internal immigration destination is economic opportunity. To read many American press reports one could be forgiven for thinking this means economic opportunity on the north side of the border. That is, perhaps, less the case now than ever.

The real magnet may be the maquiladora programs. Maquiladoras are factories in Mexico (and elsewhere) run by foreign companies exporting their products to the company's country of origin, or elsewhere, largely duty-free and tariff-free. These factories take raw materials and process them into finished products for export, often into the United States. Tijuana is a major maquiladora hub with high-tech factories lining the border east of the San Ysidro border crossing. Today's maquiladora trade in Tijuana dates back to 1964, when the Mexican government introduced the Programa de Industrialización Fronteriza.

The effect is that Tijuana's maquiladora programs have become a major internal immigration magnet. They have also had the effect of taking some of the bloom of the rosy promise of economic opportunity across the border in the Unites States. Not all of the press has taken notice. Tijuana, on the other hand, has.

As a result of these various factors, Tijuana and Baja California—much like San Diego, Los Angeles, and the rest of Southern California—have become regions consisting, in significant part, of immigrants. Tijuana is full of Tijuanenses from Mexico City, Oaxaca, Mazatlán, the Yucatán, and just about every state in Mexico, just as there are San Diegans and Angelenos from New York, Chicago, Boston, Houston, and just about every state in the United States of America.

THE IMPACT OF BAJA'S IMMIGRANT NATURE ON THE FOOD

The foods of Tijuana and Baja California—much like the foods of
San Diego and Southern California—reflect the reality of that mobile
population. Take, for example, the birria taco. It is has become, perhaps,
Tijuana's signature taco. And from Tijuana it crossed the border
(legally) and grew into a bona fide Southern California food fad (if not
trend). But birria—slow-cooked meat (originally goat but now more
commonly beef) served in its spiced broth—is not, or at least was not,
originally a Baja food. Rather, birria hails from Jalisco.

As birria moved north, it morphed. While serving a steaming bowl
of birria with excellent corn tortillas may be traditional, birria tacos
were hardly much of a thing until recently. And it was in Tijuana and
north of the border that it became something of a craze. The tortillas for
the birria taco are dipped in the birria consommé before being heated
on the flattop, lending them a deep red color. A Tijuana-style birria taco
con todo comes with the birria filling piled onto that crimson tortilla
and topped with onions, cilantro, salsa, and a notably lightly seasoned
guacamole. These birria tacos are 100 percent a Tijuana dish (whether
served north or south of la frontera) despite the undeniable fact that
the star—the birria itself—was clearly born in Jalisco.

Perhaps the most iconic mariscos dish in Tijuana is aguachile.
Aguachile is a dish of raw seafood lightly cured in a broth of chiles, lime
juice, salt, and cilantro, often with accompaniments of sliced cucumber
and onion. Aguachile differs from ceviche primarily in the degree to
which the seafood is "cooked" (actually, cured) by the spicy and acidic
brew (the "aguachile"). Aguachile was not born in Baja, though, but
rather in Mazatlán, Sinaloa. The original version, in fact, was not even
a seafood dish, but was made from beef machaca (think shredded
beef jerky), though shrimp has long since relegated the original to
history. In Baja California, aguachile is often made with yellowtail or
sparkling fresh tuna (as Javier Plascencia did at his late lamented
Bracero restaurant in San Diego). Ultimately, the defining feature of an
aguachile is not the protein but rather that "chile water" itself. And that
makes it an immigrant.

But internal immigration is not the only form of immigration
that has contributed to Cali-Baja cuisine. External immigration,
including some from homelands that might seem unexpected, has
had a significant influence on the flavors of Baja. Indeed, Asian
flavors and techniques have helped shape the way we perceive Baja
food, sometimes in unexpected and counterintuitive ways. Take, for

example, the iconic Ensenada (though San Diego tries to claim it) fish taco. While there is no definitive proof of the origin of the fish taco, and likely never will be, the odds-on best bet is that it was created by Ensenada food vendors in order to appeal—and sell—to Japanese fishing boats at the Port of Ensenada by frying fish in the batter the Japanese used for their tempura. Similarly, the incorporation of ingredients like soy sauce and fish sauce as well as Asian techniques was a hallmark of the Baja Med culinary movement of the early 2000s.

External immigration has impacted the food of Baja in different ways. Take the story of one of Baja's signature dishes: tacos adobada. The dish began its life half a world away before Lebanese immigrants brought their shawarma with them to Veracruz and Tampico on Mexico's eastern shores in the late nineteenth century. By the mid-twentieth century, the lamb of the original shawarma was replaced by pork and pita was replaced by corn tortillas. Along the way, Mexican flavors took over from the Middle Eastern originals. Thus, al pastor was born, and it would soon become a Mexico City taco icon. As Mexico City emigrants arrived in the north, they brought with them the idea of the dish and the vertical spit (called a *trompo*) upon which they were cooked. Oddly, somewhere along the way the name changed from *tacos al pastor* ("shepherd-style tacos") to the more directly descriptive name *tacos adobada*. While adobada is, for the most part, the same as al pastor, the former tends to be a bit heavier on the chiles and the latter tends to lean heavier into the sweet spices.

THE IMPACT OF ALTA CALIFORNIA ON THE FOOD OF BAJA CALIFORNIA

It is beyond reasonable doubt that Baja California has greatly impacted the food of California north of the border, and done so profoundly. It could hardly be otherwise. For one thing, every inch of the state of California was once Mexico. Immigration patterns (both legal and otherwise) have ensured that that influence continued and still continues today. Americans, whether of Mexican descent or not, continue to demand Mexican flavors and foods. There were more than forty-eight thousand Mexican restaurants in the United States as of 2022, and that number has been growing at the rate of 2.4 percent per year. And that is excluding non-Mexican restaurants that include Mexican dishes on their menus. Viewed more broadly, there are more than seventy-four thousand businesses in the larger Mexican restaurant industry in California. Americans, and Californians in particular, do seem to really like their tacos.

WHAT'S IN A NAME?

One of the problems with creating a new cuisine is figuring out what to call it. In today's media age—both broadcast and social—if people can't figure out what to call something, they likely won't bother talking about it. Everything, it seems, needs at least a nickname, if not a name. The first attempt at finding a name/nickname for Baja's new cuisine was Baja Med. At one level, it was a name that seemed to make sense. It highlighted that though the locus of the cuisine was in Baja California, it was going beyond anything traditionally associated with Baja and emphasizing the ingredient-forward aspects of the Spanish part of Mexico's heritage.

But while a number of early accounts of the cuisine used the term and it's still used occasionally, it had some problems. First, it failed to capture a lot of what the movement was about, in particular the Asian and Indigenous influences. The body of work the term purports to describe encompasses a lot more than just Baja food and Mediterranean food. Indeed, a key element is the incorporation of Asian ingredients and flavors such as soy sauce, nori, ponzu, ginger, fish sauce, and lemongrass. Second, one of the chefs cooking the cuisine—Miguel Angel Guerrero—claimed a trademark on the term (though he hardly sought to prevent others from using it). The result was that writers, commentators, and many of the chefs themselves increasingly began to look for other descriptors.

Among the candidates to replace the Baja Med tag are the simple Baja California cuisine, Nuevo Cocina de Baja (or its English translation, New Cuisine of Baja), and similarly unsexy phrases that hardly come tripping off the tongue. "Baja Med," for all its flaws, was short and catchy. Perhaps a better name—and the one used in this book—is one that may have been coined by *San Diego Magazine* and the Food Network's Troy Johnson: Cali-Baja cuisine. It concisely encapsulates the sense of place that is the hallmark of the cuisine.

While the impact of Baja California and its cuisine on the food north of the border—and specifically in Southern California—is obvious, the influence of Southern California on the food of Baja California may, at first blush, seem less so. Perhaps it should not. People, and food, cross the border in both directions.

Take, for example, the TJ Dog. It is not a single dish any more than the taco is a single dish. Rather, like tacos, the TJ Dog is a platform upon which chefs, street-cart vendors, and others can improvise. It is a wide-ranging approach to meat in tubular form served inside a bun. Put differently, it's tacos done as hot dogs: wrap the dog in bacon (or don't), then fry or grill it and pile on ingredients of your choice. There are no rules. It was when that Tijuana-born and -bred dog found a welcoming home on streets north of the border (particularly where pesky things like license status were laxly enforced) that the TJ Dog really became a "thing."

The precise provenance of the TJ Dog is disputed. Sonora (the Mexican state just to the east of Baja California) claims it as theirs, calling it the Danger Dog. While Baja and Sonora can fight a small-scale border war over the birthright claim, what is not particularly disputable is that it was when the TJ/Danger Dog arrived in Southern California, and more particularly in Los Angeles, that it became a true phenomenon. Even if the bacon-wrapped hot dog was initially created in Sonora, it did not take long for it to make its way to Tijuana. And from Tijuana it traveled north to Los Angeles, where it found both a home and, perhaps more important, a laboratory.

As Gustavo Arellano has documented in articles as well as in his 2012 book *Taco USA: How Mexican Food Conquered America*, it was in Los Angeles that the vendors of the TJ Dog "ditched bolillos in favor of giant hot dog buns [and] switched out regular franks with any type of gigantic sausage (think: kielbasa, Cajun hot link, Italian, even chorizo)." Equally, the vendors—*dogueros*—also expanded the range of toppings from Tucson's pinto beans, crema, and tomatoes to, essentially, anything the mind could conjure. Arellano notes that by the late 1990s, these dogueros had already become "a familiar presence" at Southern California weekend events ranging from soccer and baseball games to just about any opportunity to sell to "the hungry and curious and drunk." The TJ Dog has become such a "thing" that it has now become a popular street food in the city that could well be the street food capital of the world: Mexico City.

Beyond the numbers, the dishes, and the anecdotes there are a slew of chefs who have shown that they do not see the border as an obstacle. Famously, Javier Plascencia has had multiple restaurants on both sides of the border. Roberto Alcocer currently runs Valle in

Oceanside (north San Diego County) as well as Malva Restaurant in Baja's Valle de Guadalupe. Ruffo Ibarra worked for multiple San Diego restaurants (starting with Plascencia at Romesco) and now owns ORYX Capital in Tijuana. Conversely, American Chad White is an owner and was the founding chef of La Justina in Tijuana. American chef Drew Deckman—the only chef in Baja California to have helmed a restaurant with a Michelin star—owns and runs one of the Valle de Guadalupe's signature restaurants, Deckman's en el Mogor. Beyond that, it is no secret that the restaurant industry north of la línea is run on the backs of Mexican cooks and dishwashers, only a fraction of whom likely possess valid papers. They do not always get away with it. Many return to Baja and do what they were doing up north.

One of the most important contributions of California to its southern neighbor addresses a fundamental question about the old Baja Med label: where, exactly, is the "Med" in Baja? Often the answer to that question has been "the climate." After all, Baja, like the Mediterranean, is by the sea and thus offers ample seafood options. No doubt there are similarities between the Mediterranean climate and that in portions of Baja. But most of Baja is more arid than the Mediterranean (and getting more so). The same might be said about portions of the state of California.

And therein might lie the answer: California cuisine. One of the key points of the California cuisine movement kicked off by Alice Waters at Chez Panisse in Berkeley and Michael McCarty at Michael's Santa Monica in the 1970s and '80s was the shortening of the food supply chain that led to the farm-to-table movement. California cuisine chefs not only bought their produce locally, they were often intimately involved with the farmers who grew that produce, even to the point of collaborating on the specifics of the produce. And the early chefs of that so-called Baja Med movement have followed in those footsteps. The sourcing of the foodstuffs in the kitchens of Javier Plascencia, Jair Téllez, Drew Deckman, Benito Molina, and Solange Muris always was and remains remarkably carefully curated. Miguel Angel Guerrero takes it to another level, hunting (literally) for some of the proteins served in his restaurants himself. These chefs may not always know the names of the parents of a fish or pig, but you can bet they know the provenance.

It is this, in large part, that sheds light on the parallels to both Mediterranean cuisine and the California cuisine that was based on it, that explains much of the essence of the Cali-Baja culinary movement. In the span of a generation, the food of Tijuana has gone from parents telling their children they shouldn't eat the street food because "it's dirty" to the sort of crave-worthy, buzzy cuisine that has become one of the primary magnets for both tourism and immigration.

CALI-BAJA AS A CUISINE

It might seem intuitively obvious that Cali-Baja (by whatever name) is a bona fide cuisine, but an argument to the contrary is possible. Part of the problem is that it is not as easy as one might suspect to say what Mexican cuisine is and is not. For one thing, there is no single "Mexican" cuisine. Depending on how you want to split or lump them, there are as many as seven distinct Mexican cuisines (and that's just in Mexico): Norteño, Oaxaqueño, Veracruzano, Yucateco, Poblano, Jalisciense, and Bajacaliforniano. Each of these distinct cuisines features the foods of different regions with different geographies and different ingredients. If you start adding the Tex-Mex and Southwestern cuisines found north of the border, the problem grows exponentially.

Then there is this: What, exactly, is a cuisine? At its most basic level, to paraphrase Wikipedia, a cuisine is a style of cooking characterized by distinctive ingredients, techniques, and dishes, and usually associated with a specific culture or geographic region. Regional food preparation techniques, customs, and ingredients often combine to create dishes unique to a region. There are many influences that shape a cuisine—religion, history, the economy, immigration, emigration—and a number of factors that get lumped into the catchall term *tradition*.

Take, for example, the food of Oaxaca. It is an ancient cuisine, predating the Spanish conquest and, for the most part, still intact afterward in part because Oaxaca offered relatively little resistance to the Spaniards, resulting in less disruption of the regional economy and foodways. Oaxacan cuisine is, perhaps, best known for its famous seven (more accurately, more than two hundred) moles. Though the moles are served in many different dishes, it is almost always the mole itself (as opposed to the protein) that is the star of the dish. Collectively, these dishes and a panoply of other familiar ones—tlayudas, barbacoa, empanadas, and more (and drinks like aguas frescas and mezcal)— make up Oaxacan cuisine. They define it.

Compare that to Baja. Oaxacan cuisine was old before Tijuana or Loreto (in what is now Baja California Sur) were even significant population centers, much less cities or cultural capitals. And Tijuana

and Loreto were the "big" ones at the time. They were lands that were home to small Indigenous tribes, the Kumeyaay north of the border and the Kumiai south of it, which still exist today. Indeed, the food of those tribes was and remains quite similar, likely because the lands were largely the same, as were the flora and fauna. It was a form of Cali-Baja even then.

Today, there are no doubt a handful of dishes that are indelibly associated with Baja: the Ensenada fish taco, the Puerto Nuevo lobster, the TJ Dog, the Caesar salad (by those who don't mistake it for Italian), seafood tostadas, and more. But a dozen or so dishes does not a cuisine make. Most of those dishes do not predate the birth of some people reading these words.

But that does not mean that Cali-Baja is not a cuisine. It does mean Cali-Baja is not an old or traditional Mexican cuisine with roots in the land going back centuries and authoritative recipes from which a cook strays at their peril. Baja is too young for that type of tradition and too much of an immigrant culture. In many ways, Baja eschews it.

But Baja—and its extension north of la línea—has a wealth of distinctive ingredients, both protein and plant. Its chefs, street-stand vendors, and home cooks use those ingredients and flavors to create dishes from old homes elsewhere or maybe just out of the ether. They can be restaurant dishes from Tijuana's Zona Gastronómica or the Valle de Guadalupe. It can be an adaptation of Nayarit-style zarandeado, a variation of Los Angeles street food, or a dish from whatever happens to be on hand that becomes the next big thing on Avenida Revolución.

Cali-Baja cuisine is all of that and pieces of that. It is the set of ingredients: sea urchin (uni), Pismo and chocolate clams, spiny lobster, shrimp (brought over daily from Sinaloa), fish (in particular tuna, marlin, and shark), beef (from Sonora but also from northeastern Baja), quail, avocado, asparagus, beets, and so many more. It is also about a style of eating. While there are, no doubt, world-class fine-dining restaurants, Cali-Baja cuisine is often more casual than that. Many Baja eateries, from some of the best and most prestigious to beachside food stalls and zarandeado fish grilled up as you feel the sand between your toes, are set outdoors and often cooked over live fire.

Baja is, at the end of the day, an immigrant region with all the energy and innovation that flows from that nature. And the food of Baja—of the entire Cali-Baja cross-border region—reflects that reality. It is a living, breathing cuisine that will not be constrained by borders, be they temporal, traditional, or geographical.

And yet Cali-Baja cuisine is still in its relative youth. And that is one of its greatest strengths. The slightest change in a classic dish of Italian cuisine (among others) can be seen as an affront to tradition, as insolent. But while that is a phenomenon seen and heard often in the Old World and perhaps in conjunction with the older world of Mexican cuisines, it is something heard rarely in Baja. Innovation is not frowned upon, and it is not something belonging to yesteryear.

Cali-Baja cuisine is, first and foremost, expressed in the signature ingredients of Baja California and Southern California. It is thus demarcated by the land and the sea and by the spirit of innovation and invention that transformed Mexico's farthest hinterland from barely meriting statehood to one of its most important regions in barely more than a handful of decades. As new ingredients emerge and the region's chefs and street food vendors and home cooks find new ones or come up with new ways to play with the old ones, the cuisine of Cali-Baja will continue to stretch its legs, if not sow its oats.

It is, perhaps, this spirit of innovation and determination not to be bound by a hard-and-fast set of rules (and sacrosanct dishes) that most thoroughly defines Cali-Baja cuisine. While America has learned about what Baja has been doing with its food just on the other side of the border (and has begun to figure out that much the same is happening on this side too), and while American chefs have been a part of this Cali-Baja cuisine, American home cooks haven't had a lot of places to turn to for guides on how to get in on the action themselves. There are very few cookbooks dedicated to the food of Baja.

The goal of this book is, first and foremost, to fill that need. From recipes for some of the core Cali-Baja dishes to explorations of the region's signature ingredients and forms in the style of (and sometimes directly from) some of Baja's best, the intent of this book is to help you understand, see, and hopefully cook in the Cali-Baja style.

HOW TO USE THIS BOOK

I have been known to pick up a cookbook and read it cover to cover.
It has, I must admit, been a while, and I know that's not exactly the norm.
Most of you will open a cookbook and begin by looking at the photographs
or heading straight to the index. You will look for a particular ingredient
or sauce, either in search of an idea for your next meal or to seek
specific guidance on an idea or technique you already have in mind.

Say, for example, you want to do something new with chicken.
The index would lead you to Chicken Pozole Verde (page 183), Enrique
Olvera's Chicken Tinga (page 186), or Baja Roast Chicken (page 185). Or
maybe you liked an aguachile you tasted on a surfing trip to Baja or a
fishing trip to Cabo San Lucas. The index would lead you to Shrimp and
Blood Orange Aguachile (page 74), Javier Plascencia's Tuna and Carrot
Aguachile (page 77), and Californios-Style Cantaloupe Aguachile (page
71). The pages around those three recipes offer further suggestions of
related dishes: ceviches, a tiradito, a carpaccio, and cócteles.

The process of visually grazing through the book may mean you
don't end up making any of those dishes for dinner, but each of the
recipes includes at least one idea you could incorporate into that
dinner. From the use of chiles in a dish or a sauce or different ways to
infuse a dish with flavor, the book is as much a compendium of ideas
as it is a set of culinary formulas. My goal is inspiration as much as
replication. It is my genuine hope that for nearly every center-of-the-
plate star ingredient (or all of them), this book will offer interesting
and delicious flavor combinations and new-to-you techniques and
approaches to bring to your dinner table.

A few notes on particular pieces of equipment to consider:

- First, throughout this book I call for the use of a high-speed blender
  or food processor. For pureed soups or sauces, I tend to use a
  Vitamix. My basic reasons for this preference are the sheer power
  of its motor and the superior, refined texture of the puree that the
  blender's variable speed control produces. You can, however, use
  whatever you like or already own: an immersion blender, a food
  processor, a drink blender, or a Ninja. Passing the resulting puree
  through a fine-mesh strainer, although an extra step, can yield an
  equally good if not superior final product.

- Second, I live in San Diego, where the weather means it's "grilling season" all year, but that is clearly not the case everywhere. So, if it is cold where you are and you want to make a dish in which I call for smoking ingredients (for example, the Grilled Cotija and Smoked Tofu Stuffed Artichokes on page 164), I suggest using a smoking gun—a remarkably convenient gadget that quickly and efficiently infuses relatively small amounts of food with the smoky flavors of your choice, even in the dead of winter. I use the PolyScience Hand-Held Smoke Infuser.

- Third, while I love the flavor and poetry of grilling and the technical perfection of the reverse-sear method of meat cookery, my go-to for cooking steaks is sous vide. Adapted from industrial processes, the food (here, the steak) is sealed in food-grade plastic vacuum-sealer bags and cooked slowly to a specific internal temperature in a water bath heated to a consistent temperature with an immersion circulator. The primary advantage is that the entire piece of meat from its surface to its center is cooked to the exact same degree. It's all "the good part." A quick, high-temperature sear to caramelize the outside gives the perfect finish. There are a number of brands of very good home immersion circulators. Mine is made by Anova (and I highly recommend it), but Joule is also good.

HOW TO HANDLE CHILES

When most Americans think of Mexican chiles, it is usually green jalapeños, serranos, or near-nuclear bright orange habaneros that come to mind. The real workhorse chiles of the Mexican kitchen, however, are not fresh chiles but rather the panoply of dried chiles: sweet, raisinated ancho chiles (dried poblanos), mildly spicy and fruity guajillo chiles (dried mirasol), smoky chipotle chiles (dried and/or smoked jalapeños), and many more.

Fresh and dried chiles require different handling. Fresh chiles generally need to be seeded and stemmed and sometimes deveined. Contrary to popular belief, it is not the seeds of fresh chiles that house the heat. Rather, it is the veins: the white, fleshy internal membranes that house the seed pods. That said, those seeds should be removed for textural purposes. Once seeded and stemmed (and with as much of the veins removed as your taste demands), fresh chiles are good to go. The primary caution involved in preparing fresh chiles is simply remembering not to touch your eyes while handling them!

Dried chiles, on the other hand, require some more work. As with fresh chiles, the first step lies in stemming and seeding the chiles. But that is where the similarity ends. Dried chiles generally need to be brought back to life. Fortunately, that is both simple and easy. To do so, cut the dried chiles in segments and toast them in a dry sauté pan or cast-iron skillet over medium heat for about 20 seconds, until they are fragrant. Do not overtoast the chiles; it is better to go too short than too long. Place the chile segments in a bowl and pour in enough hot water to fully cover them. Soak the chiles for 10 minutes, and they will be good to go.

HOW TO WARM TORTILLAS

The two most important things to know about warming up cold (or store-bought) tortillas: First, there is nothing wrong with buying good-quality tortillas at a store, in particular if the store has a tortilleria (which many Hispanic markets do). Second, you really do need to warm them up. You are leaving a lot of flavor behind and risking catastrophic structural failure if you try to make your taco with a cold tortilla. About the only time it is OK to use tortillas cold is if you're going to cut and fry them for tortilla chips or fry them to use as the base of tostadas.

So how do you warm tortillas? There is no shortage of websites and givers of friendly advice who will happily tell you it is just fine to heat up corn tortillas in the microwave. Don't do it! The single best way to heat up yesterday's tortillas that you just grabbed out of the refrigerator is on a comal, cast-iron skillet, or sturdy sauté pan. Heat the pan dry (no fat) over medium to medium-high heat before adding a tortilla to the pan. Cook the tortilla until light brown spots form on the underside of the tortilla. Flip the tortilla and repeat on the other side. Flip once again and reheat the first side for 5 seconds. Repeat with the remaining tortillas.

Another acceptable (in my view) method for warming tortillas is to use an oven preheated to 350°F. Wrap the tortillas in aluminum foil and stick them in the oven for 5 to 10 minutes (depending on how many tortillas are in the foil). This gets the warming job done, but you lose the flavor created by the direct contact with the hot pan in the first method, and you lose some moisture and texture too.

| GF / Gluten Free | VEGAN / Vegan | VEG / Vegetarian |

BREAKFAST

BAJA EGGS "FLORENTINE"
with Lime Hollandaise and Jamón Serrano

At times it seems that apart from the city of Rosarito Beach itself, the coastline from the south end of Playas de Tijuana to Ensenada might as well be an American expat colony. There are gated communities filled with retirees, other gated communities filled with surfers attracted by world-class breaks, and restaurants, hotels, and bars that cater to one group, the other, or both. Brunch is more of a "thing" in these communities than it is north of the border.

While the classic eggs Florentine might not seem a particularly likely candidate for a Baja chef to riff on, swapping out the spinach of the original for Swiss chard is, perhaps surprisingly, a natural choice. From October through early May the chard in Baja is some of the best I've tasted anywhere. The product is good in the Calimax supermarkets but even better in the street markets and in Tijuana's remarkable Mercado Hidalgo.

Preheat the oven to 350°F and line 2 baking sheets with parchment paper.

Arrange the bolillos on one of the prepared baking sheets and brush them with the olive oil. Toast the rolls for 3 minutes, or until the sliced surface just begins to take on some color. Remove the rolls from the oven and raise the oven temperature to 400°F.

Heat the butter in a large sauté pan over medium-high heat until it foams. Add the shallot and garlic and cook for a few seconds. Add the chard by the handful as it fits in the pan. Season the chard with salt and stir frequently until wilted.

While the chard is wilting, arrange the jamón serrano in a single layer on the second prepared baking sheet and bake until crispy, 6 to 8 minutes. Remove from the oven and cool completely, then crumble into small pieces.

To make the lime hollandaise, pour water into the bottom of a double boiler and bring it to a rolling boil. In the top section of the double boiler, combine the egg yolks, water, lime juice, and salt and add a piece of the butter. Place the top section over the boiling water, being careful not to let the bottom of the top section touch the water below. Cook, stirring rapidly with a whisk, until the butter melts and the sauce

Special Equipment

double boiler

instant-read thermometer

For the Eggs Florentine

4 bolillos (Mexican rolls), top third sliced off with a bread knife

2 tablespoons olive oil

1 tablespoon good-quality butter

1 small shallot, minced

1 medium clove garlic, minced

12 ounces Swiss chard (green or red), stems removed and leaves shredded

Kosher salt

2 tablespoons distilled white vinegar

8 large eggs

For the Garnish

4 slices good-quality jamón serrano or prosciutto

For the Lime Hollandaise Sauce

3 large egg yolks, beaten

1 tablespoon water

1 tablespoon fresh lime juice

⅛ teaspoon kosher salt

½ cup (1 stick) unsalted butter, cut into thirds

begins to thicken. Add the remaining butter, one piece at a time, stirring constantly until melted. Cook the sauce, stirring, until it thickens, about 2 minutes. Immediately remove the sauce from the heat. If the sauce is too thick or curdles, immediately whisk in 1 to 2 tablespoons hot water.

Work in two batches of 4 eggs each to poach the eggs. Bring 6 cups salted water and the vinegar to a boil in a medium pot, then reduce the heat to maintain a simmer (the water should register about 200°F on an instant-read thermometer). Carefully break an egg into a small bowl, then tip the egg into the water. Swirl gently with a wooden spoon for about 10 seconds, just until the egg begins to set. Repeat with 3 more eggs. Cook, swirling the water occasionally, until the egg whites are fully set but the yolks are still soft, about 4 minutes. Carefully lift the eggs from the pot using a slotted spoon. Repeat with the second batch of 4 eggs.

To serve, place a toasted bolillo on each of 4 plates. Top each roll with the wilted chard, making two little beds for the eggs in the chard. Place an egg in each bed. Spoon some hollandaise sauce over the top of the eggs and finish with a shower of crumbled jamón serrano.

Note: Bolillos can be found at most Mexican markets. Crusty French bread is a good substitute.

HUEVOS RANCHEROS

Serves 4 / GF

Huevos rancheros is, likely, America's best-loved Mexican breakfast. It used to be a dish you'd have to get at a Mexican restaurant. No longer. These days, huevos rancheros is a regular feature on the menus of typically American breakfast joints and other eateries in Southern California, New York, and beyond. The homemade version tends to be better. And perhaps that is why huevos rancheros is still one of the Mexican farmhouse breakfasts of choice.

Warm each tortilla individually by reheating in a medium sauté pan over medium heat. Arrange a single tortilla on each of 4 plates. Top each tortilla with just enough of the refried beans to cover it in a thin layer. Sprinkle the shredded cheese over the bean-covered tortillas.

Pour the salsa roja into a small saucepan and place over medium heat. Bring to a simmer, stirring occasionally, then reduce the heat to maintain the lowest possible simmer until you are ready to serve.

Meanwhile, heat 1 teaspoon of the olive oil in the sauté pan you used for the tortillas. When the oil just starts to ripple, crack an egg and add it to the pan, taking care not to break the yolk. Fry the egg sunny-side up, lifting and tilting the pan occasionally to redistribute the oil, until the white is set but the yolk remains soft. Transfer the fried egg to one of the tortillas. Repeat with the remaining eggs.

Pour ¼ cup of the warm salsa roja over each egg and top that with ¼ cup of the salsa bandera. Garnish each plate with sliced avocado, a sprinkling of the cilantro, cheese, and hot sauce, if desired.

4 Corn Tortillas (page 228)

1½ cups Refried Beans (page 239)

½ cup shredded Oaxaca, Monterey Jack, or Real del Castillo cheese

1 cup Baja-Style Salsa Roja (page 244)

4 teaspoons extra-virgin olive oil

4 eggs

1 cup Salsa Bandera (page 242)

For the Garnish

1 medium Hass avocado, sliced

½ cup finely chopped fresh cilantro leaves and tender stems

Crumbled Cotija or feta cheese

Hot sauce (optional)

BREAKFAST BURRITO

The breakfast burrito, to be clear, is by no means Mexican food, unless "New Mexico" counts. It is, basically, a bunch of breakfast ingredients wrapped in a flour tortilla with Southwestern takes on Mexican sauces. History has lost the definitive attribution of the breakfast burrito's creation—a Santa Fe diner claims to have done so, though evidence of earlier examples abound—but the dish received the ultimate kiss of American capitalist approval in the late 1980s and early '90s when fast-food chains began selling them faster than hotcakes. Regardless, breakfast burritos remain an important gateway for many Americans on their way to full-on Mexican food addiction.

1 medium russet potato, peeled and diced

2 teaspoons extra-virgin olive oil

Kosher salt and freshly ground black pepper

½ teaspoon garlic powder

4 slices bacon

4 large eggs

1 teaspoon butter

½ cup grated cheddar cheese

2 large Flour Tortillas (page 229), warmed

¼ cup Guacamole (page 252)

½ cup Salsa Bandera (page 242)

2 tablespoons chopped fresh cilantro leaves and tender stems

Preheat the oven to 425°F. Line 2 baking sheets with parchment paper. In a large bowl, toss the potato with the olive oil and season with salt, pepper, and the garlic powder. Spread the potatoes out on one of the prepared baking sheets and transfer to the oven. Roast for about 20 minutes, turning the potatoes occasionally, until browned and crisp

At roughly the same time, arrange the bacon strips on the second prepared baking sheet, taking care that they do not overlap. Roast for 10 minutes, then rotate the pan and roast until the bacon is thoroughly browned, about 10 more minutes. Remove the bacon from the oven and transfer the strips to a paper towel–lined plate to drain. When the bacon has cooled and dried, break it up into small pieces.

Meanwhile, whisk the eggs with a large pinch of salt until thoroughly combined with no visible egg white remaining. In a medium sauté pan, melt the butter over medium heat until it foams. Add the eggs and cook, stirring constantly, until they have formed curds but remain runny, 1 to 2 minutes. Stir in the cheese and cook, stirring constantly, until the cheese has melted and the eggs are soft and fluffy, about 1 minute longer.

To assemble the burritos, arrange the warmed tortillas on a work surface and spread each with half the guacamole in an even rectangular layer at the center of the tortilla, leaving about a 2-inch border around the sides and 3 inches at the top and bottom. Top the guacamole on each tortilla with half the bacon and top that with half the egg mixture, followed by the potatoes, salsa bandera, and cilantro.

To form each burrito, fold the sides of the tortilla in over the filling. Then roll the bottom flap of the tortilla up over the filling, holding the sides tight as you roll. Continue rolling until the burrito is sealed.

HUEVOS DIVORCIADOS

In Baja restaurants this dish is perhaps more common than huevos rancheros (of which it is, essentially, a variant). Divorciados is basically huevos rancheros done with two eggs, each with a different sauce. Those two eggs and their differences account for the colorful name—*divorciados*, meaning "divorced."

This version of the dish was created by Drew Bent, the founding chef and co-owner of Lola 55, a Michelin-recognized restaurant in San Diego.

To make the salsa verde, combine all the salsa verde ingredients in a food processor or high-speed blender and process to a smooth, creamy consistency. Transfer to a bowl and rinse the food processor bowl or blender jar.

To make the roasted red salsa, heat a cast-iron skillet or other heavy pan over high heat. When it's hot, add the tomatoes and onion and pan-roast until they are well charred, 7 to 9 minutes. Transfer the charred tomatoes and onion to a food processor or high-speed blender. Add the árbol, morita, and guajillo chiles to the pan and cook until they puff up, then transfer them to the food processor or blender and process to a smooth, creamy consistency.

To cook the eggs, pour 2 tablespoons of the oil into a frying pan and heat over high heat to bring the oil to its smoking point. Crack 2 eggs into the pan and cook until the whites are set but the yolks are still runny. Transfer to a plate and repeat with the remaining eggs, adding an additional 2 tablespoons oil to the pan before each batch. The goal is puffy, even, bubbly whites with deeply caramelized, crispy edges. While classic technique might disfavor these smoky, crispy edges, they are not a flaw but rather a feature of this dish.

For each serving, place a single tortilla in the middle of a plate. Top the tortilla with 2 tablespoons of the beans and top the beans with another tortilla. Place 2 sunny-side up eggs on top of the tortilla-and-bean stack. Spoon some creamy salsa verde around the yolk of one egg and some roasted red salsa around the yolk of the other egg. Garnish with cilantro leaves and a squeeze or two of lime juice.

Note: If you cannot find gooseberries, green table grapes are a decent substitute.

For the Creamy Salsa Verde

3 ounces gooseberries (see Note)

1 medium Hass avocado, flesh scooped out

¼ medium sweet onion, roughly chopped

½ medium jalapeño chile, stemmed and seeded

½ bunch cilantro, leaves and tender stems

1 teaspoon kosher salt

Juice of 1½ large limes

½ cup water

For the Roasted Red Salsa

2 large red heirloom tomatoes

½ medium sweet onion

2 dried chiles de árbol, stemmed and seeded

2 dried morita (or dried chipotle) chiles, stemmed and seeded

1 dried guajillo chile, stemmed and seeded

For the Eggs

½ cup grapeseed, canola, or other neutral oil

8 eggs

For Serving

8 Corn Tortillas (page 228), warmed

½ cup Refried Beans (page 239)

Fresh cilantro leaves

Lime wedges

MENUDO COLORADO

Makes 4 servings / GF

North of la línea, Mexican breakfast and huevos rancheros or huevos divorciados come to mind. But for many Mexicans—and for me—a Mexican breakfast means one thing: menudo. The reason menudo is so nearly synonymous with Mexican breakfasts is simple: all the ingredients to serve a family of six would likely total little more than a handful of pesos. It is, like the great glories of many cuisines, created from what was cheap and on hand. In this case, it is made of the less gloried parts of the beasts. The sum, however, is much greater than its parts.

But why, when so much of Mexican cuisine has entered the American consciousness, has menudo remained something either unknown or exotic? One word: tripe.

The savory, delicious menudo broth of the meat and hominy stew itself and the contrasting textures between the tripe and that hominy are a wonderful way to slide into the day. In the right hands—whether at a specialist street stall or restaurant—it is the symphony of textures and warm hug of the broth that makes it a perfect breakfast. The key to making a great version comes down to proper cooking. Undercooking tripe is not necessarily bad, but leaves it a bit more al dente (in the pasta sense) than most folks like their meats. Overcooking tripe leaves it way too mushy. If it is properly cooked in a dish as strongly flavorful as this one, the tripe will give the dish body and a meaty feel that is nearly irresistible to those approaching it with an open mind. It is this careful simmering of the tripe in particular (but also the trotters) that is the first key to menudo colorado. It harvests the intrinsic goodness of the meats, leaving the tripe succulent and tender.

Place the tripe, pig's feet, calf's foot, pork hock, garlic, salt, and about 4 quarts water (enough to comfortably cover the meats with room to spare) in a large stockpot or soup pot. Bring to a boil, then reduce the heat to maintain a simmer. Simmer, uncovered, until the tripe and feet are tender but not too soft, 1½ to 2 hours. To check the tenderness of the tripe and feet, pierce them with the tip of a sharp knife; it should slide in easily.

For the Meat

2 pounds honeycomb tripe, rinsed well and cut into 1-inch squares (see Note)

2 pig's feet (trotters), halved

1 calf's foot, halved

1 large, meaty fresh (not smoked) pork hock (if not meaty, add 8 ounces pork butt, cut into 1-inch dice)

1 tablespoon kosher salt

5 cloves garlic, peeled

For the Chile Puree

5 dried guajillo chiles, stemmed and seeded

2 dried ancho chiles, stemmed and seeded

1 teaspoon cumin seeds, crushed

1 teaspoon dried Mexican oregano

3 cloves garlic, crushed

For the Stew

1 medium white or yellow onion, diced

1 medium carrot, diced

2 medium ribs celery, diced

Kosher salt

For Serving

Attractive cilantro leaves

Lime wedges

Finely chopped onion

Tortillas

RECIPE CONTINUES

To make the chile puree, about 1 hour into the simmer, toast the chiles on a dry sauté pan or cast-iron skillet over medium heat for about 20 seconds, until fragrant. Do not overtoast the chiles. It is better to go too short than too long. Place the chiles in a bowl and pour in enough hot water to fully cover them. Soak for 10 minutes, or until they are pliable. Remove the chiles from the water and place in a high-speed blender or food processor, along with the cumin, oregano, garlic, and 1½ cups of the broth from the pot of meat. Blend the mixture until very smooth, adding more broth if needed.

To make the stew, once the tripe and feet are tender, remove the pig's feet, calf's foot, and pork hock from the pot and set aside. When they are cool enough to handle, remove the fleshy parts (discard the bones and cartilage) and either tear them into small pieces or chop, then return to pot and add the onion, carrot, celery, and chile puree and simmer for about 1 hour more, until the flavors have fully melded. Season with additional salt as needed.

Serve in large bowls, with cilantro, lime wedges, onion, and tortillas at the table for each guest to take as desired.

Note: When buying tripe for menudo at a Mexican grocery store or market, do not buy *tripa*. That is a different part of the cow's intestines. While tripa is excellent for tacos, it is not what you want for menudo. What you do want is, perhaps not surprisingly, called *menudo* in Spanish. It is known as honeycomb tripe in English.

SALADS AND SOUPS

THE VICTOR SALAD

Serves 4

Almost everyone loves a Caesar salad. Tijuana and its Prohibition-era visitors from the north certainly did. But in the 1970s, then president of Mexico Luis Echeverría Álvarez increased the quantity of pesos circulating in the Mexican economy without corresponding increases in the country's wealth, resulting in a series of massive devaluations of the peso. Consequently, the price of some of the key ingredients in a Caesar salad escalated because they were imported. It was likely in response to these devaluations that Victor Rubio, a broker on the Mexican Stock Exchange and the owner of Victor's Restaurant in Tijuana, created a variation on the Caesar salad. He worked with his chef, Jose Guadalupe Moreno, and Jose Fimbres (founder of the Calimax grocery store chain) to swap out imported Parmesan cheese in favor of Mexican Cotija—though there are conflicting stories as to whether Cotija or Parmesan was used on the croutons (as opposed to directly on the salad)—and imported olive oil for readily available corn oil, which they infused with garlic. It is this garlic-infused oil that makes the Victor a garlicky, more Mexican cousin to the more Italian-inflected Caesar salad.

Keep in mind that two separate quantities of corn oil (one for the croutons and one for the salad) need to be infused with garlic overnight. This means that the recipe ought to be started the night before, though waiting until the morning of would not be the end of the world.

For the Croutons

1 clove garlic, sliced

2 tablespoons corn oil

2 tablespoons butter

1 small French baguette

2 tablespoons grated Cotija or Parmesan cheese

Paprika

For the Salad

2 cloves garlic, roughly chopped

½ cup corn oil

2 heads romaine lettuce, sliced in half lengthwise

2 large eggs

Juice of 1 lemon

1 teaspoon Mayonnaise (page 255)

1 tablespoon A.1. steak sauce

2 teaspoons Worcestershire sauce

2 dashes Tabasco sauce, plus more as needed

½ cup grated Cotija cheese

Kosher salt and freshly ground black pepper

Lightly crush the garlic slices for the croutons, place in a bowl, add the corn oil, cover, and infuse overnight.

Lightly crush the chopped garlic for the salad, place in a bowl, add the corn oil, cover, and infuse overnight.

The next day, preheat the oven to 350°F.

Remove the garlic slices from the oil for the croutons, reserving the garlic. Melt the butter in a small skillet over low heat, then mix with the garlic oil. Cut the baguette into ½-inch-thick slices and coat each slice with some of the garlic butter. Arrange on a baking sheet. Sprinkle with the cheese and some paprika. If topping the salad with the croutons, bake until crisp, 7 to 8 minutes. If serving them on the side, bake for just 3 to 4 minutes.

Separate, wash, and trim the ends off the romaine leaves. Dry the leaves with paper towels.

To coddle the eggs, bring a small pot of water to a boil. While the water is heating up, fill a small bowl with ice and water. Gently submerge the eggs in the boiling water for exactly 1 minute (if you let them go longer, the white and yolk may become too firm). Immediately remove the eggs from the pot and place in the ice bath for 1 minute.

Combine the lemon juice, peeled eggs, mayonnaise, steak sauce, Worcestershire, Tabasco, and most of the cheese—reserving some for garnish—in a large salad bowl or cazuela (clay pot) and mix well. Slowly drizzle in the garlic oil for the salad while whisking constantly. This will emulsify the dressing. Add the lettuce and coat with the dressing.

Arrange the dressed lettuce leaves on salad plates, sprinkle with the reserved cheese, and top each with a large crouton (or serve the croutons on the side). Season with salt and pepper and serve.

THE BIRTH OF THE CAESAR SALAD IN TIJUANA'S GOLDEN AGE

There is something about the crisp freshness and slight bitterness of the romaine lettuce; the soothing umami of the Parmesan cheese; the textural contrast of the big, garlicky croutons; and the way the acidity, richness, and mysteriously funky flavors of the dressing manage to achieve simplicity and depth at the same time. It's the elegant perfection of a few good ingredients combined in just the right proportions.

But as delicious as it may be, it's doubtful that the Caesar (or the Victor) would exist if it weren't for Tijuana's golden age in the 1920s. That, together with a string of controversies and competing claims about nearly anything touching on the salad's history, have built up a rich mythology around the Caesar.

One of the few things that seems beyond reasonable doubt is that the salad was created at Caesar's Restaurante Bar at the Caesar Hotel in Tijuana, owned at the time by Cesare Cardini. But who created it? Was it Cardini himself, Cardini's brother, his partner Paul Magiora, or Livio Santini, the restaurant's cook? Each of them—along with a totally unrelated Chicago restaurateur—have claimed it.

But that Caesar did more than just taste good. It was a reason for Prohibition-era Hollywood celebrities to head south. We likely wouldn't remember the salad if it weren't for those celebrities Cardini served it to as they chased booze across the border. Those celebrities and their star power lent the Tijuana of the time a certain mystery and elegant glow. Subsequent incarnations of the city would trade on that aura long after the shine had worn off, many of the institutions were gone, nearly all those celebrities had left, and Prohibition had ended.

GRILLED VENISON LOIN SALAD

Serves 4 / GF

Chef Miguel Angel Guerrero is known for many things. He trademarked the term Baja Med (as one might expect a guy with a law degree to do) and helped popularize the term and the style. He is also known to be an avid hunter who brings the catch into his restaurants. This recipe is, essentially, one of his tacos done up in salad form. If you cannot get access to venison, there is no reason not to substitute beef. Filet mignon or rib eye would be excellent cuts to use.

Season the venison with the spice blend. Cover and refrigerate for at least 2 hours or up to overnight.

When ready to cook, make a hot fire in a charcoal grill or set a gas grill on high heat. Grill the venison loin, without moving it, until nicely browned on the bottom, 4 to 5 minutes. Rotate the venison 90 degrees (but do not flip it yet) and leave it for just a minute more to make grill marks. Flip the meat and cook for 4 to 5 minutes, again rotating the venison if grill marks are desired. You want to aim for a good, deeply charred outside with a rare or medium-rare inside. Transfer the venison to a cutting board and let rest for at least 10 minutes.

To make the dressing, combine the shallots, garlic, thyme, rosemary, honey, and lime juice in a small bowl and whisk to combine. Add the olive oil, whisking again to emulsify the dressing.

Thinly slice the venison against the grain. Dress the arugula and arrange it on a plate. Arrange the sliced venison atop the salad and top with the queso fresco, beans, and avocado. Drizzle with a bit more dressing and garnish with rosemary flowers.

For the Venison

1½ pounds venison loin

2 tablespoons Cali Baja Spice Blend (page 261)

For the Salad and Dressing

2 small shallots, finely chopped

4 cloves garlic, minced

1 teaspoon fresh thyme leaves, finely chopped

2 teaspoons fresh rosemary leaves, finely chopped

1 teaspoon honey

Juice of 2 limes

3 tablespoons extra-virgin olive oil

1 bunch arugula, torn into bite-size pieces

⅔ cup crumbled queso fresco

1 cup cooked black beans or pinto beans

2 medium Hass avocados, sliced

Rosemary flowers, for garnish

ARUGULA, HEART OF PALM, AND CRAB SALAD

Serves 4 / GF

Mexican cuisine is not known for its salad wizardry. Perhaps it should be. While the Caesar salad is, clearly, the most famous Mexican salad, it is certainly not the only one. In Baja—indeed, in much of Mexico—combining the freshest and most delicious ingredients and tying them together by little more than a simple dressing and some greens is a natural way of constructing a dish. It is, perhaps, the main thing Baja's cuisine inherited from California cuisine north of the border.

In this salad one of Baja's signature proteins—crab—is paired with arugula, hearts of palm, and a lime vinaigrette. The result is simple, delicious, and refreshing. The key to the dressing is de-flaming the shallot slices by soaking them in water for ten minutes.

For the Salad

2 medium shallots, thinly sliced

1 (14-ounce) can hearts of palm, drained

1 pound crabmeat (picked from about 6 blue crabs, or good-quality canned)

5 ounces arugula, roughly chopped

1 cup red cherry tomatoes, halved lengthwise and salted

For the Dressing

2 tablespoons apple cider vinegar

2 tablespoons fresh lime juice

2 teaspoons Dijon mustard

½ teaspoon kosher salt

¼ teaspoon freshly ground black pepper

½ cup extra-virgin olive oil

In a small bowl, soak the shallot slices in cold water to cover for 10 minutes, then drain them. While the shallots are soaking, slice the hearts of palm into ½-inch segments.

To make the dressing, combine the vinegar, lime juice, mustard, salt, and pepper in a large bowl and whisk to combine. Stream in the olive oil, whisking vigorously to emulsify the dressing.

Combine the hearts of palm and crabmeat in a medium bowl, toss to combine, and dress with some of the vinaigrette. In a separate bowl, dress the arugula.

Divide the arugula among 4 salad plates. Divide the hearts of palm and crab mixture on top. Garnish with the tomatoes.

MEXICAN AJO BLANCO

Serves 4 to 6
VEGAN

Growing up in San Diego, I ate a lot of Mexican food. One of my favorites—whether in Tijuana or north of the border—was gazpacho, the classic cold soup based on sweet red pepper, tomato, and cucumber with olive oil and bread. It would be years before I learned that gazpacho was a Spanish (Andalusian, to be specific) dish that had been adopted in Mexico.

It would also be years before I learned that the red gazpacho I knew and loved was only one variety of gazpacho. In fact, white gazpacho—*ajo blanco*—may be far closer to the origins of the soup. It has also become a favorite in my household. This version features a final flourish in the form of a Mexican take on amba sauce, a mango concoction referencing the dish's possible Jewish and/or Muslim roots.

Combine the almonds, 3 cups water, and the garlic in a high-speed blender or food processor and blend, starting on low and gradually increasing the speed—stopping periodically to scrape down the sides—until you get a milky liquid. Add the bolillos and blend until very smooth. Season with salt, then blend in the vinegar and olive oil. Transfer the soup to a container, cover, and refrigerate until very well chilled, at least 2 hours or up to 2 days.

To serve the soup, thinly slicing the grapes lengthwise. Give the soup one last spin in the blender or food processor. Check the soup's consistency and thin with cold water if needed. Check the seasoning, adding more salt or vinegar, if desired. Pour the soup into chilled serving bowls. Arrange 3 to 5 grape slices in the center of each bowl and top with a mint leaf. Drip dots of amba sauce around the grape slices.

Ingredients:

1 cup (about 6 ounces) Marcona almonds

1 or 2 medium cloves garlic (depending on how strong you want the garlic flavor to be), peeled

4 or 5 bolillos (Mexican rolls), cut into 1-inch cubes (about 8 ounces or 3 cups)

Kosher salt

1½ teaspoons sherry vinegar, plus more as needed

1½ tablespoons extra-virgin olive oil, plus more for garnish

4 to 6 seedless green grapes

4 to 6 attractive mint leaves

Mexican Amba Sauce (page 253)

MEXICAN LEEK AND POTATO SOUP

Serves 4
GF / VEGAN

The combination of leeks and potatoes in a soup is a familiar idea. From the potage Parmentier of classic French cuisine to the even more familiar pureed version of the soup, vichyssoise, the pairing of these two ingredients is a tried-and-true formula. It is also one that crosses national borders and cultures.

Mexico's version, eaten throughout the country, is homey, a comforting dish that is equally good in the summer as it is in the winter. In the summer, serve it cold. In the winter, puree it (almost like a vichyssoise) and serve it warm. A dollop of Mexican crema can be a perfect finishing element. But if the crema is excluded, the dish is vegan.

Heat the olive oil in a medium soup pot or Dutch oven over medium heat. When the oil ripples, add the leek rings and cook until translucent, 3 to 4 minutes. Add the garlic and cook for an additional minute. Add the potato, stirring to coat with the oil. Season with salt and pepper and cook for an additional 3 minutes, stirring constantly.

Add the stock to the pot and bring to a boil, stirring and scraping up any bits from the bottom of the pot. Add the tomato paste and bay leaf and stir until the tomato paste dissolves into the stock. Reduce the heat to low and simmer until the potatoes are completely cooked, about 20 minutes.

Serve the soup hot or cold, garnished with oregano leaves and topped with a dollop of Mexican crema, if desired.

3 tablespoons extra-virgin olive oil

1 medium leek, white part only, washed and sliced into thin rings

1 clove garlic, minced

1 large russet potato, peeled and cut into ½-inch dice

Kosher salt and freshly ground black pepper

8 cups Vegetable Stock (page 235) or Roasted Vegetable Stock (page 236)

2 tablespoons tomato paste

1 bay leaf

Fresh Mexican oregano leaves

Mexican Crema (page 255) for serving (optional)

CHARD AND CHOCHOYOTE SOUP

Serves 4 / GF

Chochoyotes are corn masa dumplings originating from Oaxaca. Classically they're served with a mole or thick black bean soup. Pairing them with a broth made from green chard, one of Baja California's signature vegetables, plants the dish squarely in Baja. Some of the best chard I've had was from the Monday morning Rosarito Beach *mercado sobre ruedas* ("market on wheels"). They were the most colorful, fluffy, and sweet chard leaves I'd ever seen, and they inspired me to create this recipe.

For the Chochoyotes

1¾ cups masa harina

1 teaspoon kosher salt

2 tablespoons lard

1 cup cold water

For the Soup

8 cups Chicken Stock (page 232)

2 bunches green Swiss chard, stems removed

½ cup Pink Pickled Onions (page 259), brunoised

To make the chochoyotes, in a large bowl, combine the masa harina and salt. Work in the shortening with your fingertips until it's fully incorporated. Add the water and mix with your hands until combined.

Use a tablespoon to scoop out the dough, rolling it very well in between your hands to make a smooth ball. Use your thumb to make a crater in the center halfway through each ball (this will help them cook evenly). Place the chochoyotes on a sheet pan as you form them and cover with a damp, clean kitchen towel to keep them from drying out. You should have about 25. Set aside, covered, while you make the soup.

To make the soup, pour the stock into a soup pot or Dutch oven and bring to a boil over high heat. Add the chard, lower the heat to medium, and cook just until it wilts.

While the soup cooks, fill a large, wide saucepan with a few inches of water and bring it to a simmer. (Use a large Dutch oven to cook the dumplings in bigger batches, or a small saucepan for smaller batches.) Reduce the heat so the water is just below a simmer. (Chochoyotes will disintegrate if the heat is too high or the water is simmering aggressively.) Working in batches (or all at once if your pot is at least 6 quarts), gently add the chochoyotes and poach, undisturbed, for 20 minutes, until tender and cooked through. To check for doneness, scoop out a chochoyote, cut it open, and taste; it should feel soft and creamy on the outside but firm inside.

Remove the soup from the heat. Carefully pour the chard and broth into a high-speed blender or food processor, working in batches if necessary, and blend to a smooth puree.

Arrange 5 or so chochoyotes at the bottom of each serving bowl. Garnish each chochoyote with some of the pickled onions. Carefully pour or ladle an equal amount of broth into each bowl around the chochoyotes.

TOMATO-CHILE BROTH
with Poached Egg and Microwave "Fried" Cilantro

Serves 4 / GF

This dish, *huevos rabo de mestiza* in Spanish, is a classic recipe from San Luis Potosi. Traditionally, it is eggs poached in a hearty sauce of tomatoes and fire-roasted poblano chiles. This Cali-Baja approach to the dish lightens it by sweating a classic mirepoix (onion, celery, and carrot) and incorporating diced tomatoes (essentially making a Catalan sofregit) before adding the poblanos and the broth. Poaching the eggs in this heady (more than hearty) broth yields a more delicate dish, and the final touch is a garnish of cilantro "fried" in the microwave with just the slightest kiss of grapeseed oil. The result is a soup that honors the depth of flavor and profile of the classic but is lighter with a contemporary feel.

To make the broth, combine the olive oil, onion, leek, carrot, and fennel in a large soup pot and place over low heat. Season with salt and pepper and sweat for 5 minutes.

Meanwhile, char the chiles. The best way to accomplish this is over an open flame on a gas stovetop. Place the chiles directly on the grate covering the burner and let the fire blacken the skin. When one side has blackened, use tongs to turn the chile and blacken another side. (This can also be done with a broiler, but be very careful not to overcook the chiles; they should still be somewhat firm.) Once the chiles are blackened all over (it's OK if a few green spots remain), place them in a paper bag or thick plastic bag, close the bag, and let them steam in their own heat for a few minutes. When the chiles are cool to the touch, remove them from the bag. Working over the sink, use your fingers or a damp paper towel to strip off the blackened skin. Try to avoid running the chiles under water, as the water will dilute the flavor. Once you have peeled them, slice open the chiles and cut out and discard the stems, seeds, and inner veins (if you prefer more heat, you can leave the veins intact). Cut the chiles into long strips, about 1 inch wide.

Add the chile strips and the tomatoes to the soup pot and season with salt. Raise the heat to medium and cook for 5 minutes, or until the tomatoes break down. Add the stock, raise the heat to high, and bring to a boil. Reduce the heat and simmer for 30 minutes. Strain the broth and return it to the cleaned pot.

For the Broth

1 teaspoon extra-virgin olive oil

1 medium white or yellow onion, diced

1 leek, white parts only, washed and sliced into thin half-moons

1 medium carrot, diced

1 medium bulb fennel, diced

Kosher salt and freshly ground black pepper

6 poblano chiles

10 medium plum tomatoes, diced

8 cups Chicken Stock (page 232) or Vegetable Stock (page 235)

For the Microwave "Fried" Cilantro

Grapeseed, canola, or other neutral oil

4 sprigs fresh cilantro

For the Poached Eggs

4 eggs

To make the microwave "fried" cilantro, wrap a dish in plastic wrap and brush the top with grapeseed oil. Arrange the cilantro sprigs on top of the plate. Microwave the cilantro at 800 watts for about 2 minutes, until it lies flat. The precise strength setting will depend on the total maximum wattage of your microwave oven; for me it was 6. Consult the instruction manual of your microwave as to how to adjust the wattage of your equipment. If you lost your original instruction manual, it is likely available online. (If you cannot find yours in either hard copy or online, it is fine to simply use fresh cilantro leaves instead.)

Return the broth to a simmer. Carefully break each of the eggs into the broth (do not break the yolks) and poach until the whites are just set, about 1½ minutes for each egg. Remove the eggs from the broth (they continue to cook off the heat) and, using a paring knife, trim the fly-away whites (unless, of course, you like the look of them).

Place a poached egg in the bottom of each soup bowl. Ladle some of the broth around each egg. Garnish by floating a piece of the "fried" cilantro in the soup.

CRAB
with Pickled Asparagus in Guajillo-Pork Broth

Serves 4 / GF

Pork and crab are among the most-used proteins in Baja cookery. Both are rich and deeply flavored but cry out for something to tie them together: the smokiness and mild spice of cascabel chiles—hollow round balls filled with seeds that rattle when shaken, giving the chile its name—is just what's needed in this soup. It is a simple dish to make—just remember to pickle the asparagus a day in advance.

The day before you plan to serve the soup, make the pickled asparagus. Combine the peppercorns, garlic, dill, and asparagus in a sterilized 1-pint canning jar. Combine the vinegar, water, salt, and sugar in a medium saucepan and bring to a boil over medium heat, stirring until the salt and sugar have dissolved. Carefully pour the hot vinegar mixture over the asparagus in the jar, filling the jar to ½ inch from the top. Let cool, then seal the jar and refrigerate for 24 hours.

To make the guajillo-pork broth, toast the chiles in a large sauté pan over medium heat until they just begin to develop dark marks, about 30 seconds. Flip the chiles and toast the other side. Transfer the chiles to a bowl with hot water to cover and soak for 10 minutes, or until they are tender and pliable. Transfer the chiles and their soaking liquid to a high-speed blender or food processor. Blend to a smooth puree.

Heat the oil in a medium Dutch oven over high heat until the oil ripples. Add the onion, celery, carrots, garlic, and tomatoes and season well with salt. Cook until the tomatoes just start to break down, then add the pork bones, pureed chiles, and 4 cups water. Bring to a boil over high heat, then reduce the heat to low and simmer for 4 hours. Pour the broth through a fine-mesh strainer into a large bowl, discarding the solids.

To cook the crabs, pour 2 gallons water into a large pot, add the salt, and bring to a boil. Add the crabs and cook for 18 to 20 minutes, depending on their size. The crabs are done when they turn orange and the meat flakes when tested with a fork. When the crabs are almost done, fill a large bowl with ice and water. Remove the crabs from the pot and move them to the ice bath to cool. Clean the crabs of their

For the Pickled Asparagus

½ teaspoon whole black peppercorns

1 clove garlic, cut in half lengthwise

2 sprigs dill

8 ounces asparagus (about 10 medium spears), trimmed and cut into ½-inch segments

1½ cups distilled white vinegar

2 cups water

2 tablespoons kosher salt

2 teaspoons granulated sugar

For the Guajillo-Pork Broth

3 guajillo chiles, stemmed, seeded, and cut into 1-inch pieces

2 cascabel chiles, stemmed, seeded, and cut into wedges

2 tablespoons grapeseed, canola, or other neutral oil

1 medium white or yellow onion, roughly chopped

2 ribs celery, roughly chopped

2 medium carrots, roughly chopped

RECIPE AND INGREDIENTS CONTINUE

meat, reserving the shells and innards (except the lungs) for another purpose. You should end up with about 12 ounces of crabmeat. Mix the crabmeat with the green onions and set aside.

Divide the crab mixture among 4 serving bowls and top with the pickled asparagus spears. Carefully ladle the strained broth into the bowls, taking care to disturb the crab as little as possible. Garnish with cilantro leaves.

Note: To roast the pork bones for the broth, preheat the oven to 350°F. Drizzle olive oil over the bones and arrange them in an even layer in a roasting pan. Transfer to the oven and roast, turning once or twice, until the bones begin to brown, about 15 minutes.

3 cloves garlic, peeled

2 medium plum tomatoes, cored and quartered

Kosher salt

2 pounds pork bones, roasted (see Note)

2 tablespoons apple cider vinegar

For the Crab

3 tablespoons kosher salt

6 blue crabs (about 2 pounds)

4 green onions, finely chopped

For the Garnish

4 to 8 attractive cilantro leaves

BAJA TORTILLA SOUP

Serves 6 / GF/ VEG

Tortilla soup is perhaps the most commonly available Mexican soup north of the border. Featuring crunchy baked or fried tortillas, the soup is traditionally made with chicken broth. For this Baja version, I replaced it with a vegetable-based stock and paired the soup with two of Baja California's most prominent crops: asparagus and tomato.

6 Corn Tortillas (page 228)

4 tablespoons extra-virgin olive oil

Kosher salt

1 large dried ancho chile, stemmed, seeded, and cut into 1-inch pieces

2 tablespoons grapeseed, canola, or other neutral oil

1 medium white onion, sliced ¼ inch thick

3 large cloves garlic, peeled

1 (15-ounce) can diced tomatoes (preferably fire-roasted), with their juices

8 cups Vegetable Stock (page 235) or Roasted Vegetable Stock (page 236)

6 to 8 medium asparagus spears, trimmed

1 large Hass avocado, cut into ¼-inch cubes

1½ cups (6 ounces) crumbled queso fresco (optional)

2 medium limes, cut into 3 wedges each

Preheat the oven to 400°F. Line a baking sheet with parchment paper.

Cut the tortillas into 1-inch squares, place in a large bowl, toss with 2 tablespoons of the olive oil, and season with salt. Arrange the tortilla squares on the prepared baking sheet, place in the oven, and bake until the squares are crisp, 10 to 12 minutes. Set the tortilla squares aside.

Heat a large sauté pan over medium heat. Toast the chile in the pan until it just begins to develop charring, about 30 seconds. Flip the chile and toast the other side. Transfer to a high-speed blender.

Heat the remaining 2 tablespoons oil in a medium saucepan over medium-high heat. Add the onion, garlic, and 1 teaspoon salt and cook, stirring frequently, until the vegetables are golden, about 7 minutes. Using a spatula or wooden spoon, scoop up the onion and garlic, pressing them against the side of the pan to leave behind as much oil as possible. Transfer the onion and garlic to the blender with the chile, then add the tomatoes. Starting on low speed and gradually increasing to high, blend to a smooth puree.

Increase the heat under the sauté pan to medium-high and heat until hot. Add the puree and cook, stirring constantly, until thickened to roughly the consistency of tomato paste, about 6 minutes. Add the stock to the pan, bring to a simmer, then reduce the heat to medium-low and simmer until the flavors come together, about 15 minutes. Taste and season with more salt if needed.

While the broth is simmering, fill a medium pot with water, add 1 tablespoon salt, and bring to a boil. Fill a large bowl with ice and water. Add the asparagus to the boiling water, cover the pot, and boil until it turns bright green and is crisp-tender, 3 to 4 minutes. Immediately transfer the asparagus to the ice bath to stop the cooking. When the asparagus is cool, place it on a plate with a double layer of paper towels and pat dry. Slice the asparagus into ½-inch segments.

Divide the tortilla squares among 6 serving bowls and top with the avocado. Arrange the asparagus segments around the tortilla squares. Ladle the broth into the bowls, sprinkle with the cheese, if desired, and serve immediately, with the lime wedges alongside for squeezing.

CILANTRO AND SPINACH SOUP

Serves 4 to 6 / GF

Cilantro is, famously, loved by some and abhorred by many. To some, cilantro offers a citrusy taste. To others, it tastes like soap or, perhaps even worse, dead bugs (I've always wondered how those who say the latter can identify that flavor!). It is not cilantro's fault. Rather, it is the fault of the genetics of the cilantro haters. They have a variation in a group of olfactory receptor genes that enables them to strongly perceive the soapy-flavored aldehydes in cilantro leaves.

As a child I was no fan of cilantro, but this classic Mexican cilantro soup changed my mind! Perhaps no herb more thoroughly says "Mexico" than cilantro. It speaks of freshness. And it was the fresh quality of the herb in this soup that converted me. The classic Mexican version includes dairy ingredients—Mexican crema or even cream cheese—but I wanted the freshness of the cilantro to shine, with only stock and spinach there to round out the flavors.

In a large soup pot, sweat the onion, leek, and carrot in the oil over low heat until just translucent, about 3 minutes. Add the chile, potato, and stock and bring to a boil over high heat. Reduce the heat to maintain a simmer and cook for 15 minutes. Add the cilantro and spinach to the broth and simmer for another 5 minutes.

Working in batches, carefully pour the soup into a high-speed blender or food processor and blend until thoroughly pureed. Taste the soup and adjust the seasoning with salt or a squeeze of lime juice, if needed.

Ladle the soup into bowls. Garnish each with a dollop of crema and top with a cilantro leaf.

1 medium white or yellow onion, chopped

1 large leek, white parts only, washed, quartered lengthwise, and thinly sliced

1 medium carrot, chopped

2 tablespoons grapeseed, canola, or other neutral oil

1 large poblano chile, roasted, peeled, and seeded (see page 33)

1 medium russet potato, peeled and quartered

8 cups Chicken Stock (page 232) or Roasted Vegetable Stock (page 236)

2 cups fresh cilantro leaves and finely chopped stems, plus 4 to 6 attractive leaves for garnish

½ cup spinach leaves

Kosher salt (optional)

Fresh lime juice (optional)

Fresh Mexican crema

CALIFORNIOS-STYLE CANTALOUPE AGUACHILE

Serves 4

Chef Val Cantu of Californios in San Francisco has earned and kept two Michelin stars. That makes him the most Michelin-honored Mexican chef in the world. One of Cantu's signature dishes is his elegant take on aguachile using watermelon juice in the aguachile liquid. From October to June, it's cantaloupe season in Baja, but if you get the urge to make this dish in the summer, by all means use watermelon as Cantu does.

Combine the cantaloupe juice, lime juice, soy sauce, and agave syrup in a large bowl and whisk to combine thoroughly. Line a strainer with a coffee filter and set it over another large bowl. Pour the liquid into the coffee filter, then place in the refrigerator and allow to strain for about 2 hours. Remove the strainer and coffee filter, add the quartered jalapeño to the strained liquid, and steep in the refrigerator for 1 hour.

Just before serving, cut the fish into ⅛- to ¼-inch-thick slices and arrange on a serving plate with the sliced jalapeño and the basil. Pour over enough of the chilled aguachile liquid to just cover the fish. Sprinkle with salt and a couple of drops of olive oil and serve immediately.

1¼ cups cantaloupe juice

½ cup fresh lime juice

⅓ cup white soy sauce (shiro shoyu)

1 tablespoon agave syrup

2 medium jalapeño chiles: 1 stemmed and quartered, 1 stemmed, seeded, and thinly sliced

4 micro basil leaves

1 pound sashimi-grade tuna

Maldon salt

Extra-virgin olive oil

VAL CANTU AND CALIFORNIOS

I did not grow up thinking of Mexican food as fine dining or upscale any more than I thought of Jewish cuisine in those terms. Delicious? Yes. Often—perhaps more often than not—it was what was for dinner. But even as a child I sensed Mexican food was somehow not generally regarded as fancy.

While my family would go to Tijuana rather frequently, it was, both culinarily and in many other ways, a very different place then than it is today. There was good food in Tijuana at the time, but not in that sort of way. There was no real sense of a Baja cuisine. The Valle de Guadalupe as a food and wine destination was decades in the future.

It was not until a trip to Mexico City that I first had a chance to see Mexican cuisine in a different light. Fast-forward a few decades, and today Mexico City's Pujol and Quintonil are ranked among the top ten restaurants on the planet, according to The World's 50 Best. The food may or may not be much better now than it was when I was a child, but such a thing would have seemed unthinkable at the time.

And the idea of fine-dining Mexican cuisine in the US was, plainly, nonexistent when I was a child. It is a different story today. Taco María in Costa Mesa has a Michelin star. And the Mexican restaurant with the most Michelin stars in the world is in San Francisco: Val Cantu's Californios with its two Michelin stars.

Of course, one can and perhaps should acknowledge that the only reason Pujol and Quintonil (and arguably Maximo Bistrot and others) do not have more stars is because Michelin ignores the entire nation of Mexico, except, perhaps, for selling tires. But that doesn't take anything away from Cantu and Californios. The food is everything my perception of Mexican food growing up was not: precise flavors, carefully and artfully presented in ways that challenge the diner to think creatively, even poetically about Mexican cuisine.

SHRIMP AND BLOOD ORANGE AGUACHILE

Serves 6 to 8

Aguachiles are ubiquitous on Baja's Pacific coast. Superficially similar to the more well-known ceviche, aguachile classically features raw seafood, most often shrimp, in a spicy, acidic, and utterly delicious sauce. Hence the name *aguachile*, which translates as "chile water." The critical difference is that ceviches are chemically "cooked" in their acidic sauce, whereas the seafood in aguachiles does not spend enough time in the sauce to cook. This makes an enormous and delicious difference in the end result.

This particular dish is my take on one I helped Chad White plate for a dinner in Rosarito, south of Tijuana. His first James Beard Award nomination, coming half a decade after his run on *Top Chef*, showed the world that Cali-Baja cuisine thrives outside both California and Baja. White's Zona Blanca carries on the type of food he cooked at his restaurants in San Diego: simple Baja cuisine elevated to another level through the use of imagination and technique.

While most aguachiles are made with raw shrimp or fish, not all are! Indeed, the original aguachiles of Sinaloa were made with beef machaca (think beef jerky). It is the sauce, not the protein, that defines a dish as an aguachile.

Rinse the shrimp and dry them thoroughly. Transfer the shrimp to a food processor and process until smooth. Add the egg white, process again until very smooth, then cover the food processor bowl and refrigerate for 30 minutes.

Combine the egg, Marmite, MSG, and fish sauce in a bowl and whisk to combine. Cover and refrigerate the mixture for at least 30 minutes.

Preheat the oven to 350°F. Bring a large pot of water to a simmer and bring a separate small pot of water to a boil. Line a terrine mold with plastic wrap (wet the mold so that the wrap sticks better).

Fill the lined terrine mold with the shrimp. Fold the plastic wrap over the shrimp and cover with a lid or foil. Set the terrine mold in a roasting pan and pour the simmering water into the pan so that it comes three-quarters of the way up the sides. Put the roasting pan in the oven and cook until the terrine reaches an interior temperature

Special Equipment

terrine mold (approximately 8¼ x 5½ x 3½ inches)

blowtorch

For the Shrimp

1 pound shrimp, peeled and deveined

1 large egg white

1 large egg

1 tablespoon Marmite (or Vegemite or soy sauce)

½ teaspoon MSG

1 teaspoon fish sauce

For the Aguachile

Juice of 3 blood oranges

Juice of 4 key limes, or 2 large ripe Persian limes

1 or 2 serrano chiles, stemmed, seeded, and roughly chopped

2 cloves garlic, crushed

Kosher salt

For the Garnish

3 Persian cucumbers, thinly sliced

3 radishes, thinly sliced

6 to 8 attractive cilantro leaves

12 to 16 strips Pink Pickled Onions (page 259)

Sea salt

Extra-virgin olive oil

of 135° to 140°F. Remove the terrine from the oven and then from the terrine mold. Refrigerate for at least 30 minutes to cool.

To make the aguachile, combine the blood orange juice and lime juice with half of one of the chiles (you can always add more, and probably should) and the garlic in a high-speed blender or food processor, season with salt, and blend to a smooth puree. Taste the aguachile sauce, testing for seasoning as well as heat and sweet-acid balance. Adjust the flavors according to your taste and heat tolerance.

When the terrine is cool, cut it into even cubes. Using a culinary blowtorch, sear the top surface of all the pieces (or sear in a hot sauté pan). While this step is optional, it improves the flavor, texture, and appearance of the finished product.

Pour enough of the aguachile into each bowl to just cover the bottom. Place a cube of terrine in each of the bowls. Arrange slices of cucumber and radish along with a leaf of cilantro and 2 strips of pickled onion attractively around and over each piece of terrine. Sprinkle salt on the terrine cubes and drizzle or pour dots of olive oil around the cubes.

Note: If blood oranges are out of season, use navel oranges (or whatever orange variety is available) and add about 1 teaspoon grenadine to adjust the color.

JAVIER PLASCENCIA'S TUNA AND CARROT AGUACHILE

Serves 4 / GF

Javier Plascencia is quite likely the highest-profile Baja California chef and the standard-bearer for Cali-Baja cuisine. His Misión 19 restaurant in Tijuana's Zona Gastronómica (since sold) opened the eyes of many to the new cuisine of Baja California. Plascencia's Bracero Cocina de Raíz gave San Diego a taste of what was happening in Tijuana without the need to drive south. Others, including Roberto Alcocer at Valle Restaurant in Oceanside, have continued carrying that torch.

One of the best and most creative dishes at Plascencia's Bracero was his decidedly upscale take on a classic Baja aguachile. Instead of shrimp in a nearly raw state, Plascencia married raw tuna and sea scallops with carrot in two different ways to create a bright and memorable starter.

Combine the carrot juice and chile in a high-speed blender or food processor and blend until smooth. Strain the resulting liquid through a fine-mesh strainer into a medium bowl.

Mix the lemon juice and lime juice into the bowl with the carrot juice. Toss the red onion, cucumber, and salt in the juice mixture. Add the tuna and scallops to the bowl and mix together gently.

Transfer to a serving dish. Garnish with the green onions, cashews, carrot slices, roe, and fennel fronds and flowers, if desired.

Ingredients:

4 cups carrot juice

2 ghost chiles or habanero chiles, stemmed

Juice of 4 large lemons

Juice of 4 key limes

1 medium red onion, julienned (about 40 slices)

2 medium Persian cucumbers, sliced

¼ cup kosher salt

8 ounces ahi tuna

8 ounces dry-packed sea scallops

8 green onions, chopped

¾ cup cashews, toasted and crushed

8 slices carrot (sliced lengthwise on a mandoline)

1 teaspoon salmon roe

Fennel fronds and flowers for garnish (optional)

JAVIER PLASCENCIA AND TIJUANA'S ZONA GASTRONÓMICA

It is difficult to overstate the importance of Javier Plascencia on where the cuisine of Baja is today. No, Plascencia did not invent the cuisine by himself. He does not own a trademark on it. A case could be made that he is not its greatest practitioner.

But there is absolutely no argument that the cuisine of Baja would not be what it is today had Plascencia not opened Misión 19 in Tijuana. It was groundbreaking. It was the right restaurant at the right time, and it caught the world's attention.

And the food! I wrote, at the time, "The best restaurant in our region may not be in San Diego . . . it may not even be in this country." Its food embraced not only Mexico, not only the Mediterranean influences that Baja had begun to recognize, but Middle Eastern and Far Eastern influences as well. From the labne in Misión 19's parfait to the use of soy and other Asian ingredients, Plascencia sought to incorporate the manifold diverse influences that make up the fabric of life in Northern Baja.

More important, however, the world began taking notice of Baja cuisine and, more specifically, of Plascencia, its unlikely ambassador. There is a shyness about Plascencia that belies his public face. But his personal warmth and generosity are what the world—in the form of the *New York Times* and other major media outlets—seems to have recognized in nominating him as the face of this then-new culinary phenomenon.

The impact on Tijuana has been significant. The city, once again, is a food and beverage destination. As Anthony Bourdain observed in his Baja episode of *No Reservations*, Plascencia and Misión 19 were at the vanguard of Tijuana reframing its tourist industry from American-focused to Mexican-focused. Instead of depending on attracting dollars from the north, Baja began concentrating on internal tourism, in particular from crime-ravaged parts of Mexico's mainland. In doing so, it helped a new Tijuana emerge.

DREW DECKMAN'S KUMIAI OYSTERS
with Pink Peppercorn Mignonette

Serves 4 / GF

One of the great joys of living in Northern Baja is the festival season that runs roughly from spring through fall. Two of the most popular are Vendimia (a tribute to the grape harvest in the Valle de Guadalupe and surrounding valleys) in late July and August and the Baja Culinary Fest in Tijuana in October. My favorite, though, is the celebration that kicks off the season: the Festival de las Conchas y el Vino Nuevo (festival of shellfish and new wines) in Ensenada in the spring.

While the festival is different every year, one can only hope Drew Deckman, chef-owner of the eponymous Valle de Guadalupe restaurant, is shucking oysters and serving them with his take on a classic mignonette. I remember once asking him how many oysters he'd shucked in his life. He favored me with a dirty look and just a hint of a wry smile and said something along the lines of: "I lost count last year." His shucking technique, reflected in this recipe, is (needless to say) impeccable.

Special Equipment
oyster knife

1 medium shallot, minced

½ cup red wine vinegar

1 teaspoon ground pink peppercorns

Coarse salt for serving

12 Kumiai (or other) oysters

Extra-virgin olive oil

Borage flowers for garnish

Combine the shallot, vinegar, and pink peppercorns in a bowl and mix to combine. Let the mignonette stand for at least 10 minutes or up to overnight. This will not slow you down because unless you are an expert already, it will take you longer than that to shuck all the oysters.

Coat the bottom of 4 small plates with coarse salt.

Just before serving (and not a moment sooner), shuck the oysters using an oyster knife. Start by setting an oyster belly-side down on a folded towel with its hinge facing toward the hand with the knife. Fold the towel, leaving the hinge exposed. Place your non-knife hand on top of the oyster (covered by some towel) to hold it steady. Patiently work the oyster knife into the hinge, but do not force it. Find the sweet spot where the knife can gain penetration without forcing it.

Once you do, wiggle the knife in and around until you feel like you can exert some pressure against both the top and bottom shells at once by twisting and prying the knife. Work the knife up and down while twisting and rotating it until you feel (more than hear) a slight "pop" as the oyster gives up the ghost. Once the hinge pops, twist the knife so that the broad flat of the blade pries the shells apart even more. Pry the shells open and sever the muscle that connects to both the top and bottom shells by sliding the blade across the oyster starting from the hinge end and keeping the blade flat the entire way. When you get about two-thirds of the way around the oyster, you'll feel the muscle. Cut it. When you do, you should be able to pull off the top shell. Discard the top shell and inspect the oyster by looking at it and smelling it. Discard the oyster if it does not smell fresh. Remove any bits of shell. Free the oyster from the bottom shell by sliding the knife under the oyster, severing the muscle connecting it to the bottom shell. Push the oyster around to make sure it is totally free in the shell. Repeat with the remaining oysters.

Arrange 3 oysters sitting freely in their bottom shells on the salt on each plate. Pour a teaspoon of the mignonette sauce on each oyster along with a drop of olive oil. Garnish each oyster with a borage flower.

SEARED CALLO DE HACHA
with Avocado Crema and Salsa Negra

Serves 4 / GF

It looks like a scallop. It's shaped like a scallop. It has the texture of a scallop, tastes like one, and eats like one. But the callo de hacha is, in fact, a different kind of mollusk that grows in a shell that looks like a fan. It is also one of Baja California's (and Sinaloa's) signature ingredients.

Unfortunately, the callo de hacha is not easy to obtain outside Mexico. But since it is so similar to the scallop, almost any dish made with the fan-shaped pen shell mollusks can be made with their more readily available cousins. Raw (or acid-cooked) dishes like aguachiles, carpaccios, tiraditos, and ceviches are common. But the callo de hacha, like the scallop, takes well to cooked preparations. Here it is given classic Baja treatment: quickly seared and then paired with avocado and a dark, brooding sauce with its twin punches of acid and sweetness.

2 tablespoons grapeseed, canola, or other neutral oil

12 large callos de hacha or sea scallops

Kosher salt and freshly ground black pepper

Avocado Crema (page 254)

Carlos Salgado's Salsa Negra (page 243)

Microwave "Fried" Cilantro (see page 60)

Heat the oil in a large sauté pan over medium-high heat until the oil ripples. Meanwhile, season the callos de hacha with salt and pepper. When the oil comes to temperature, sear the callos until caramelized on the bottom, 1½ to 2 minutes. How long it will take depends on the properties (in particular the water content) of the individual scallops. Flip once and sear on the other side until just barely cooked through.

Swipe some avocado crema on each plate and top each with 3 scallops. Spoon some of the salsa negra on top of each scallop and garnish with "fried" cilantro.

GEODUCK GREEN CEVICHE
with Watermelon Radishes

Serves 4 / GF

This ceviche is a riotous combination of textures, colors, and flavors built around the largest burrowing clam in the world. And yet it is entirely possible that anyone who sees that clam prior to the preparation of the dish will focus on the fact that it looks a lot like a massive phallus. What they ought to focus on instead is the geoduck's flavors and various textures, depending on which parts of the siphon the meat comes from. If you enjoy sushi or sashimi, you may have tasted geoduck: it is called mirugai in Japanese. As mirugai sushi and sashimi demonstrate, geoduck shines in raw preparations, so ceviche is a natural choice. As good as this ceviche is on its own, it would also make an excellent topping for a tostada.

1 geoduck clam (1 to 2 pounds)

1 medium tomatillo, husked, rinsed, and quartered

½ cup fresh lime juice

Handful fresh cilantro leaves and tender stems

4 cloves garlic, minced

4 green onions, chopped

2 serrano chiles, stemmed, seeded, ribs removed and finely chopped

Kosher salt

3 watermelon radishes, julienned

2 medium Persian cucumbers, cubed

8 cherry or grape tomatoes, quartered

Attractive cilantro leaves for garnish

Bring a pot of water large enough to accommodate the geoduck to a boil. Fill a large bowl with ice and water. Submerge the geoduck in the boiling water for about 30 seconds to blister and loosen the tough outer skin. Transfer the geoduck to the ice bath to stop the cooking.

To clean the geoduck, start by slicing along the shell on one side. Pry open the shell and pull all the meat out. Discard the shell and pull the tough skin away from the geoduck's siphon (the phallic portion sticking out of the shell). Cut the breast of the geoduck away from the siphon, reserving the breast. Trim the end of the siphon until the edge is clean. Cut the thick base meat away from the narrower tip of the siphon. Slice the tip open lengthwise and rinse out any sand or pebbles. Rinse the breast to remove sand.

Chop the geoduck meat into ½-inch dice.

Put the tomatillo, lime juice, cilantro, garlic, green onions, and chiles in a high-speed blender or food processor and blend to a smooth puree. Pour the puree over the geoduck meat in the bowl. Cover and refrigerate for at least 1 hour or up to overnight.

Divide the geoduck ceviche into 4 bowls. Arrange the julienned radish, cucumber cubes, and tomato quarters on top of the ceviche. Garnish with cilantro leaves.

Note: Look for tomatillos with a husk that covers the fruit tightly and with no signs of tearing. It's OK if a bit of the tomatillo peeks out from the bottom. The fruit inside should be firm but not rock-hard.

MARISCOS

There are nearly seven thousand miles of coastline in Mexico, depending on how you count them. More than forty-five hundred miles of that coastline face the Pacific Ocean. More than two thousand of those miles are the Baja California peninsula alone. Not surprisingly, then, both Baja California and Baja California Sur are well-known as fishing destinations. What is surprising, perhaps, is that the fruits of those seas don't readily come to mind when many of us think of Mexican cuisine. Indeed, the most famous Mexican mariscos dish—ceviche—is almost surely not even Mexican but rather Peruvian or Ecuadorean (or both) in origin.

But mariscos are a critical, indeed, profoundly characteristic, part of Baja cuisine. From street carts to food trucks, beachside stalls and shacks to high-end restaurants, seafood tends to be the star. At the most basic level, the Spanish word *mariscos* translates to English as "seafood." A bit more specifically, the word *mariscos* is generally understood to refer to any edible marine invertebrate intended for food consumption, especially crustaceans and mollusks. But, of course, the menus at mariscos food trucks, carts, and stands as well as brick-and-mortar restaurants—on both sides of the border—will often include Ensenada-style fish tacos as well as finfish ceviches. It is crustaceans and mollusks, however, that are at the core of the Mexican seafood menu.

Raw fish dishes in particular are ubiquitous in Baja. It is these dishes, perhaps more than any others, that capture the essence of Cali-Baja food, whether beachside, streetside, or in the temples of gastronomy.

BAJA-STYLE MUSSELS

Serves 4

Mussels are plentiful along Baja's Pacific coastline, seemingly growing out of every crack in every rock to which they can conceivably cling. They're offered at roadside choros stands lining the free road south of Rosarito Beach and were among the first themes Cali-Baja chefs turned their attention to, highlighting the parallels between the climates and bounties of Northern Baja and Mediterranean Europe. It was one of the original inspirations for the term "Baja Med."

    This version highlights another Baja influence, and another parallel: Asia. In particular, this variation highlights the Asian influences on Baja's cuisine and culture and the similarities to some of the flavors of Southeast Asia, in particular Thailand.

Using a stiff brush, scrub the mussels under cold running water. Tap on the mussels and see if they close. If they don't, discard them. You do not want to eat them. Just before cooking the mussels, remove the hairy, wiry "beards" by either pulling them out of the shell with your hands or cutting them close to the shell.

    Melt the butter in a large straight-sided sauté pan or shallow pot over low heat. Increase the heat to medium, add the garlic, shallots, and tomato, and simmer until the garlic and shallots are fragrant and just starting to brown, 2 to 3 minutes. Add the stock, wine, fish sauce, lemongrass, and ginger and bring to a boil over high heat. Reduce the heat to medium-low and simmer for 15 minutes, or until reduced by half.

    Raise the heat to medium-high and add the jalapeño and Fresno chiles and the mussels. Cover and simmer until the mussels open, 2 to 3 minutes. Divide the mussels among 4 bowls, discarding any that haven't opened. Garnish with the cilantro leaves, lime wedges, and hot sauce and serve with toasted bolillos, if desired.

1 pound fresh mussels (either black or New Zealand green-lipped)

2 tablespoons salted butter

6 cloves garlic, minced

2 medium shallots, finely chopped

1 medium plum tomato, diced

½ cup Chicken Stock (page 232)

½ cup dry white wine, such as Lechuza Vineyard unoaked chardonnay

2 tablespoons fish sauce

1 stalk lemongrass, white section only, trimmed, cut into 2-inch pieces, and lightly smashed

1 (1-inch) knob fresh ginger, cut into ⅛-inch-thick slices

1 medium jalapeño chile, stemmed, seeded, and finely chopped

2 Fresno chiles, stemmed, seeded, and finely chopped

For Garnish

½ cup fresh cilantro leaves

Lime wedges

Chiltepin Hot Sauce (page 247)

Bolillos (Mexican rolls), split and toasted (optional)

TACOS

MAKO SHARK TEMPURA TACOS

This take on the fish taco would likely be recognizable to anyone who has had a Rubio's taco or enjoyed a taco at any of the many excellent stands and carts on the streets of Ensenada. But this version hearkens back to one of the fish taco's apocryphal origin myths: the idea that it's directly derived from Japanese tempura. It is, basically, an Ensenada fish taco with tempura batter substituted for the beer batter.

Fish tacos can be made using just about any fish. Angelito is common in Ensenada, but the best fish tacos in town seem to be made from mako shark. It is about as meaty and savory as fish gets, and the classic seasoned beer batter brings out its inherent sweetness. This tempura batter will do that too, but it also gives the fish an addictive lightness.

To make the tempura batter, sift the flour into a small bowl once or twice to remove any clumps and to make it light and soft. In a medium bowl, gently beat the egg until the yolk and white are just barely incorporated. Add the ice water, then add the sifted flour and lightly work in the flour using chopsticks. Be careful not to overmix the batter.

To fry the fish, pour enough oil into a heavy skillet to fill it to a depth of 1½ inches. Heat the oil to 370°F. While the oil is heating, cut the fish into pieces about 3 inches long and ½ inch wide. Using tongs, pick up a piece of fish, dip it completely into the batter, then lay it in the hot oil. Repeat with a few more pieces of fish, taking care not to overcrowd the pan. Fry, turning the pieces regularly, until golden and crisp, about 4 minutes. Drain on paper towels and keep warm in a low oven on a wire rack set over a sheet pan while you fry the rest of the fish.

To make the white sauce, put all the ingredients in a medium bowl and whisk to combine. Cover and refrigerate until ready to serve.

Assemble the tacos by laying 2 pieces of the fish on each tortilla. Top with a sprinkling of shredded cabbage, some pickled onions, and salsa and drizzle each taco with 2 tablespoons of the white sauce. Pass the hot sauce for the brave and serve with lime wedges.

For the Tempura Batter

1 cup all-purpose flour

1 large egg

1 cup ice water

¼ teaspoon kosher salt

For the Fish

Grapeseed, canola, or other neutral oil for frying

1 pound mako shark fillet, or other shark or firm fish like halibut

For the White Sauce

½ cup sour cream

½ cup Mayonnaise (page 255)

1 tablespoon fresh lime juice

¼ teaspoon ground cumin

¼ teaspoon garlic powder

Kosher salt

For Serving

10 Corn Tortillas (page 228), street taco size, warmed

¼ medium head green cabbage, cored and finely shredded

Pink Pickled Onions (page 259)

Salsa Bandera (page 242)

Chiltepin Hot Sauce (page 247)

Lime wedges

RALPH RUBIO AND THE FISH TACO

It's settled: Fish tacos neither originated in San Diego nor emerged from Ralph Rubio's head like Athena from that of Zeus. Nor is it likely that what we think of today as the prototypical fish taco originated in San Felipe where Rubio found them on a 1974 spring break trip. In fact, even the idea that the "original" fish taco was the one Rubio riffed on seems unlikely.

The more likely origin story is placed in the Port of Ensenada and dates back to the 1920s, when Japanese fishermen supposedly brought tempura with them to the Northern Baja coast. Japanese fishing boats tied up at the port and local food vendors supposedly tried, mostly unsuccessfully, to sell to those fishermen. One eventually got the idea of frying the fish in the kind of batter the Japanese were using for their tempura. Add a tortilla, and those Japanese fishermen were being handed pretty much the same stuff handed to every Ensenada fish taco customer today.

But as Matthew Jaffe wrote in *Sunset Magazine* years ago, "People have been eating fish tacos in the coastal areas of Mexico for . . . thousands of years [since] indigenous North American peoples first wrapped the plentiful offshore catch into stone-ground-corn tortillas." The fish in those original fish tacos was not fried in tempura batter; in fact, it was not fried at all.

Today, when you hear the term *fish taco*, one thing comes to mind: fried beer-battered white fish (or shark) with white sauce, salsa, and shredded cabbage on a corn tortilla. Think Rubio's or innumerable superior versions in every hamlet, town, or metropolis of Northern Baja California (and some north of the border). Ralph Rubio would be the first to tell you he didn't invent the fish taco. But the fish tacos he found and brought to the masses have become nearly synonymous with the term.

ORIGINAL HOME OF RUBIO'S FISH TACOS

Rubio's®

SUMMER SUN
SURF AND
FISH TACOS!

Rubio's
FRESH MEXICAN GRILL

TUESDAY
SPECIALS

GROUND YELLOWTAIL TACOS

Makes 8 tacos / GF

While fish tacos are indelibly associated with Ensenada-style fried fish tacos and their Southern California manifestations, it is highly unlikely that the first fish tacos featured battered fish. Were the fish wrapped in those long-ago corn tortillas grilled by Indigenous folk? Or were they grilled up on a plancha?

San Diego fishmonger Tommy Gomes (star of the Outdoor Channel television series *The Fishmonger*) once told me that he regularly found something similar fishing off Baja in the 1970s. When a Pacific storm came in, their commercial vessel would tie up with the crew, taking shelter in one of the many shanty shacks dug into the sand up and down the coast for just such purposes. Each was stocked with canned goods, cabbage, and tortillas. They would chop the fish and cook them on the firepit or stove, pop them on the tortillas with shredded cabbage and bottled Herdez salsa, and thus make it to the end of the storm.

Heat the oil in a large sauté pan over high heat. Add the ground fish and season with salt. Cook the fish until the raw pinkish color is almost gone. Add the onion, celery, and carrot, reduce the heat to medium, and cook until the onion is translucent, about 2 minutes. Add the jalapeño and Fresno chiles and season with the ancho and guajillo chile powders, onion powder, garlic powder, and 1 teaspoon salt. Cook until the vegetables have given up their water and the seasoning is incorporated.

To assemble the tacos, lay 2 tablespoons of the fish mixture on each tortilla, top with a tablespoon of the salsa and a sprinkling of cabbage, and drizzle with hot sauce.

Notes: To grind the fish, cut it into ½-inch cubes and pass the cubes through a meat grinder (or the meat grinder attachment for a stand mixer), or (more challenging) mince the fish using a sharp chef's knife. Or ask your fishmonger to grind the fish for you.

Ancho and guajillo chile powders can be found at most Mexican markets. Of the two, guajillo chile powder can be a bit harder to source. Feel free to substitute California chile powder for the guajillo.

2 tablespoons grapeseed, canola, or other neutral oil

1 pound ground Mexican yellowtail (or pretty much any fish or mix of fish you have on hand; see Note)

Kosher salt

1 medium white onion, finely chopped

1 medium rib celery, finely diced

1 medium carrot, finely diced

1 medium plum tomato, seeded and diced

1 medium jalapeño chile, stemmed, seeded, and diced

1 Fresno chile, stemmed, seeded, and diced

1 teaspoon ancho chile powder (see Notes)

1 teaspoon guajillo chile powder (see Notes)

1 teaspoon onion powder

1 teaspoon garlic powder

8 Corn Tortillas (page 228), warmed

For the Garnish

½ cup Salsa Bandera (page 242)

¼ medium head green cabbage, finely shredded

Chiltepin Hot Sauce (page 247)

TACOS 95

BRAISED OXTAIL AND GUAJILLO GUISADO

Serves 4 to 6 / GF

One part of Mexican culture that first captivated me has begun to fade away: bullfighting. I would later that the first bullfight I saw featured the greatest matadors of successive generations: Luis Miguel Domínguín, El Cordobés, and Eloy Cavazos.

Near almost every bullfighting arena, there is a restaurant that features rabo de toro, a braised bull tail dish. The tails in question are traditionally those of the bulls from the ring.

There is far less bullfighting in Tijuana than there was when I was a child, and I couldn't tell you the name of a Tijuana restaurant today featuring rabo de toro. But combined with guajillo chiles, boned, and offered in a warm corn tortilla with traditional accompaniments, this dish makes for a wonderful taco guisado.

Trim off any excess fat from the oxtails. Combine the trimmed oxtails, 2 of the garlic cloves, 1 quarter of the onion, and 6 cups water in a large Dutch oven. Bring to a boil over medium-high heat and season with salt and pepper. Reduce the heat to medium-low and cook, covered, until the beef is tender, about 4 hours. Using tongs, move the oxtails to a bowl and refrigerate to cool. Strain the cooking liquid into a separate bowl and discard the solids. Set the cooking liquid aside.

Meanwhile, toast the guajillo chiles in a large sauté pan over medium heat until they just begin to develop dark marks, about 30 seconds. Flip the chiles and toast the other side. Place the chiles in a bowl with hot water to cover and soak for 30 minutes, or until pliable. Transfer the chiles and their soaking liquid to a high-speed blender or food processor with the remaining garlic, onion, and the tomato. Blend to a smooth puree.

Once the oxtails are cool enough to handle, strip the meat off the bone by digging your fingers into the meaty sections.

Heat the oil in a large saucepan over medium-high heat. Add the chile puree and cook, stirring constantly, until slightly reduced, about 8 minutes. Stir in 2 cups of the oxtail cooking liquid, then return the oxtail meat to the pot and bring to a boil. Reduce the heat to medium-low and cook, stirring occasionally, until the cooking liquid and chile puree take on a beefy flavor, about 20 minutes. Season with salt and pepper and serve either as a stand-alone dish with Mexican Rice (page 237) and lime wedges or as the filling for a taco guisado.

Ingredients

1½ pounds beef oxtail segments (four or five 2-inch segments)

6 cloves garlic, peeled

1 small white onion, quartered

Kosher salt and freshly ground black pepper

4 guajillo chiles, stemmed, seeded, and cut into 1-inch pieces

1 large or 2 small plum tomatoes, cored and quartered

2 tablespoons grapeseed, canola, or other neutral oil

TACOS DE GUISADOS

The word *taco* dates back to Mexico's silver mines in the eighteenth century. The term analogizes corn tortillas wrapped around a protein to the little pieces of paper-wrapped gunpowder miners used to excavate ore. Tacos themselves go back further, though. Anthropological evidence shows that Mesoamerican Indians in the valley now occupied by Mexico City ate tortillas filled with small lake fish.

Not so long ago, many Americans thought tacos were hard preformed shells filled with ground beef, Day-Glo "cheese," diced tomatoes, iceberg lettuce, and an utterly impotent "taco sauce." Then, somewhere in the last decade, some folks got the bright idea of taking tacos upscale. And while those creating (if not slinging) those tacos may have had fine-dining training and credentials, something of the soul of a taco was lost when $6 apiece became the starting price. Next came Food Network, Bourdain, Rick Bayless, and a relentless, if somewhat philosophically futile, search for something called "authenticity."

Whether in Baja or San Diego, tacos rarely get more "authentic" (a word I despise because it obscures more than it explains) or truer to the soul of a taco than guisados. Often described as "grandmother food," guisados go back to the stewed and sometimes grilled fare mothers and grandmothers traditionally made at home. They can be offered in the form of tacos, tortas (sandwiches), or burritos, but are always warm and comforting.

Prior to the COVID-19 pandemic, our town south of Rosarito in Northern Baja was home to a nearly prototypical tacos guisados stand called Tacos Varios Mar y Tierra (many such stands have some variation on the "Tacos Varios" name). Whether there or at Corazón de Torta (co-owned by Antonio Ley, Anthony Bourdain's "fixer" for the Baja episode of *No Reservations*), the menus at these restaurants are often similar. The beef barbacoa guisado at Tacos Varios was quite similar to the beef short ribs with guajillo chiles from Corazón de Torta. And that is not all that different from the oxtail taco at Wes Avila's Guerilla Tacos in Los Angeles.

Nearly any dish could be the star of a taco guisado along with accompaniments like shredded cabbage, finely chopped onions, chopped cilantro (both leaves and tender stems), and your choice of various salsas, like Salsa Bandera (page 242), Árbol Chile Salsa (page 243), Baja-Style Salsa Roja (page 244), or Salsa Taquera (page 246). Among the dishes that could play the filling role are the oxtails from Braised Oxtail and Guajillo Guisado (page 96), the lentils from Lentil Guisado with Marinated Mushroom Chips (page 162), or the Pork Stew in Salsa Verde (page 101). In fact, there are elements of most dishes in this book that could deliciously do that trick.

Guisados are a warm hug in culinary form. It's the food your mother would have made if she was Mexican and the stuff you probably grew up with if she was.

PORK STEW IN SALSA VERDE

Serves 4 to 6

Before the COVID-19 pandemic, the low-key crown jewel of the town near our house in Baja was a little guisados stand called Tacos Varios Mar y Tierra. Without a doubt my favorite taco there was the pork in salsa verde. The pork was simple and direct, but the acidity lent by the tomatillos made it the star of a perfectly balanced taco.

Still, it would be months before my wife turned to me one Saturday afternoon as I was eating the taco and asked: "Why don't you go home and re-create it yourself?" I looked at her, wondering why I hadn't thought of doing so. This recipe was the result.

Stir the flour, salt, pepper, and cumin together in a large bowl. Place the cubed pork in the mixture and stir well to coat the meat.

Heat the olive oil in a Dutch oven over medium-high heat until the oil shimmers. Working in batches, place the pork in the pot in a single layer and sear until browned on all sides, about 15 minutes. Transfer the pork to a bowl and cover to keep warm.

Reduce the heat to medium, add the onion and more olive oil, if needed, and cook until the onion is translucent and just beginning to brown around the edges, about 7 minutes. Return the meat to the pot and stir in the garlic, tomatillos, poblano and jalapeño chiles, oregano, chopped cilantro, and lager. Check the seasoning and add more salt if needed. Cover and simmer over low heat, stirring occasionally, until the meat is tender, about 1 hour. Skim excess fat off the stew, then spoon into bowls and garnish with the crema and a cilantro sprig. Alternatively, serve as the filling for a taco guisado.

½ cup all-purpose flour

1 teaspoon kosher salt, plus more if needed

1 tablespoon freshly ground black pepper

½ teaspoon ground cumin

3 pounds boneless pork shoulder roast, trimmed of excess fat and cut into 1-inch cubes

2 tablespoons extra-virgin olive oil, plus more if needed

1 large white onion, chopped

3 cloves garlic, minced

2 cups chopped fresh tomatillos

1 poblano chile, roasted (see page 33), peeled, and chopped

2 medium jalapeño chiles, stemmed, seeded, and chopped

2 teaspoons dried Mexican oregano

½ cup chopped fresh cilantro, plus 4 to 6 sprigs for garnish

1 cup Mexican lager, such as Tecate

2 tablespoons Mexican Crema (page 255)

ROY CHOI-STYLE KOREAN SHORT RIB TACOS

Serves 6

Korean and Mexican cuisines might not, at first blush, seem like kissing cousins. Roy Choi and his Kogi BBQ food truck proved otherwise. Lines extending around the block from his fleet of food trucks showed the marriage of Korean and Mexican flavors was a happy and counterintuitively natural one. It was also one that Choi recognized growing up in Los Angeles where the Koreatown and Mexican neighborhoods are right next door to each other.

While Choi may best be remembered for kicking off the gourmet food truck craze, it is ultimately his fusion of Mexican and Korean flavors and forms that made that happen. This Korean short rib taco shows why. The big flavors of Korean food—soy sauce, gochugaru (chile flakes) and garlic—presented in a simple, quintessentially Mexican form are a match that feels completely natural and organic. It is as if they were next- door neighbors.

Put the short ribs in a large resealable plastic bag. Combine the soy sauce, garlic, onion, ginger, brown sugar, sesame oil, gochugaru, and half the can of cola in a high-speed blender or food processor (drink the remaining cola, if you like, or reserve it for another marinade), and blend until smooth. Pour the marinade over the meat, seal the bag, and massage the bag to distribute the marinade. Refrigerate for at least 2 hours or up to 8 hours.

When ready to cook the ribs, preheat the oven to 300°F.

Drain the meat and place it in a single layer in a large Dutch oven or soup pot. Place the pot in the oven and braise the meat until fork-tender, 2½ to 3 hours.

2 pounds boneless beef short ribs

For the Marinade

½ cup soy sauce

4 cloves garlic, crushed and roughly chopped

¼ medium white onion, roughly chopped

1 (1-inch) knob fresh ginger, peeled and roughly chopped

2 tablespoons brown sugar

2 tablespoons toasted sesame oil

1 teaspoon gochugaru (Korean chile flakes)

1 (12-ounce) can cola

RECIPE AND INGREDIENTS CONTINUE

While the meat is braising, make the slaw. Combine the soy sauce, vinegar, lime juice, garlic, brown sugar, sesame oil, and ginger in a jar or resealable plastic bag, cover or seal, and shake vigorously to emulsify. Combine the cabbage, carrots, green onions, and cilantro in a large bowl and toss with the dressing. Set aside or cover and refrigerate until ready to serve.

Carefully drain the cooking liquid from the meat into a clean saucepan and skim off the fat. Bring the liquid to a rapid boil, then reduce the heat to maintain a simmer and cook until the sauce has reduced by one-third. Shred the still-hot meat with 2 forks and moisten it with a few spoonfuls of the reduced sauce.

Serve the meat on warmed corn tortillas and top each with a generous spoonful of the slaw. Sprinkle with sesame seeds and drizzle with sriracha, if desired.

For the Slaw

¼ cup soy sauce

3 tablespoons rice vinegar

1 tablespoon fresh lime juice

1 clove garlic, crushed and minced

1 tablespoon brown sugar

2 tablespoons toasted sesame oil

1 (1-inch) knob fresh ginger, peeled and finely grated

1 large head napa cabbage, quartered lengthwise, cored, and thinly sliced crosswise

2 medium carrots, coarsely grated

2 green onions, thinly sliced

¼ cup fresh cilantro leaves, torn or roughly chopped

For Serving

12 (6-inch) Corn Tortillas (page 228), warmed

Toasted sesame seeds

Sriracha sauce (optional)

EL YAQUI-STYLE TACOS

Makes 6 tacos

Felipe Núñez, a Yaqui Indian from Zacatecas in Northern Mexico, took the carne asada taco to new heights starting in 1984. Núñez settled in Rosarito after deciding that making his "fortune" in the United States (and remitting much of it back home) was not the life he wanted. The menu at his Tacos El Yaqui is short—very short: tacos perrones—essentially a carne asada–stuffed quesadilla. They are flour tortillas filled with cheese and cooked briefly on the flat top—there's your quesadilla—then filled with guacamole, pinto beans, chopped white onion, fresh cilantro, a bit of salsa, and carne asada.

Essential to the perrones is the use of Sonoran arrachera, the Mexican cut of skirt (or hanger) steak, the highest grade in use for carne asada in Mexico. And instead of grilling over charcoal, Núñez grills the meat over mesquite wood, adding another layer of flavor.

Combine the olive oil, adobo seasoning, orange juice, lime juice, and garlic in a large bowl and whisk to combine. Add the skirt steak to the marinade and marinate in the refrigerator for 1 to 3 hours. Do not marinate the steak longer than 3 hours or the acidity of the marinade will break down the meat and result in a mushy texture.

Make a hot fire in a charcoal grill or set a gas grill on high heat. Alternatively, heat a cast-iron skillet or grill pan on the stovetop over high heat until very hot. Grill the meat for 3 to 4 minutes on each side, then let it rest for 5 minutes. Slice it against the grain into ½-inch-thick strips, then slice the strips crosswise to make ½-inch cubes.

Place a slice of cheese into the fold of each tortilla, like you would for a quesadilla, followed by a serving of meat (6 to 8 pieces), then 1 tablespoon of the salsa roja, some beans, onion, guacamole, and cilantro. Serve 2 or 3 tacos for each diner with the jalapeño toreados on the side.

2 tablespoons extra-virgin olive oil

2 tablespoons Red Adobo Seasoning (page 261)

Juice of 1 orange

Juice of 1 lime

2 cloves garlic, minced

12 ounces skirt steak

6 (8-inch) Flour Tortillas (page 229), warmed

6 thin slices Real del Castillo or Monterey Jack cheese

For the Garnish

6 tablespoons Baja-Style Salsa Roja (page 244)

Peruano beans (see page 238)

1 medium white onion, chopped

Guacamole (page 252)

Finely chopped fresh cilantro

Jalapeño Toreados (see page 208)

TIJUANA STREET FOOD AND TACOS KOKOPELLI

Tijuana is, straight up, one of the world's great street food cities. Living in the shadow of Mexico City, though, it doesn't always get the credit it deserves. But long before foodies were known as foodies and well before Tijuana was recognized as a bona fide foodie destination, Tijuana's street food game was both long and strong.

The tortas (think Mexican sandwiches) are great, the mariscos (ceviche, seafood tacos, and the like) are excellent, and there's so much more. Mariscos Rubén, for example, made *Food & Wine* and *Travel + Leisure* magazines' globe-spanning short lists of "the best restaurants that travelers must visit right now." Similarly, the carne asada tortas at the oddly named Tortas Washmobile are what every little carne asada torta wants to be when it grows up. And then there are the TJ Dogs at the very appropriately named Hot Dogs right below the great arch at the base of Avenida Revolución. All are wonderful Tijuana street food options.

But the royal family of Tijuana street food is the tacos. Following Anthony Bourdain's visit for *No Reservations*, perhaps the most legendary tacos in town are to be found at a strip of six taquerias known as Taco Alley or Las Ahumaderas. Bourdain ate Tacos El Paisa on camera, and you could do a lot worse. Or ask for the combination birria and tripa—yes, tripe (you know, intestines)—tacos at Tacos Fitos outside the Mercado Hidalgo.

But perhaps Tijuana's most creative street food came out of the Tacos Kokopelli street cart opened in 2012 by Chef Guillermo "Oso" Campos Moreno (a Tijuana Culinary Art School graduate with experience at three- Michelin-star Oud Sluis restaurant in the Netherlands and as executive chef at the Parque Bicentenario in Guanajuato). Kokopelli was so successful as a street cart that it now sits parked in the lot of Campos's brick-and-mortar restaurant, Tras/Horizonte, on Avenida Río Colorado. From a taco of portobello mushroom and cilantro pesto to a mesquite-grilled octopus taco and a remarkable escargots burrito, Campos has taken street food to a new level.

DUCK CONFIT TACOS
with Lightly Pickled Red Cabbage
and Charred Tomatillo-Orange Salsa

Serves 4 to 6 / GF

One of the favorite tacos in Northern Baja and Southern California is pork carnitas. North of the border it is hardly unusual for the pork to be braised in water, then cooked on the plancha in lard or oil, but that would be sacrilege south of the border. Originally from the Mexican state of Michoacán, carnitas are supposed to be made by braising pork in lard.

It occurred to me that carnitas are, basically, pork confit. So why not do the same thing with duck? The biggest problem with making duck confit at home is that few people just happen to have half a pound of duck fat in the fridge. But lard (manteca) is readily available in just about every supermarket, and that brings it right back to its origins.

I pair the duck confit with lightly pickled cabbage for a burst of color, and a sauce that plays on the classic duck-orange combination. The sauce is based on one by San Diego's James Beard Award–nominated chef Claudette Zepeda-Wilkins.

Pat the duck legs dry with paper towels. Using the tip of a sharp boning or paring knife, prick the skin of the duck all over. The idea is to pierce the skin covering fat but not pierce the meat itself. To do this, insert the knife tip at an acute angle over the drumstick and the center of the thigh. The purpose is to give the fat that lies under the skin a place to seep out so the skin will get nice and crispy.

Spread 2 tablespoons salt over the bottom of a dish large enough to hold the duck in a single layer. Nestle the duck legs, skin-side up, over the salt, then sprinkle with another 2 tablespoons salt. Transfer the dish with the salted duck legs to the refrigerator, uncovered, and leave for at least 20 minutes or up to 1 hour.

Melt ¼ cup of the lard in a small soup pot or Dutch oven (just large enough to hold all the legs) over low heat. Remove the duck legs from the refrigerator and add them to the pot along with the lime, bay leaves, and garlic.

Set the oven to 300°F, immediately transfer the pot to the oven, and leave for 30 minutes, or until the duck legs are partially submerged in rendered duck fat. Add the remaining lard and cook the duck legs in the oven for 1 hour more.

For the Duck Confit

4 to 6 duck legs
(1 per person)

Kosher salt

8 ounces lard, plus
more if needed

1 lime, sliced
horizontally

2 bay leaves

6 cloves garlic, peeled

**For the Charred
Tomatillo-Orange
Salsa**

2 tomatillos, husked
and rinsed

1 large plum tomato

1 small white or
yellow onion, halved

½ orange, peeled and
quartered

2 medium jalapeño
chiles, stemmed
and seeded

2 teaspoons
extra-virgin olive oil

2 tablespoons
finely chopped
fresh cilantro

Juice of 1 key lime

Kosher salt

For the Tacos

8 to 12 Corn Tortillas
(page 228), warmed

4 to 6 tablespoons
Pickled Red Cabbage
(page 258)

While the duck legs are cooking, make the salsa. Toss the tomatillos, tomato, onion, orange quarters, chiles, and olive oil in a large bowl. Heat a large cast-iron skillet or other heavy sauté pan over medium-high heat. Add the tomatillo mixture and cook until each ingredient is charred in spots, transferring them to a cutting board as they reach that point. It should take 5 to 8 minutes for the orange quarters and chiles and 8 to 10 minutes for the tomatillos, tomato, and onion. Roughly chop each, transfer to a food processor, and pulse to a coarse consistency. This is not the dish for a smooth, elegant puree. Pour the salsa into a bowl and add the cilantro and lime juice. Mix thoroughly and let cool. When the salsa has cooled, taste it and adjust the seasoning with salt as needed.

An hour after adding the remaining lard, check the duck legs. They should be fully submerged in the fat and the skin should be starting to get crisp. If the legs are not submerged, add more lard. If the skin is not beginning to crisp, cook for an additional 15 to 20 minutes, until they begin to crisp. Increase the oven temperature to 375°F to brown the skin. Roast until most of the duck skin is golden brown, 15 to 20 minutes. Remove the duck from the oven and let cool on the counter for 10 to 15 minutes. Once the meat is cool enough to handle, separate the skin from the meat. Shred the meat and slice the skin into thin strips.

Assemble the tacos by topping each warm tortilla with 2 tablespoons of the duck confit, then 1 tablespoon of the lightly pickled cabbage, and 1 tablespoon of the charred tomatillo-orange salsa. Garnish with the strips of duck skin.

Note: As unpopular as it may be north of the border, for some relatively (but not entirely) dubious health reasons, lard tends to be the fat of choice south of the border. For many purposes olive oil or grapeseed oil or even butter can be used where a recipe calls for lard. This, however, is not one of those recipes.

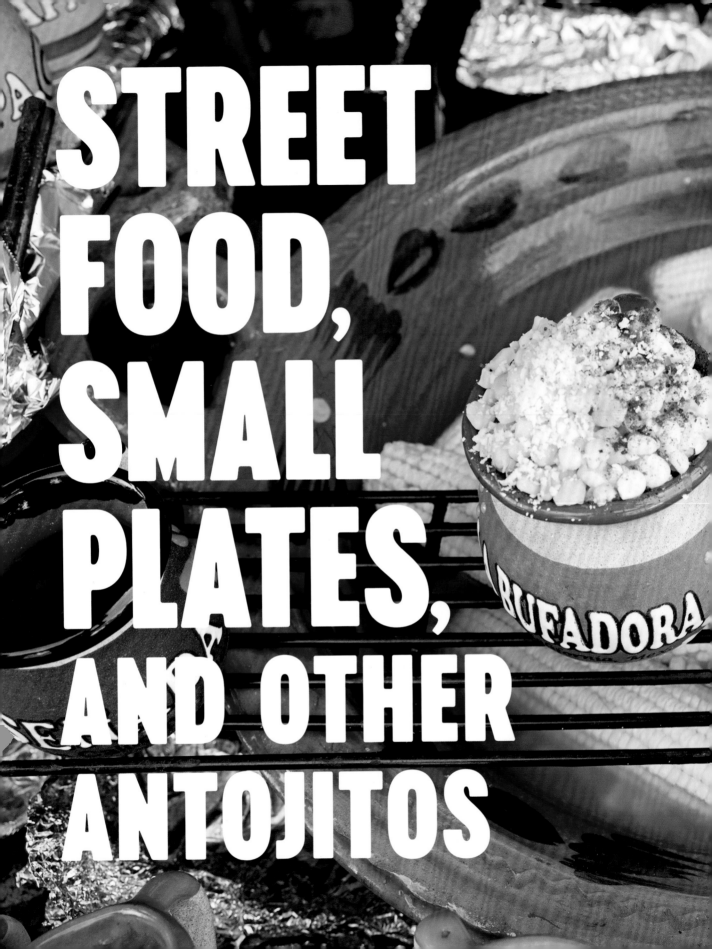

STREET FOOD, SMALL PLATES, AND OTHER ANTOJITOS

CARNE ASADA TORTAS

Makes 4 tortas

Along with tacos, tortas are at the very core of Mexican street food. From the *torta ahogada* ("drowned torta") of Guadalajara to the incredible creativity of Mexico City's street vendors to the carnivorous festival that is the torta cubana (no particular relationship to the similarly named Cuban sandwich), tortas are Mexico's answer to the sub sandwich. But where subs are about multiple layers of ingredients on an enormous roll, tortas are generally focused on one or more meats with accompaniments like avocado, pickled vegetables, and salsa on telera rolls. They are, in essence, tacos done up in sandwich form.

Perhaps my favorite torta is the carne asada torta at Tortas Washmobile in Tijuana. Their menu consists of carne asada tortas, carne asada tortas, and, as a demonstration of their commitment to variety, carne asada tortas. Carne asada tortas is what they do—it's the only thing they do. And when a restaurant makes the call to do one thing and only one thing, they must do it very well. Washmobile does carne asada tortas very, very well.

2 pounds Carne Asada (page 203)

4 telera rolls, large bolillos, or small ciabatta buns, split

½ cup grapeseed, canola, or other neutral oil

½ cup Avocado Mayonnaise (page 254)

½ cup Habanero Pickled White Onions (page 259)

Salsa Taquera (page 246)

Cut the carne asada into large bite-size pieces, taking care to gather all the juices that run off the beef. Add the cut meat to the juices.

Heat a comal, griddle, or large cast-iron pan over medium-high heat. Brush the cut side of each roll with 1 tablespoon of the oil. When the comal is hot, place the rolls on the pan, oiled-side down, and grill until they take on a bit of char. Swipe a generous tablespoon or two of the avocado mayonnaise on the cut surface of each roll. Pile the carne asada high on the bottom halves of the rolls, top with the habanero pickled onions, and drizzle with salsa taquera.

TORTA CUBANA

Makes 1 sandwich

The assumption of many Americans, based on the name of the sandwich, would logically be that the Mexican torta cubana would have something to do with the Florida-style Cuban sandwich (aka the cubano—note the last letter). It is not so. Rather, the torta cubana derives its name from being created on Mexico City's Calle República de Cuba. It's named for the street, not the country, and not the American-Cuban sandwich of that so-similar name.

The torta cubana has found a particularly welcoming home in Tijuana and features on the menu of just about any place you can get tortas in town (except Tortas Washmobile). In fact, there is no single definitive recipe for the sandwich. At base, it is a buttered and pan-fried telera roll (think of a Mexican bolillo stretched and on steroids) filled with various meats, cheeses, condiments, sauces, and more. The meats could be slices of supermarket ham, roast pork, carnitas, chorizo, carne asada (see page 203), or some combination of the above. Condiments could include refried beans, avocado, guacamole, and American-style cheese. Sauces might include a chipotle crema.

1 telera (or kaiser) roll

2 tablespoons salted butter

¼ cup Avocado Mayonnaise (page 254)

3 to 4 tablespoons Refried Beans (page 239)

½ cup loose Mexican chorizo

2 carrots slices from Carrot, Jalapeño, and Cauliflower in Escabeche (page 256)

1 medium Hass avocado, sliced

2 jalapeño slices from Carrot, Jalapeño, and Cauliflower in Escabeche (page 256)

3 thin slices cooked ham

Heat a heavy sauté pan over high heat. Slice the roll in half, spread the butter on the cut surfaces, and place the roll buttered-side down on the pan. Cook until the bread is golden brown on the cut sides. Swipe half the avocado mayonnaise on the cut sides of the roll. Divide the refried beans evenly between the top and bottom halves of the roll.

On the bottom half of the roll, nestle the chorizo into the beans. Top the chorizo with the sliced carrots and layer the avocado slices on top of that. Top the avocado slices with the jalapeños and layer the ham on top of that. Place the top half of the roll over the ham to finish.

PUERTO NUEVO-STYLE LOBSTER ROLL TORTAS

Makes 4 tortas

Perhaps the most famous form of mariscos just south of the border in Baja is Puerto Nuevo lobster. These are not the big-clawed creatures of Maine lobster rolls but, rather, spiny lobsters that look more like crawdads on steroids. In the early parts of the twentieth century, the waters off Puerto Nuevo were silly with them, and the town grew up around the trade. In time, though, that trade became more about export, particularly to the Far East (and especially to China). Along the way, Puerto Nuevo became something of a parody of itself. But tourists still flock there for frozen imported split lobsters deep-fried in lard and doused in melted margarine, offered with large flour tortillas, refried beans, and two hot sauces.

In some ways, Puerto Nuevo's lobster tails are not that different from those of New England's touristy lobster rolls. While the lobsters of New England are different from those of Puerto Nuevo, both are delicious. And while Pacific spiny lobsters are not as readily available as Maine lobsters, the latter work equally well in most applications.

While lobster salad–based Maine lobster rolls are New England's best-known version of the sandwich, this dish is essentially a cross between the slightly less familiar Connecticut-style butter-based lobster roll and the Puerto Nuevo–style lobster dish.

2 lobsters (Maine or spiny), about 1½ pounds each

4 tablespoons (½ stick) butter

4 telera (or kaiser) rolls, sliced in half lengthwise

8 tablespoons Refried Beans (page 239)

¼ cup thinly sliced green onions or Mexican onions (green parts only), or chives

Kosher salt and freshly ground black pepper

Salsa Bandera (page 242)

Árbol Chile Salsa (page 243)

Dispatch each lobster by pressing the tip of a heavy chef's knife in the crack just behind the eyes in the center of the lobster's carapace. Press down firmly, then split the head in half. Using kitchen towels, twist off the tail, claws (not an issue if you are using spiny lobsters), and knuckles from the carapace. Reserve the carapace for another use. Press each tail flat against the cutting board and insert wooden skewers along their entire length to keep them straight.

Place a steamer insert in the bottom of a large lidded stockpot and add 1 inch of water. Bring to a boil over high heat. Add a single layer of lobster tails and legs (about half the lobster to the steamer) and cover the pot. Steam the tails and legs for 2 minutes, then transfer to a large bowl. Set the bowl under cold running water. Return the water in the pot to a boil and repeat with the remaining lobster.

As soon as the lobster is cool enough to handle, pick the meat from the shell using kitchen shears, lobster crackers, and/or the back of a heavy cleaver to help crack the shells. Roughly chop the lobster meat into bite-size pieces and set on paper towels to drain.

Melt 1 tablespoon of the butter in a 12-inch heavy-bottomed skillet over medium-low heat. Swirl to coat the pan. Add 2 rolls, cut-side down, and toast, gently pressing on the rolls until golden brown on the cut side. Repeat with the remaining rolls.

Melt the remaining 3 tablespoons butter in a large skillet over medium heat. As soon as the butter has melted, add the lobster meat. Cook, tossing constantly and using a spoon to gently flip the meat and nap it with butter, until the meat is mostly opaque, about 3 minutes. At no point in the process should the butter sizzle, much less brown. Add the green onions and cook until the lobster meat is cooked through, about 1 minute longer. Season with salt and pepper.

Swipe the bottom half of each roll with 2 tablespoons of the refried beans. Scatter one-quarter of the lobster meat on top of the beans on each roll. Spoon some of the excess juices and salsa bandera over the lobster and drizzle some árbol chile salsa on top. Close the tortas with the top halves of the rolls.

CORN RIBS ESQUÍTES-STYLE

Serves 4 / GF / VEG

Esquítes is Mexican street corn salad—kernels of corn slathered in mayonnaise; tossed with crumbled cheese, lime juice, chile powder, and cilantro; and served up in a cup. Esquítes may not be on every street corner in Tijuana, but every *other* street corner might not be too much of a stretch. When I staged at La Justina on Tijuana's Avenida Revolución, esquítes was one of the dishes I was responsible for.

That was only a few years before New York's Momofuku Ssäm Bar first brought corn ribs—a deep-fried strip of corn kernels held in place by a sliver of the corncob—to the attention of America's dining public. TikTok took it from there and made corn ribs a bona fide fad. Fried, baked, or grilled, they suddenly seemed to be everywhere. And they seemed to me like a natural delivery vehicle for corn done up esquítes-style.

Preheat the oven to 425°F. Line a baking sheet with parchment paper.

Lay the corn ears on a cutting board and halve them crosswise using a sharp knife so that you have 8 roughly equal-size segments. Cut the stem off the bottom of each of the 4 bottom segments. Stand each segment vertically (with the wider portion from which you just sliced off the stem on the cutting board). With each of the segments standing, slice down the middle, halving each. Lay each segment flat and, once again, slice down the middle of each, yielding 16 segments. Place the segments on the prepared baking sheet and season with salt. Roast until the corn is nicely charred and the "ribs" begin to curl, 18 to 20 minutes.

Meanwhile, combine the cheese, green onions, cilantro, jalapeño, garlic, mayonnaise, lime juice, and chile powder to taste in a large bowl and whisk to thoroughly combine. When the ribs are cooked, add them to the bowl and toss to coat. Taste and adjust the seasoning with salt and more chile powder, if needed. Serve immediately.

4 ears fresh corn, shucked

Kosher salt

2 ounces Cotija, feta or Parmesan cheese, finely crumbled (or grated, if using Parmesan)

½ cup thinly sliced green onions (green parts only)

½ cup finely chopped fresh cilantro leaves and stems

1 medium jalapeño chile, stemmed, seeded, and finely chopped

1 or 2 medium cloves garlic, crushed and finely chopped

2 tablespoons Mayonnaise (page 255)

1 tablespoon fresh lime juice

Chile powder (guajillo, ancho, or a mixture)

BACON-POACHED SHRIMP AND PINK PICKLED ONION AVOCADO TOAST

Serves 12

Let's admit it. Avocado toast is basically a bougie American take on the tostada. So the avocado goes on toasted bread instead of a fried tortilla? It, perhaps like Baja cuisine itself, is just another example of the same dish divided by a border.

This take combines the theme of avocado toast with the wonderfully fresh shrimp readily available throughout Baja California. Oddly, they're not among the top of the region's harvests. Shrimp are, however, one of the top (legal) "harvests" in Sinaloa, just across the Sea of Cortez from Baja. As such they make their way to San Felipe and then truck across the peninsula to Popotla, Ensenada, and Tijuana on a daily basis.

Instead of grilling or sautéing the shrimp, I chose to amp up their flavor by poaching them in bacon fat. The richness of that and the avocado is perfectly cut by the acidity of the pink pickled onions.

2 pounds sliced bacon

24 medium shrimp, peeled and deveined

2 small Hass avocados

1 tablespoon fresh lime juice

Kosher salt and freshly ground black pepper

1 sourdough baguette or loaf French bread, lightly toasted, then cut into 12 slices

12 attractive cilantro leaves with about ¼ inch of stem

36 Pink Pickled Onions (page 259)

Maldon salt (or other flaky finishing salt)

Heat a large skillet over medium-low heat and, working in batches, cook the bacon until the fat is rendered and the bacon is golden and crisp, 8 to 10 minutes per batch. After each batch, drain off the rendered fat, pouring it through a fine-mesh strainer into a saucepan just large enough to hold the shrimp. Reserve the bacon for use as an optional garnish.

Place the saucepan over medium heat and add the shrimp to the fat. Poach the shrimp in the fat until they are pink and just cooked through, about 5 minutes. Use a slotted spoon to transfer the shrimp to paper towels to drain and cool. When they are cool enough to handle, slice the shrimp in half lengthwise.

Pit the avocados, scoop the flesh into a small bowl, and add the lime juice. Mash with a fork until relatively (but not totally) smooth and season with a heaping ½ teaspoon kosher salt and a few grinds of pepper.

Build the avocado toast by spreading the mashed avocado over the toasted baguette segments. Top each with 4 shrimp segments. Top the shrimp with 3 slices of pink pickled onions, some bacon (if using) and a cilantro leaf. Sprinkle with Maldon salt to finish.

GRILLED CHICKEN LIVERS
with Salsa Taquera

Serves 2 to 4 / GF

There is no better way to enjoy chicken livers than just after they've taken a quick cook on a grill. A little bit of magic happens. It is down to those browned parts with big savory and sweet flavors that develop when the external temperature is significantly higher than the internal temperature. It's called the Maillard reaction, and it is the basic reason grilling is so good. Chicken livers are especially good candidates for the grill because they cook so quickly, yielding a bit of char on the outside while remaining tender and pink inside.

This version of grilled chicken livers reflects the offerings at taco stands lining just about any major roadway in Northern Baja from the border down to Ensenada. The salsa taquera pulls together the earthy flavors of the liver and the acidic pop of the pickled cabbage.

Special equipment

wooden or metal skewers

1 pound chicken livers, trimmed

Kosher salt and freshly ground black pepper

1 tablespoon lard or butter

1 medium white onion, halved and thinly sliced

2 cloves garlic, minced

2 to 4 Corn Tortillas (page 228), warmed

2 to 4 tablespoons Salsa Taquera (page 246)

Pickled Red Cabbage (page 258)

4 to 8 attractive cilantro leaves

Soak wooden skewers in hot water for at least 30 minutes prior to use (or use metal skewers). Prepare and start the grill according to your setup, setting it to moderate heat. Thread the livers onto the skewers, using 2 skewers for each set of livers. This gives you more control of them as they cook. Leave a little space between the livers on the skewers. Season with salt and pepper.

Grill the livers over moderate heat (indirect heat is best), turning once, until just charred outside and still slightly pink within, about 5 minutes. Carefully remove the chicken livers from the skewers.

While the livers are cooking, heat the lard in a medium sauté pan over medium heat. Add the onion and cook for 2 to 3 minutes, until it is just starting to take on color. Add the garlic and cook until the onion is just soft, another 2 to 3 minutes.

To serve, top each warm tortilla with a layer of the onions and garlic. Top that with the chicken liver. Spoon a tablespoon of the salsa over the liver and garnish with pickled red cabbage and cilantro leaves.

TJ POLISH DOG

Makes 6 dogs

Baja and Sonora compete for ownership of the bacon-wrapped hot dogs known as Sonora Dogs or Danger Dogs and by those in Baja as TJ Dogs.

The TJ Dog is not so much one specific kind of hot dog as it is meat in tubular form inside a bun. Put differently, it's tacos done as hot dogs. Wrap the dog in bacon, then grill or fry it and pile on ingredients of your choice. There are no rules.

It was when that Mexican-born-and-bred dog found a welcoming home on the streets of Los Angeles that it really became a "thing." And it's when the dog crossed the border back to Tijuana that it truly became an art form.

Here I've swapped out the traditional hot dog for Polish kielbasa segments (hardly a stranger to TJ Dogs) and accompanied them with their natural partner: sauerkraut. Mustard, in two forms—stone-ground swiped on the brioche bun and Dijon in the chile-mustard sauce—completes the picture.

Wrap 1 slice of bacon around each kielbasa segment, securing the bacon to the sausage with toothpicks at each end. Heat the oil in a large sauté pan over medium heat. When the oil ripples, add the wrapped kielbasa and cook until the bacon is browned and cooked through, about 5 minutes per side. During the last 2 minutes of cooking, add the buns to the pan to toast, if desired.

To make the sauce, toast the ancho chiles on a dry sauté pan or cast-iron skillet over medium heat for about 20 seconds, until fragrant. Do not overtoast the chiles. Place the chiles in a bowl and pour in enough hot water to fully cover them. Soak them for 10 minutes, or until they are pliable. Drain.

Combine the stock, tangerines, chipotle and adobo sauce, and the soaked ancho chiles in a medium saucepan and bring to a boil over high heat. Reduce the heat to low and simmer until the sauce thickens and reduces by half, about 15 minutes. Transfer the sauce to a high-speed blender or food processor along with the Dijon and crema and blend until it is completely smooth. Taste the sauce and season with salt as needed.

To serve, swipe 1 teaspoon of the stone-ground mustard over the bottom of each bun. Top with 1 tablespoon of the sauerkraut. Nestle a sausage segment atop the sauerkraut. Finish with some of the sauce and top each with 1 teaspoon each of the pickled onions and jalapeños.

For the Polish Dogs

6 thick-cut slices bacon

2 (1-pound) Polish kielbasas, cut into thirds

1 tablespoon grapeseed, canola, or other neutral-flavored oil

6 brioche hot dog buns

For the Ancho-Chipotle-Mustard Sauce

3 ancho chiles, stemmed and seeded

4 cups Chicken Stock (page 232)

2 tangerines or oranges, peeled and roughly chopped

1 chipotle chile (from a can of chipotles in adobo), plus 1 teaspoon adobo sauce from the can

2 tablespoons Dijon mustard

2 tablespoons Mexican Crema (page 255)

Kosher salt

For Serving

6 teaspoons stone-ground mustard

6 tablespoons sauerkraut

6 teaspoons Pink Pickled Onions (page 259)

6 teaspoons Pickled Jalapeño Chiles (page 260)

LA GUERRERENSE-STYLE SEA URCHIN AND CLAM TOSTADAS

Makes 4 tostadas

Sabina Bandera's signature tostada of sea urchin and Pismo clams is all about great, fresh, local ingredients elevated with Bandera's light touch. It is simple, direct, and delicious and a dish I have trouble not ordering at her La Guerrerense food truck.

If you have access to sea urchin (try your closest Japanese market) and clams (even if they are not Baja's Pismos), you can make it in your own home.

To cook the clams, pour the wine into a pot large enough to fit the clams, add the butter and salt, and bring to a boil over medium-high heat. Gently add the clams, cover, and steam until fully opened, about 5 minutes. Drain the clams (discard any that have not opened) and refrigerate until ready to use.

To make the sea urchin paste, in a bowl, combine the onion, lime juice, sherry, soy sauce, and olive oil and whisk to combine. Add the sea urchin, season with salt and pepper, and set aside to marinate while you make the tostadas.

To cook the tostadas, preheat the oven to 250°F.

Arrange the tortillas on a baking sheet. When the oven comes to temperature, place the pan in the oven for 10 to 12 minutes, until the tortillas are dry. This will make them fry better. Pour enough oil into a sauté pan to come ¼ inch up the sides. Heat over medium-high heat until the oil is sizzling but not smoking. Using tongs, add a single tortilla at a time to the hot oil. Bubbles should form on the surface of the tortilla immediately as you put it in the oil. If they do not, the oil is not hot enough. Fry the tortilla until golden brown, stiff, and crisp, 30 seconds to 1 minute per side. Remove the fried tortilla using the tongs, letting excess oil drain back into the pan as you do so. Transfer the tortilla to a paper towel–lined plate to absorb excess oil and immediately sprinkle with salt. Repeat to fry the remaining tortillas.

To build the tostadas, using a fork, lightly mash the sea urchins with the marinade in the bowl to make a non-uniform paste. Top each tostada with about ¼ cup of the sea urchin paste. Arrange 5 clams on top of each tostada. Spoon 1 to 2 tablespoons (depending on your heat tolerance) of the salsa macha around the clams and garnish each tostada with pickled onions and the cilantro.

For the Clams

½ cup white wine, such as unoaked chardonnay from the Valle de Guadalupe

20 littleneck clams, scrubbed

2 tablespoons butter, melted

2 cloves garlic, minced

For the Sea Urchin Paste

½ small white onion, minced

1 tablespoon fresh lime juice

1 tablespoon dry sherry

1 teaspoon soy sauce

2 tablespoons extra-virgin olive oil

12 sea urchin (uni) tongues

Kosher salt and freshly ground black pepper

For the Tostadas

4 Corn Tortillas (page 228)

Grapeseed, canola, or other neutral oil for frying

Kosher salt

6 to 8 tablespoons Salsa Macha (page 241)

Pink Pickled Onions (page 259)

12 attractive cilantro leaves

THE BEST STREET CART IN THE WORLD

When it comes to street food in Baja, Tijuana tends to get most of the love. But not all of it. There's good street food in most, if not all, Baja cities. Then there's La Guerrerense. Located in Ensenada at the corner of 1st and Alvarado, Zona Centro, it's at another level altogether.

Anthony Bourdain supposedly described it as "the best street cart in the world." While he's widely quoted as having called it that, he was actually quoting someone else. But he did call it "Le Bernardin quality seafood in the street," and Rick Bayless described it as "one of the best places to eat in Mexico."

And they were neither kidding nor wrong.

The owner, Sabina Bandera, has a certain quiet charisma. Her diminutive stature belies, in a sense, the drive and confidence that helped her take a little street cart serving seafood tostadas to worldwide fame. She's your grandmother if your grandmother had the guts of a prizefighter and cooked like Éric Ripert.

The mariscos Bandera serves at her street cart (and at her slightly more expensive but more comfortable eponymous restaurant across the street) are truly remarkable. Take, for example, her tostada de erizo con almeja: sea urchin (aka uni or, in Spanish, *erizo*)—one of Baja's best products—and Pismo clam tostadas with a squeeze of lime, hot sauce, and thin slices of still-firm avocado at peak ripeness. At one level, it is a dead simple dish: a crisp corn tortilla with a bunch of seafood on top. Of course, the seafood came from the nearby Mercado Negro, Ensenada's fresh seafood market, that morning. And the uni is in the form of a paste atop the tortilla, providing both a structural matrix for the clams and a tier of deep umami warmth with more than a hint of sweetness. The Pismo clams offer intriguing, implausible textural interest: tender, toothsome, and with a suggestion of crunch. A squeeze of lime, a few dashes of hot sauce, and some thin slices of avocado complete the dish. Like so many great dishes, it is both simple and complex.

STREET FOOD FEST
CEVICHE DE ERIZO CON ALMEJA
CEVICHE DE CARACOL CON
1ST
PATÉ DE PESCADO CON CALLO DE HACHA
FISH PATE WITH SCALLOPS
LA GUERRE RENSE
Carreta

TOSTADAS DE SIERRA

Baja—both Baja California and Baja California Sur—are well-known fishing destinations. Among the most sought-after species is mackerel (*sierra* in Spanish). This rich, oily fish is full of flavor and benefits from many styles of preparation. One of my favorites is the Japanese-style pickling that marries the mackerel's natural depth and richness with the acidity of the brine. It makes for a wonderful tostada. Alternatively, save time by buying pickled mackerel at a local Japanese market.

To make the pickled mackerel, start by removing any pin bones from the fish. Place the fish in a dish or nonreactive pan with sides and dust the fish liberally on both sides with salt, covering it completely (you'll use about ⅓ cup). Cover and refrigerate for 1 hour.

Combine 1 cup of the vinegar, the kombu, and sugar in a small saucepan, bring to a simmer over medium heat, and simmer until the sugar has dissolved. Remove from the heat and let steep for 3 minutes. Add the remaining 2 cups vinegar.

Remove the fish from the refrigerator, rinse off the salt with cold water, and pat the fish dry. Rinse the dish and return the fish to the dish. Discard the kombu from the vinegar mixture, then pour the mixture over the fish so it is completely submerged. Cover and refrigerate for 1 hour.

Remove the fish from the vinegar mixture, pat it dry, wrap in plastic wrap, and refrigerate for up to 12 hours.

To make the tostadas, preheat the oven to 250°F. Arrange the tortillas on a baking sheet. When the oven comes to temperature, place the pan in the oven for 10 to 12 minutes, until the tortillas are dry. Pour enough oil into a sauté pan to come ¼ inch up the sides. Heat over medium-high heat until the oil is sizzling but not smoking. Using tongs, add a single tortilla at a time to the oil. Bubbles should form on the surface of the tortilla immediately. If they do not, the oil is not hot enough. Fry the tortilla until golden brown, stiff, and crisp, 30 seconds to 1 minute per side. Remove the fried tortilla using tongs, letting excess oil drain back into the pan. Transfer the tortilla to a paper towel–lined plate to absorb excess oil and immediately sprinkle with salt. Allow the tortillas to cool fully before assembling the dish.

To assemble, cut the pickled mackerel into ¼-inch dice. Arrange the cooked tostadas on a cutting board. Spread avocado crema generously on each, top with the diced mackerel and sprinkle with the red onion. Garnish with the cilantro leaves.

For the Japanese-Style Pickled Mackerel

1 mackerel fillet (about 1 pound), skinned

Fine sea salt

3 cups unseasoned rice vinegar

1 (6-inch) piece kombu

½ cup sugar

For the Tostadas

4 Corn Tortillas (page 228)

Grapeseed, canola, or other neutral oil for frying

Scant ½ cup Avocado Crema (page 254)

¼ medium red onion, finely chopped

12 attractive cilantro leaves

SMOKED EGGPLANT, MUSHROOM, AND FRESH HERB TOSTADAS

Makes 4 tostadas
GF / VEGAN

Tostadas, in a very real sense, are an edible plate. They're a delivery system for an infinite variety of flavor combinations. And while the most famous tostadas in Baja tend to have a protein—often seafood—as their focal point, there is no reason they cannot be meat- and seafood-free. This tostada is inspired by a dish at a pop-up dinner in San Diego that amazed me. It was a collaboration of three hot young gun chefs. The combination of smoked eggplant and fresh herbs was beguiling and sexy. It also transported me south of the border in unexpected ways.

To make the garlic confit, place the garlic cloves in a small saucepan with enough oil to cover by 1 inch. Heat over medium heat until small bubbles rise in the oil. Reduce the heat to its lowest possible setting and gently simmer the garlic, stirring occasionally, for 40 minutes, or until the cloves are very tender and pale golden. Remove from the heat and let the garlic cloves cool in the oil. Store in an airtight container in the refrigerator for up to 1 week.

To make the tostada toppings, remove any leaves from around the stems of the eggplants, taking care to leave the stems attached. Pierce the eggplants several times with the tines of a fork. Place the eggplants in a plastic freezer bag, leaving it unsealed, and place the bag in the microwave. Microwave on high until the eggplants begin to soften, about 5 minutes.

Meanwhile, in a medium bowl, whisk together the soy sauce, vinegar, and sesame oil. Add the mushrooms and set aside to marinate while you grill the eggplants, flipping them periodically.

Using tongs, remove the eggplants from the bag and lay them directly over a medium-high flame on the stovetop. Cook until the bottom begins to fully char, about 3 minutes. Gently turn the eggplants with tongs and repeat the 3-minute char on the other side. (Alternatively, use a commercial or culinary blowtorch to char the eggplants for 3 minutes per side.) Set the eggplants aside to cool for 15 minutes.

For the Garlic Confit

4 cloves garlic, peeled

Extra-virgin olive oil

For the Tostada Toppings

2 medium globe eggplants

¼ cup soy sauce or tamari

2 tablespoons red wine vinegar

1 tablespoon toasted sesame oil

1 cup sliced (¼-inch) button mushrooms

Kosher salt

1 tablespoon extra-virgin olive oil

For the Tostadas

4 Corn Tortillas (page 228)

Grapeseed, canola, or other neutral oil for frying

Kosher salt

¼ cup fresh cilantro leaves

¼ cup fresh mint leaves

Pink Pickled Onions (page 259)

RECIPE CONTINUES

Working with one eggplant at a time, use tongs to hold the eggplant by its stem as you gently peel the skin away from the flesh using a knife (a butter knife will work) or spoon. Try to get as much of the burnt skin off as you can, but if you miss a little bit, it will just enhance the smoky flavor of the resulting puree. Transfer the eggplant flesh to a food processor. Add 4 garlic confit cloves, season with salt, and pulse to thoroughly combine. The goal is not a silky puree but a slightly rustic, textured product.

Heat the olive oil in a sauté pan over medium heat. Remove the mushrooms from the marinade, add them to the pan, and cook until they just begin to soften and release their liquid but keep their texture, about 5 minutes.

To cook the tostadas, preheat the oven to 250°F.

Arrange the tortillas on a baking sheet. When the oven comes to temperature, place the pan in the oven for 10 to 12 minutes, until the tortillas are dry. This will make them fry better. Pour enough oil into a sauté pan to come ¼ inch up the sides. Heat over medium-high heat until the oil is sizzling but not smoking. Using tongs, add a single tortilla at a time to the hot oil. Bubbles should form on the surface of the tortilla immediately as you put it in the oil. If they do not, the oil is not hot enough. Fry the tortilla until golden brown, stiff, and crisp, 30 seconds to 1 minute per side. Remove the fried tortilla using the tongs, letting excess oil drain back into the pan as you do so. Transfer the tortilla to a paper towel–lined plate to absorb excess oil and immediately sprinkle with salt. Repeat to fry the remaining tortillas.

To build the tostadas, top each tortilla with about ¼ cup of the eggplant topping. Arrange about ¼ cup of the mushrooms on top of the eggplant. Scatter the cilantro and mint leaves over the mushrooms and garnish with the pickled onions.

ENSENADA-STYLE YELLOWTAIL CEVICHE TOSTADAS

Makes 4 tostadas / GF

Contrary to popular belief (at least in some quarters), ceviche was not originally a Mexican dish. But if ceviche wasn't born in Mexico, one could be forgiven for believing it was lovingly adopted by Baja parents. At the center of Ensenada's iconic foods, from the quintessential fried fish tacos to Sabina Bandera's tostadas (see page 128), there is a directness born of excellent ingredients and simple, careful execution.

If you can't find perfectly fresh yellowtail, do not hesitate to make this with tuna or whatever fish you would be happy to eat raw. If you cannot find one, then turn the page and try the next fish tostada! That's probably what they would do in Ensenada.

To make the ceviche, in a large bowl, combine the yellowtail and enough lime juice to cover. Set aside to marinate for 20 minutes. Drain the fish, reserving ½ cup of the lime juice.

In a large bowl, combine the drained yellowtail with the onion, jalapeño, cilantro, tomatoes, and carrot. Add the reserved lime juice, season with salt, and stir gently to combine. Chill thoroughly.

To make the tostadas, preheat the oven to 250°F. Arrange the tortillas on a baking sheet. When the oven comes to temperature, place the pan in the oven for 10 to 12 minutes, until the tortillas are dry. This will make them fry better. Pour enough oil into a sauté pan to come ¼ inch up the sides. Heat over medium-high heat until the oil is sizzling but not smoking. Using tongs, add a single tortilla at a time to the oil. Bubbles should immediately form on the surface of the tortilla as you put it in the hot oil. If they do not, the oil is not hot enough. Fry the tortilla until golden brown, 30 seconds to 1 minute per side, until golden brown, stiff, and crisp. Remove the fried tortilla using the tongs, letting excess oil as you do so. Transfer the tortilla to a paper towel–lined plate to absorb excess oil drain back into the pan and immediately sprinkle with salt. Repeat to fry the remaining tortillas.

To make the cilantro mayonnaise, in a food processor, combine the cilantro, lime juice, and salt and pepper to taste. Pulse until the cilantro is very finely chopped and a paste begins to form. Add the mayonnaise and process to combine thoroughly.

To assemble, spread a thin layer of the cilantro mayonnaise on each tostada. Top with the seafood ceviche and garnish with avocado slices.

For the Ceviche

1 pound boneless, skinless yellowtail, cut into ¼-inch dice

About 1 cup fresh lime juice

½ medium red onion, finely diced

1 jalapeño chile, stemmed, seeded, and finely diced

¼ bunch cilantro, leaves and tender stems, finely chopped

2 medium plum tomatoes, finely diced

1 medium carrot, finely diced

Kosher salt

For the Tostadas

4 Corn Tortillas (page 228)

Grapeseed, canola, or other neutral oil for frying

For the Cilantro Mayonnaise

1 bunch cilantro, leaves and tender stems, roughly chopped

Juice of 1 lime

Kosher salt and freshly ground black pepper

½ cup Mayonnaise (page 255)

For the Garnish

Sliced avocado

TOSTADAS
$ 35 c/u

EL BARRIO
$85 c/u Sazondado

TOSTADAS
Beverly Hills
$ 40 c/u

SRIRACHA
$ 100 c/u

Jugo Maggi
$ 50 pz

Fresh Harvest
$ 35 pz

Sazonador
CHUXHEMAN
$ 90 pz

Pimienta Molida
$ 60 pz

Sazonadores
$ 32 pz

Hule·   Tapatio cn. $25   Guacamaya   Valentina   MAYONESA

TOSTADAS
$35 c/u

CRUCHEMAN ACEITE
$95

MÉXICO LINDO
$25 pz

CHUCHEMAN
$25 pz

LA PERRONA
$25 pz

anegra va.
$25 pz

a Sauce
25 pz

CATSUP
CHICA GRANDE
$25 pz $38 pz

Clamato chico
$18 pz

Clamato Med.
$28 pz

Clamato Gde
$45 pz

Clamato
más grande
$65 pz

REFRIED BEAN, SWEET CORN, AND PICKLED RED CABBAGE SOPES

Makes 4 sopes / GF

Masa (nixtamalized ground corn flour), it is fair to say, is a foundation of Mexican cuisine. That is true both literally and figuratively. With the possible exception of tostadas, that is nowhere clearer than with sopes: fat tortillas with a little ridge ringing the top for the express purpose of helping to contain the myriad combinations of ingredients that can top a sope. Refried beans make a frequent appearance and pair naturally with corn and the acidity of pickled cabbage, which also adds a dash of color.

To make the sweet corn, heat the oil in a large nonstick sauté pan over high heat until shimmering. Add the corn kernels, season with salt, toss once or twice, and cook, undisturbed, until charred on one side, about 2 minutes. Toss the corn, stir, and repeat until charred on the other side, about 2 minutes more. Continue tossing and cooking until the corn is well charred all over, about 10 minutes total. Transfer to a large bowl and add the cheese, green onions, cilantro, garlic, and lime juice. Toss to combine.

To build the sopes, spread 2 tablespoons of the refried beans evenly over the top of each sope. Top the beans with 2 to 3 tablespoons of the corn and scatter the pickled red cabbage on top. (The exact amounts will depend on the size of your sopes.) Garnish with cilantro leaves.

For the Sweet Corn

1 tablespoon grapeseed, canola, or other neutral oil

Kernels from 1 ear fresh corn, (about 3 cups)

Kosher salt

1 ounce Cotija, feta, or Parmesan cheese, finely crumbled

¼ cup thinly sliced green onions (green parts only)

¼ cup finely chopped fresh cilantro leaves and stems

1 medium clove garlic, crushed and finely chopped

1 tablespoon fresh lime juice

For Serving

4 Sopes (page 230)

½ cup Refried Beans (page 239)

¼ cup Pickled Red Cabbage (page 258)

Attractive cilantro leaves for garnish

CHORIZO, BLACK BEAN, AND QUESO FRESCO SOPES

Makes 4 sopes / GF

The Spanish left behind many gifts (and the opposite thereof) in Mexico, but their charcuterie was not necessarily one of them. While Mexican chorizo bears little resemblance to its Spanish namesake, it possesses its own charms. Mexican chorizo is neither better nor worse than Spanish chorizo, it's just different —fattier, crumbly, and more acidic. And those differences make it a perfect sope topping. The black beans serve as a grounding element and the queso fresco as a mild refreshment.

Heat the oil in a medium sauté pan over medium-high heat. When the oil ripples, add the chorizo and cook until the meat is crispy and just cooked through, 10 to 12 minutes.

To build the sopes, spoon 2 tablespoons of the beans on top of each sope. Arrange the chorizo in and around the beans. Scatter crumbled cheese on top and garnish with cilantro leaves.

2 tablespoons grapeseed, canola, or other neutral oil

½ cup loose Mexican chorizo

4 Sopes (page 230)

½ cup cooked black beans (see page 238)

Crumbled queso fresco

Fresh cilantro leaves

OYSTER SOPES

Makes 8 sopes / GF

Oyster sopes are a classic take on the theme from Nayarit, home of my photographer for this book, Cintia Soto. Beyond using the best, most locally available (and hence freshest) ingredients, the pairing of earthy masa and the ethereal, oceanic product is both intriguing and delicious.

Bring a medium pot of water to a boil over high heat. Fill a bowl with ice and water. Blanch the oysters in the boiling water for 35 to 40 seconds, then immediately transfer them to the ice bath to stop the cooking.

Place 3 oysters in each sope and spoon 1 tablespoon of the onion around the oysters. Garnish the sopes with the avocado and cilantro.

24 fresh medium oysters, shucked (see page 80)

8 Sopes (page 230)

½ cup finely chopped red onion

2 medium Hass avocados, diced, for garnish

1 sprig cilantro, finely chopped

SWISS ENCHILADAS

Makes 15 enchiladas
GF

As much as I've always enjoyed tacos, it was enchiladas—corn tortillas wrapped around a delicious filling and covered with a savory sauce—that were my first antojito love. I first encountered them in the form of enchiladas suizas (Spanish for "Swiss") as a seven-year-old boy in a restaurant just off Avenida Revolución in Tijuana. It was my first meal south of the border, and all I could do was wonder what the Swiss could have to do with this Mexican dish. Apparently, I was not the only one. There are, as happens with these types of things, multiple accounts.

Perhaps the most common story is that enchiladas suizas were first introduced at Sanborn's Restaurant in Mexico City in 1950 as a tribute of sorts to Swiss cuisine. That, supposedly, explains the dish's use of lots of cheese and cream. It seems like a bit of a stretch. According to other accounts, the green and light brown of the enchiladas topped by the white of the cheese and crema reminded people of the Alps. That account is so poetically Euclidean it cannot possibly be true.

I did not get far in my inquiries as a seven-year-old because the meal arrived, but the enchiladas suizas immediately became my favorite enchiladas.

Adjust the oven racks to the lower middle and upper middle positions and preheat the broiler. Line a baking sheet with parchment paper.

Put the tomatillos, onions, garlic, and serrano and guerito chiles on the prepared baking sheet. Roast for 4 to 5 minutes, until the tomatillos soften and start to darken. Flip everything over with a pair of 12-inch tongs and roast for another 4 to 5 minutes. Take care that the vegetables do not burn. Remove from the oven and let the vegetables cool. Set the oven temperature to 400°F.

Transfer the contents of the baking sheet to a high-speed blender or food processor and blend until smooth.

Pour 1½ tablespoons of the oil into a large Dutch oven and heat over medium-high heat. Add the contents of the blender to the pot. Cook, stirring the bubbling, sizzling liquid often, until it takes on a darker hue, about 3 minutes. Pour in the stock and crema, turn the heat down to medium-low, and stir until the mixture is smooth. Cover the pot with the lid ajar and simmer for 30 minutes. Season the sauce with salt.

Ingredients

1 pound tomatillos (about 8 medium), husked and rinsed

2 medium white onions, sliced ¼ inch thick

6 cloves garlic, peeled

2 serrano chiles, stemmed

1 guerito (yellow) chile, stemmed

3½ tablespoons grapeseed, canola, or other neutral oil, plus more as needed

4 cups Chicken Stock (page 232)

½ cup Mexican Crema (page 255)

Kosher salt

3 cups shredded cooked chicken breast (from about 1 pound raw)

15 Corn Tortillas (page 228)

⅓ cup shredded Oaxaca cheese or other Mexican melting cheese

½ cup chopped fresh cilantro leaves and tender stems

Heat the remaining 2 tablespoons oil in a medium sauté pan over medium-high heat. Add the tortillas and fry until golden but still pliable, about 10 seconds per side, adding more oil if needed. Transfer to paper towels to soak up excess oil.

Spread ⅓ cup of the sauce over the bottom of a 13 x 9 x 2-inch glass baking dish. Place the tortillas on a work surface. Divide the shredded chicken evenly among the tortillas and roll each up like a cigar. Arrange the rolled tortillas in a single layer, seam-side down, snugly inside the dish. Pour the rest of the sauce over the tortillas and sprinkle the cheese all over.

Bake until the cheese is melted and starting to brown in spots, about 30 minutes. Serve 3 enchiladas per plate and garnish with the cilantro.

EGG ENCHILADAS
with Pepita Sauce and Tomato-Lime Sauce
PAPADZULES

Serves 4 / GF

This is an adaptation of an old Aztec dish that has been referred to as Montezuma's "food of the gods." The two sauces—each quite simple—combine with the egg enchiladas to form a complex and many-layered dish. The pepita sauce—which may well have been a precursor to mole verde (also known as *pipián*)—is a simple suspension of pumpkin seeds in stock. The two sauces can be made a day ahead and refrigerated.

Some would say that papadzules are not technically enchiladas, but rather their ancestor. They might be right, but in my book, papadzules look like enchiladas and eat like enchiladas.

To make the pepita sauce, put the pepitas in a large frying pan and toast over medium-high heat, stirring constantly, until they begin to color and pop, about 5 minutes. Transfer the pepitas to a food processor or high-speed blender, periodically scraping down the sides, until they achieve the consistency of beach sand. With the motor running, pour in the stock through the hole in the top in a steady stream and process until the sauce reaches the consistency of thin mayonnaise. Season with salt.

To make the tomato-lime sauce, combine the tomatoes, oil, stock, oregano, lime juice, and chile in a medium sauce pan and bring to a boil over high heat. Reduce the heat to maintain a simmer, cover the pan, and cook until the tomatoes break down, about 20 minutes. Working in batches, carefully transfer the sauce to a food processor or high-speed blender and puree. Season with salt.

To make the enchiladas, preheat the oven to 350°F. Dip one tortilla in the pepita sauce and transfer to a plate. Fill the tortilla with 2 tablespoons of the chopped egg. Roll the enchilada and place it in a baking dish. Repeat with the remaining tortillas, then cover the dish with foil. Bake just long enough for the enchiladas to heat through, about 5 minutes.

To plate the dish, arrange 3 enchiladas on each plate, aligning them diagonally. Spoon a line of the pepita sauce along the diagonal, passing through the center of each enchilada. Spoon a line of the tomato-lime sauce along the opposing diagonal and garnish with the minced egg and cilantro.

For the Pepita Sauce

3 cups shelled raw pepitas (pumpkin seeds)

3 cups Vegetable Stock (page 235)

Kosher salt

For the Tomato-Lime Sauce

6 ripe medium tomatoes, halved

2 tablespoons grapeseed, canola, or other neutral oil

2 tablespoons Vegetable Stock (page 235)

2 tablespoons finely chopped fresh Mexican oregano

Juice of 4 limes

¼ habanero chile, stemmed, seeded, and minced

Kosher salt

For the Enchiladas

6 hard-boiled eggs, peeled and chopped

12 Corn Tortillas (page 228), warmed

Grapeseed, canola, or other neutral oil

For the Garnish

2 hard-boiled eggs, peeled and minced

Fresh cilantro leaves

CALIFORNIA BURRITO

Makes 4 burritos

The California burrito is a San Diego icon. Many San Diegans see fish tacos as the signature San Diego dish, but Ensenada would have a pretty good misappropriation lawsuit. Ensenada's case, however, would not be nearly as good as the one San Diego would have if anyone elsewhere tried to lay claim to the Cali burrito.

Iconic as San Diego's California burrito is, and as indelibly associated with the town as it might be, the specifics of its origins are entirely unclear. Many say it was created at Roberto's Taco Shop, and most agree it was created at one of San Diego's various taco shop chains whose names include the suffix *–berto's*, but none can pinpoint the specific origin or date. Not even any of the –berto's owners.

To make the carne asada, in a large bowl, combine the lime juice, garlic, orange juice, cilantro, salt, pepper, oil, chile, and vinegar. Whisk to thoroughly combine the marinade. Add the skirt steak and get in there with your hands to fully coat it with the marinade. Cover and refrigerate for at least 2 hours or up to overnight.

To make the potatoes, preheat the oven to 400°F. Line a baking sheet with parchment paper. In a large bowl, toss the potatoes with the olive oil, then sprinkle with the red adobo seasoning and salt. Spread the potatoes evenly over the baking sheet and roast until crisp, about 30 minutes, turning the potatoes occasionally and checking to make sure they are cooking evenly. Remove from the oven and set aside.

Heat an outdoor grill—charcoal, gas, or pellet—to high heat. Remove the steak from the marinade and discard the marinade. Grill the steak for 4 to 5 minutes per side. Remove from the grill and let rest for 10 minutes. Slice against the grain and set aside.

To assemble the burritos, lay a tortilla flat on a clean work surface, like a cutting board or large plate. Spread a little cheese on the first third of the tortilla, leaving some of the margins clear (where you will fold it later). Then drop a few spoonfuls of refried beans in a line along the cheese. Finally, add layers of the carne asada, potatoes, salsa, and avocado crema. Fold the two side flaps of the tortilla toward the center but not all the way to the middle. Roll up the tortilla, starting from the side with the filling, to enclose all the filling. Repeat to assemble the remaining burritos.

For the Carne Asada

Juice of 2 limes

4 cloves garlic, crushed

½ cup orange juice

1 cup chopped fresh cilantro

½ teaspoon kosher salt

¼ teaspoon freshly ground black pepper

¼ cup grapeseed, canola, or other neutral oil

1 jalapeño chile, stemmed, seeded, and minced

2 tablespoons apple cider vinegar

2 pounds skirt steak

For the Potatoes

2 medium russet potatoes, diced

2 tablespoons olive oil

1 tablespoon Red Adobo Seasoning (page 261)

½ teaspoon kosher salt

For the Burritos

4 large Flour Tortillas (page 229)

1 cup shredded Oaxaca or Monterey Jack cheese

Refried Beans (page 239)

Salsa Bandera (page 242)

Avocado Crema (page 254)

BURRITOS

Burritos are two dishes sharing the same name divided by a common border. At its most basic level, a burrito is a flour tortilla wrapped around various ingredients, then grilled, steamed, or cooked on a griddle or in a dry pan. That, however, is where the similarities between the dishes end.

North of the border, burritos tend to be massive gut bombs, vaguely torpedo-like shapes stuffed to immense proportions. Take, for example, San Diego's signature California burrito: carne asada, french fries, a boatload of cheese, salsa fresca, sour cream, and guacamole. And that's just the basic model. Beans may join the party, as might meats or salsas. But if there's one property that characterizes the north-of-the-border approach to burritos, it is a conviction that size matters and bigger is better. It may take a village to raise a child, but it would probably take only one California burrito to feed that village.

South of the border, though, it's very different. Baja-style burritos are much smaller, simpler, and more direct. What Californians call burritos would be called burros in Baja (and quite probably would not involve french fries). Instead of massive torpedo shapes, Baja burritos tend to be slightly flattened (and often elongated) packets that have received the benefit of a caramelizing trip on a griddle. They feature a few fresh, tasty ingredients, prepared perfectly, instead of a cornucopia of prepared fast-food products. They are, dare I say, an improvement on the north of the border original.

But the burritos of Pocha LA are something else entirely. They may sport the proportions of a California burrito, but they also possess something of the directness of the south-of-the-border version, offering a sense of generosity and soul. They're not trading on the notion of a burrito, but celebrating that notion in their own way.

CRAB BURRITOS
with Pickled Fresno Chiles and Chipotle-Avocado Sauce

Serves 4

It was on one of my first trips to the Valle de Guadalupe, Mexico's wonderful wine region, that I discovered how different Baja's burritos were from those north of the border. We pulled up to a little wine bar off the side of the road to get our bearings and a bite to eat. We figured one burrito would work for the two of us.

But instead of loading rice and beans and/or french fries into a massive flour tortilla along with the "star" protein, we discovered that Baja burritos are smaller affairs that showcase a single protein along with a few other ingredients that highlight that protein's star power. They are of human, not Herculean, proportion. And they make the rest of the day possible without a nap or three. This dish is my attempt to capture the essence of that burrito, combining Baja-style crab with pickled chiles and a sauce based on one of Baja's signature chiles.

To make the burrito filling, heat the olive oil in a large sauté pan over medium heat. Add the onion and garlic and cook until the onion is translucent, about 2 minutes. Transfer the onion and garlic to a large bowl and, in the following order, fold in the cheese, crabmeat, pickled chiles, and cilantro. Combine thoroughly.

Heat a dry stainless-steel skillet over medium heat and warm the tortillas one at a time for about 30 seconds on each side. As each tortilla is warmed, swathe it in a clean dish towel or tortilla warmer.

To assemble the burritos, place about ½ cup of the filling on the bottom half of a tortilla. Fold the bottom of the tortilla up and over the filling and pull the filling back toward the bottom third of the tortilla. Fold in the sides and then roll up the tortilla from the bottom, using the tips of your fingers to tuck and press the tortilla into a tight cylinder, enclosing the filling. Place the burrito seam-side down on your work surface and, using the palm of your hand, press downward to create flat surfaces on both the top and bottom of the burrito.

To make the sauce, scoop the avocado flesh into a small bowl and mash it. Transfer the mashed avocado to a food processor and add the chipotle and adobo sauce, olive oil, and lime juice. Process to a smooth puree. Taste the sauce and adjust the seasoning with salt or additional lime juice as needed.

When the sauce is done, heat a skillet over medium-high heat. Place a burrito in the pan, seam-side down, and toast just until the seam

For the Burritos

1 tablespoon extra-virgin olive oil

½ medium white onion, finely chopped

2 cloves garlic, minced

1 cup shredded Oaxaca or mozzarella cheese

1 pound crabmeat (picked from about 6 blue crabs, or good-quality canned)

2 tablespoons finely chopped pickled Fresno chiles (made according to the method for Pickled Jalapeño Chiles, page 260)

2 tablespoons chopped fresh cilantro

4 large Flour Tortillas (page 229)

For the Chipotle-Avocado Sauce

1 medium Hass avocado, flesh scooped out

1 chipotle chile (from a can of chipotles in adobo), minced, plus 2 tablespoons adobo sauce from the can

1½ tablespoons extra-virgin olive oil

Juice of ½ key lime, plus more as needed

Kosher salt

seals and you can smell the flour cooking, about 1 minute. Do not let it burn. Flip the burrito and toast until you can once again smell the flour cooking, about another minute. Again, do not let the tortilla burn or get hard. Transfer to a cutting board. Repeat with the remaining burritos.

Cut the burritos in half on the bias and lean the two parts up against each other in the center of a plate. Create a swoosh of the sauce at the bottom of each plate.

TAMALES OF RAJAS CON QUESO

Serves 6 / GF

Rajas con queso is a basic Central Mexican dish that can stand on its own or serve as the filling for just about any masa-based delivery system such as tacos or, as here, tamales. The essence of the dish is the combination of relatively mild poblano chiles (*rajas* are strips of poblanos) and cheese, in particular Oaxaca cheese. If you can't find Oaxaca cheese, Monterey Jack is a good substitute.

But the star of this dish is the tamale itself. Any decent brand of *masa harina* (corn flour) will do, but *masa harina para tamales* is ideal.

Place the corn husks into a large bowl and cover with warm water. Set aside to soak while you continue with the recipe. Prepare a steamer or set a steamer basket in a large stockpot. Fill the pot with water to just below the bottom of the steamer basket.

To make the masa, melt the lard in a small pan and allow it to cool , but not so much that it solidifies again. Put the masa harina in a large bowl and add the baking powder and salt. Pour in the stock while mixing with your hands little by little until you achieve a soft dough, about 3 minutes. Add the melted lard and mix until you have a slightly sticky dough. Taste and adjust with salt if needed.

To make the filling, place the chiles directly on the stove's flame (or over an open or charcoal fire, or blacken them using a blowtorch) and roast until the skin is fully blackened. Place the blackened chiles in a resealable bag and set aside to steam for about 5 minutes. Working over a sink, use your fingers or a damp paper towel to strip off the blackened parts. Try to avoid running the chiles under water, as the water will dilute the flavor. Cut the flesh into strips and set aside.

To assemble the tamales, drain the corn husks and pat them dry with a kitchen towel. Strip off 6 to 8 strings (it is always good to have a couple extra in case 1 or 2 of the strips break) of the corn husks to use as ties.

Ingredients

6 large dried corn husks, plus extra to tie the tamales and for the steaming pot

For the Masa (Tamale Dough)

⅓ cup lard or vegetable shortening

3 cups masa harina (preferably masa harina para tamales, if you can find it)

2 teaspoons baking powder

1½ teaspoons kosher salt

1 cup Chicken Stock (page 232), warmed, plus more as needed

For the Filling

2 poblano chiles

1 cup diced Oaxaca cheese

½ cup Roasted Tomatillo Salsa Verde (page 242)

Place 2 to 3 tablespoons of tamale dough in a corn husk and, using the back of a spoon, spread it in the middle. Add about 1 tablespoon of the salsa verde over the masa and top with 4 or 5 strips of the roasted chiles. Top with 2½ tablespoons of the cheese. Fold the right side of the corn husk to the center l and repeat with the left side. Take the narrow end of the husk and fold it toward the center. Use the strips of corn husk to tie off the top of the tamal.

Place the tamal standing upright in the steamer with the open side up. If necessary, use crinkled wads of foil to fill gaps and help the tamales stand up. Repeat until all the ingredients have been used and the steamer is filled up.

To cook the tamales, bring the water in the steamer to a boil over high heat, then reduce the heat to low, cover, and cook for about 1 hour 15 minutes, checking occasionally and adding more water when needed. To check if the tamales are done, remove one using kitchen tongs, place it on a plate, and let it rest for 5 minutes. Remove the husk; if it doesn't stick to the filling when removed, the tamales are ready.

TAMALES OF DUXELLES AND CORN with Black Bean Sauce and Roasted Poblano Crema

Makes 18 to 20 tamales / GF

Many who obsess about Mexican food focus on tacos, or maybe enchiladas. For me, though, tamales have been my personal obsession. The rich flavor of fresh masa harina (corn flour) and the resulting masa (tamale dough) was one of the foundational flavors of my childhood. And it was those tamales that really captured my imagination: a hint of sweetness and a deep earthiness that said this was something profound. I've been looking for it ever since.

That search is at the core of this dish, along with two more basic ideas: that ① black beans can be a sauce, and ② a tamal can be spherical in shape. The first of these was a discovery on a trip to Mexico City during which I enjoyed a remarkable meal at Quintonil, where I was incorrectly under the impression that Chef Jorge Vallejo used beans in that way. After learning my mistake, I asked myself another question: Why not do just that? The idea for the spherical shape came upon our return from that trip when we drove past CECUT, Tijuana's cultural center, which features a spectacular spherical dome housing an IMAX theater. Why not make tamale in that shape and pair them with a black bean sauce inspired—however incorrectly—by Quintonil?

To make the masa, combine the shortening, baking powder, and salt in the bowl of a stand mixer fitted with the paddle attachment (or, alternatively, in a food processor) and beat on medium-high speed until well whipped, about 1 minute. Add one-quarter of the masa harina at a time, beating each addition until thoroughly incorporated before adding the next. Add the stock and beat until the dough is light and has a soft, spreadable, hummus-like texture. Cover the masa with plastic wrap and refrigerate for 1 hour. Remove the masa from the refrigerator and beat again, adding additional stock 1 tablespoon at a time, if needed, to return the masa to its original texture.

To make the black bean sauce, combine the beans, onion halves, and stock in a large saucepan and bring to a boil over high heat. Reduce the heat to low and simmer until the beans are tender, about

For the Masa (Tamale Dough)

8 ounces vegetable shortening or lard

2 teaspoons baking powder

2 teaspoons kosher salt

3 cups masa harina (preferably masa harina para tamales, if you can find it)

1 cup Chicken Stock (page 232), plus more as needed

For the Black Bean Sauce

1 cup dried black beans, soaked in water to cover by a few inches overnight, then drained

1 large white onion, cut in half

5 cups Chicken Stock (page 232), Vegetable Stock (page 235), or Roasted Vegetable Stock (page 236)

1 tablespoon dry white wine, such as albariño

Kosher salt

For the Poblano Crema

2 poblano chiles

1 cup Mexican Crema (page 255)

1 teaspoon kosher salt

RECIPE AND INGREDIENTS CONTINUE

3 hours. Transfer the beans to a high-speed blender, reserving their cooking liquid, and add the wine. Blend, adding just enough of the reserved liquid to achieve a fine, sauce-like texture. Season with salt.

Meanwhile, to make the poblano chile sauce, place the chiles directly on your stove's flame (or over an open or charcoal fire, or blacken it using a blowtorch) and roast until the skin of the chiles is fully blackened. Place the blackened chiles in a resealable bag to steam the skin free from the flesh for about 5 minutes. Peel the skin from the chile using as little water as possible. Remove the seeds and membranes. Place the poblano flesh, crema, and salt in a food processor (clean the bowl if you used it for the masa) and puree. Transfer the sauce to a bowl and set aside.

To make the duxelles-corn filling, working in batches, finely chop the mushrooms in the food processor. Combine the mushrooms, shallot, and olive oil in a large sauté pan and season with salt and pepper. Cook over medium heat until the mushrooms have given up their liquid and the liquid has nearly all boiled away. Add the corn, season again with salt and pepper, and cook for 2 to 3 minutes, until the raw flavor is just off the corn.

To form the tamales, take a 1½- to 2-inch ball of the masa and, using your thumb, push a hole into the middle of it. Stuff the hole with about 1 teaspoon of the filling, then close it up, molding the masa back into a perfect tamale ball. Take a large square of plastic wrap and poke holes in it using the tip of a knife. Surround the tamale ball with the plastic wrap and twist the bottom to close it off. Repeat with the remaining masa and filling.

To cook the tamales, fill the bottom layer of a Chinese-style steamer set-up with water and bring to a boil. Meanwhile, line the bottom of each layer of the steamer baskets with cabbage leaves. Place the plastic-wrapped tamales on top of the cabbage leaves, set the steamer over the boiling water, and steam until the tamales are cooked through and the outside layer takes on a slightly hardened texture, about 45 minutes.

Pour a circle of the black bean sauce in the center of each plate. Top the sauce with 1 to 3 tamales, depending on when in the meal the dish is being served, and top them with the roasted poblano crema. Garnish with the beet microgreens.

For the Duxelles-Corn Filling

8 ounces button mushrooms

2 tablespoons finely minced shallot

2 tablespoons extra-virgin olive oil

Kosher salt and freshly ground black pepper

Kernels from 2 ears fresh sweet corn (white, yellow, or bicolor)

For the Tamales
Large cabbage leaves

For the Garnish
Red beet microgreens

HUITLACOCHE QUESADILLA

Serves 4 / GF / VEG

For much of my life, my primary relationship with the quesadilla was as the Mexican answer to the grilled cheese sandwich: cheese inside a folded corn tortilla fried in a pan. It was an ultimate comfort food for my sister and me as children, just as it was for my daughter. It would be some time before I saw that the quesadilla (and its cousin/doppelganger, the sincronizada) could be something of an art form in and of itself.

Here the comfort food of my childhood is taken to a new level by the incorporation of a singularly Mexican ingredient: huitlacoche. Known variously as corn truffle or, far less poetically, corn smut, huitlacoche is a fungus that attacks ears of corn, resulting in a mind-blowingly delicious (if not particularly pretty) ingredient that tastes like the happy union of corn and mushrooms.

It is difficult to find fresh huitlacoche north of the border, but it is available in Tijuana's Mercado Hidalgo. Huitlacoche is also regularly available in canned form at most Mexican markets, and the quality of the canned huitlacoche north of the border often exceeds that available in Baja.

Heat the oil in a large sauté pan over medium heat. When the oil ripples, add the onion and tomatoes and cook until the color of the tomatoes changes and they just start to lose their texture. Add the huitlacoche and epazote and cook until the huitlacoche is just heated through. Season with salt and set aside.

Lay out 4 of the tortillas on a cutting board. Top each with a scant tablespoon of the cheese and top that with 2 tablespoons of the huitlacoche mixture. Top with the remaining 4 tortillas.

Heat a large sauté pan over medium heat. Place a quesadilla in the pan and cook until the bottom tortilla just starts to turn golden, then flip and cook until the other side is golden and the cheese is fully melted. Transfer to a plate and repeat with the remaining quesadillas. Slice each quesadilla in half, garnish with pink pickled onions, and add some árbol chile salsa to the plate for dipping.

2 tablespoons grapeseed, canola, or other neutral oil

½ medium white onion, finely chopped

2 large tomatoes, diced

1 clove garlic, crushed and minced

12 ounces canned huitlacoche, such as Goya brand

4 fresh epazote leaves, or 8 fresh Mexican oregano leaves, finely chopped

Kosher salt

8 Corn Tortillas (page 228)

12 ounces shredded Oaxaca or Real del Castillo cheese

Pink Pickled Onions (page 259)

Árbol Chile Salsa (page 243)

SQUASH BLOSSOM AND MUSHROOM SINCRONIZADA

Serves 2 / GF / VEG

Once upon a time it was clear how quesadillas and sincronizadas differed. First, quesadillas were folded, while sincronizadas were stacked. Second, the former were made with corn tortillas (except north of the border, particularly in Texas), while the latter were made with flour tortillas. Now, though, the lines have blurred. Indeed, they have done so to the point that the real distinction between the two is just what they're called. It is pretty much like hoagies versus grinders versus subs on the East Coast of the US.

Squash blossoms—also known as zucchini flowers—are both beautiful and delicious. While they have a reputation as something of a luxury ingredient north of the border, when in season they are readily available at markets in Mexico. They're delicious battered and fried but are also used as a classic filling for quesadillas. A little cheese and some mushrooms complete the picture.

1 tablespoon grapeseed, canola, or other neutral oil, plus more for brushing

½ medium yellow onion, diced

2 cloves garlic, crushed and minced

8 ounces cremini or button mushrooms, sliced

1 cup squash blossoms (about 15 blossoms), stems and stamens removed, roughly chopped

Kosher salt and freshly ground black pepper

4 Corn Tortillas (page 228)

1 cup grated Oaxaca cheese

Heat 1 tablespoon of the oil in a large sauté pan over medium heat. When the oil ripples, add the onion and garlic and sauté until the onion just begins to lose its texture, 2 to 3 minutes. Add the mushrooms and cook for another 2 minutes. Add the squash blossoms and season with salt and pepper. Cook until most of the liquid has evaporated, another 4 to 5 minutes. Transfer to a metal bowl, cover with foil, and set aside.

Wipe the pan clean and heat over medium-high heat. Brush one side of a tortilla with oil and cook, oiled-side down, for 1 to 2 minutes, brushing the other side with oil as it cooks. Flip the tortilla and top it with 2 tablespoons of the cheese, one-quarter of the mushroom mixture, then by another 2 tablespoons of the cheese.

Fold the sincronizada in half and cook until the tortilla is well toasted and the cheese has melted, about 3 minutes on each side. Transfer to a plate and repeat with the remaining tortillas and filling.

MAIN COURSES

GOLDEN BEET POZOLE

Serves 4 / GF / VEGAN

In California—both Baja and Alta California—as well as throughout Mexico, the decision of how to make pozole for dinner might as well be a matrix. Traditionally, there were a couple of major factors:

Do you want chicken or pork?

Do you want a red, green, or white broth?

Your recipe turned on where among the six squares of the matrix your answers to those questions landed you. But today, whether in Baja or north of the border, there are more options. Pozole need not be meat-based. In fact, as this dish shows, it can be vegan.

It is the complex flavor of beets—one part sweet, one part earthy—that make them a perfect candidate for the pozole treatment. Golden beets offer a stunning visual contrast to the red hues of the guajillo and ancho chile–based sauce.

To roast the beets, preheat the oven to 375°F.

Fold a 12 by 24-inch sheet of aluminum foil in half to form a square. Crimp two open sides to seal and form a pouch. Toss the beets with the olive oil in a medium bowl until the beets are coated. Season with salt. Put them in the foil pouch and crimp the remaining side to seal. Transfer to a rimmed baking sheet and place in the oven. Roast until the beets are completely tender and a toothpick or knife tip inserted into a beet through the foil meets little to no resistance, about 1½ hours.

While the beets are cooking, make the broth. Heat a large sauté pan over medium heat. Toast the chiles in the pan until they just begin to develop dark marks, about 30 seconds. Flip the chiles and toast the other side. Place the chiles in a bowl with hot water to cover and soak for 30 minutes, or until they are tender and pliable.

Meanwhile, combine the olive oil, onion, fennel, and garlic in a soup pot and sweat the vegetables over low to medium heat until they release their water. Add the bay leaves and stock and bring to a boil over high heat. Reduce the heat to maintain a simmer and cook for at least 45 minutes and up to 90 minutes (the longer in this range the better), until the broth takes on a rich flavor that says "VEGETABLES!"

For the Beets

12 medium golden beets, greens removed, scrubbed

1 tablespoon extra-virgin olive oil

Kosher salt

For the Broth

5 dried guajillo chiles, stemmed and seeded

2 dried ancho chiles, stemmed and seeded

1 tablespoon extra-virgin olive oil

1 medium white onion, diced

1 medium fennel bulb, diced (fronds reserved)

3 cloves garlic, crushed

2 bay leaves

6 cups Roasted Vegetable Stock (page 236)

1 (30-ounce) can hominy, drained and rinsed

For the Garnish

Shredded green cabbage

Thinly sliced red radishes

Fresh cilantro leaves

Lime wedges

Drain the chiles and transfer them to a high-speed blender or food processor. Blend until pureed and add the puree to the soup pot, then add the hominy and bring to a boil. Reduce the heat to maintain a simmer and cook for 20 minutes, or until the hominy is soft.

Remove the beets from the oven and allow to cool. When cool enough to handle, peel the beets by gently rubbing away their skin under cold running water. (The cooked beets can be stored in the refrigerator for up to 5 days.)

Ladle the pozole into soup bowls, arrange 3 beets in each bowl, and garnish with cabbage, radishes, cilantro, and the reserved fennel fronds. Pass lime wedges at the table.

MIXED MUSHROOM MIXIOTE

Mushrooms are magic. There are so many kinds, each with its own flavor, texture, and other properties. Carnivores and omnivores alike revel in the mushroom's ability to add new dimensions to dishes or complement the star protein.

Mixiotes are a traditional dish of meat—perhaps most classically rabbit, but also chicken, lamb, pork, or a combination—wrapped in maguey leaves and pit-barbecued. But mushrooms can and should be afforded the opportunity of a turn. That is what this dish is all about.

Cut four 12-inch squares of parchment paper, loosely roll them together, submerge them in a large bowl of water, and weight them with a light plate. Soak for 30 minutes.

To make the four-chile sauce, toast the dried chiles on a dry sauté pan or cast-iron skillet over medium heat for about 20 seconds, until fragrant. Do not overtoast the chiles. Transfer the chiles to a large saucepan, then add the chipotles, onion, garlic, cumin, allspice, cinnamon, and water to cover. Bring to a simmer over high heat, then reduce the heat and simmer until the chiles, onions, and garlic are soft and fragrant. Transfer to a high-speed blender or food processor and blend until the mixture is smooth and thick, adding more water as needed. Pass through a fine-mesh strainer.

Preheat the oven to 325°F. While the oven is heating, combine the bacon and ¼ cup water in a sauté pan and cook medium heat until the water evaporates and the bacon fat renders, about 10 minutes. Add the onion and cook until it begins to turn translucent. Add the garlic and mushrooms and cook until the mushrooms just begin to give up their water, about 3 minutes. Transfer the contents of the pan to a large bowl, add 1 cup of the four-chile sauce, and stir to combine. (Extra sauce can be used with tacos.)

Lay the soaked parchment pieces out on a work surface. Place a corn husk in the center of each parchment square. Scoop a portion of the mushroom mixture into the center of each parchment piece and season with salt. Gather up the corners of the parchment to form a pouch. Pinch the parchment together just above the mushrooms and tie securely with a piece of kitchen twine.

Place the pouches on a baking sheet, then slide into the oven. Bake for 30 to 45 minutes, until the mixture is bubbling vigorously in the packages. Serve with fresh tortillas and lime wedges to squeeze.

For the Four-Chile Sauce

4 dried guajillo chiles, stemmed and seeded

2 dried ancho chiles, stemmed and seeded

10 dried chiles de árbol, stemmed and seeded

3 ounces chipotle chiles (from a can of chipotle chiles in adobo)

1 medium white onion, roughly chopped

10 cloves garlic, peeled

1 teaspoon ground cumin

½ teaspoon ground allspice

½ teaspoon ground cinnamon

For the Mushrooms

2 medium-thick slices bacon, cut into ¼-inch-wide strips

1 medium white onion, sliced

3 cloves garlic, peeled

1 pound assorted mushrooms, such as oyster, shiitake, porcini, and cremini, sliced

For Assembly and Serving

4 dried corn husks

Kosher salt

Corn Tortillas (page 228), warmed

Lime wedges

LENTIL GUISADO
with Marinated Mushroom Chips

Serves 6 / GF / VEGAN

Lentils may not be the first legume to come to mind when thinking about Mexican cuisine. But sopa de lentejas is common throughout the country, in particular in Northern Baja, and was a fixture of my childhood. This guisado captures the essence of the classic Mexican lentil soup, but the mushroom chips add heft and textural contrast. You can serve it as a main course, but it can also be the star of a wonderful vegetarian or vegan taco.

Combine all the mushroom chip ingredients in a large bowl and toss to combine. Marinate the mushrooms in the refrigerator for 1 hour.

When the mushrooms are almost done marinating, preheat the oven to 300°F and line a baking sheet with parchment paper.

Arrange the marinated mushroom on the prepared baking sheet and roast, turning or stirring them a few times, until the mushrooms are golden brown and crisp, 45 to 60 minutes.

To make the lentil guisado, sort through the lentils to eliminate any small rocks or pebbles, then rinse them in cold water, drain, and place in a large saucepan along with the carrot, onion, and stock. Bring to a boil, then lower the heat to maintain a simmer and cook until the lentils are soft, about 30 minutes.

Once the lentils are on the stove, place a sauté pan over medium heat and add the oil. When the oil is hot, add the garlic and cook to lightly brown it and infuse its flavor into the oil. Remove the garlic and reserve for another purpose. Add the chopped onion to the garlic oil and cook until translucent, taking care not to brown the onion, about 1 minute. Add the tomato, raise the heat to high, and cook, stirring and scraping the bottom of the pan with a wooden spoon, until the mixture reduces to a sauce, 3 to 5 minutes.

Add the tomato sauce and chiles to the lentils, season with salt, and cook over medium heat for up to 30 minutes more, until the lentils soften. Add the cilantro and cook until the guisado takes on the flavor of the cilantro, 3 to 5 minutes.

Ladle the guisado into serving bowls, top with mushroom chips, and garnish with cilantro and mint leaves.

For the Mushroom Chips

20 white button mushrooms, thinly sliced lengthwise

¼ cup extra-virgin olive oil

⅓ cup fresh orange juice

Juice of 2 limes

4 cloves garlic, minced

1 chipotle chile (from a can of chipotles in adobo), chopped

1 teaspoon smoked paprika

Generous pinch of kosher salt

For the Lentil Guisado

1 cup dried small brown lentils

1 medium carrot, cut into ¼-inch dice

1 large white onion, quartered

8 cups Vegetable Stock (page 235)

3 tablespoons grapeseed

2 cloves garlic, peeled

1 medium white onion, finely chopped

1½ cups finely chopped plum tomatoes

Kosher salt

2 jalapeño chiles, stemmed and seeded

2 tablespoons roughly chopped fresh cilantro

For the Garnish

¼ cup fresh mint leaves or cilantro leaves

GRILLED COTIJA AND SMOKED TOFU STUFFED ARTICHOKES

Makes 8 artichoke halves / GF / VEG

8 medium globe artichokes, prickly tops trimmed

3 limes

6 tablespoons extra-virgin olive oil

¼ cup brunoised Smoked Tofu (page 237; cut into ¹⁄₁₆-inch cubes)

2 cloves garlic, crushed and minced

½ cup Tortilla Crumbs (page 231)

2 tablespoons chopped fresh cilantro

¼ cup grated Cotija cheese

2 tablespoons white wine, such as Monte Xanic Chenin Colombard

Kosher salt

Artichokes are not a typical Mexican ingredient. I have only rarely seen them in markets south of the border. North of the border, though, is a different story. Artichokes are one of California's most iconic crops and are readily available year-round in both globe and baby form.

In this dish I treat globe artichokes with the typically Baja flavors of smoke and Cotija cheese with wine from the Valle de Guadalupe. Tofu is a wonderful blank canvas for absorbing the flavors of smoke and soy to add a strongly umami element akin to what people love in meat.

Fill a large pot three-quarters full with water. Squeeze in the juice from 2 limes, then toss in the squeezed limes. Remove the tough outer leaves of an artichoke until you get to the somewhat lighter and more tender inner leaves. Slice the artichoke in half and core out the choke (the furry part above the heart). Immediately place the artichoke in the pot of water, then repeat with the remaining artichokes. Cover the pot and bring the water to a rapid boil. Turn off the heat and let the artichokes sit in the covered pot for 5 to 7 minutes. Remove the artichokes from the water and drain. Press a paper towel against them to gently press out excess water.

Place the artichokes in a large baking pan, cut-side up, and drizzle 3 tablespoons of the olive oil on top, along with the zest and juice of the remaining lime. Flip the artichokes over, cover, and refrigerate the pan until ready to use.

Heat 1 tablespoon of the remaining oil in a medium sauté pan over medium heat. Add the smoked tofu and garlic and cook until the garlic just begins to crisp, about 2 minutes.

Combine the tortilla crumbs, smoked tofu, cilantro, remaining 2 tablespoons oil, the cheese, wine, and a dash of salt in a food processor. Pulse until everything is thoroughly chopped and combined but not pureed. Be careful not to overprocess.

Turn the artichokes over so they are once again cut-side up and gently press a small mound of stuffing into the cavity of each. Sprinkle with salt.

Prepare a grill for indirect heat. If using a charcoal grill, light the charcoal with a chimney starter, and when the coals are ready, pour them in an even layer over half of the bottom grate. If using a gas grill, light the burners on one side of the grill only. Place the artichoke halves cut-side down on the side of the grill grate that is not over the heat. Cover and grill until the outer leaves pull readily from the body of the artichoke, about 10 minutes. If you do not have a grill, a grill pan or even a sauté pan can work, but you won't get the same flavor or appearance. Use a pastry brush to brush the artichokes all over with the herb-infused oil. Sprinkle with salt and serve.

TOMATO AND REAL DEL CASTILLO QUESO FUNDIDO

with Soy Chorizo

Serves 2 / GF / VEG

One of my favorite family dinners when I was a kid was fondue. Whether dipping bread in a cauldron of roiling cheese or skewered meat morsels in boiling oil, there was always something fun and festive about this Swiss way of dining. It was, in my mind, the ultimate family meal.

Until recently, it did not occur to me that Mexico had an adopted (and adapted) cousin of cheese fondue: queso fundido. Here I use Valle de Guadalupe white wine along with one of Mexico's best cheeses—Real del Castillo cheese from the Ramonetti Cheese factory at La Cava de Marcelo in Ojos Negros, east of Ensenada—to go back in time. At least in my mind.

To make the queso fundido, roughly grate the garlic and rub the grated garlic around the inside of a pot large enough to hold at least 6 cups and place over medium heat. Pour in the passata and wine and bring to a boil.

Add a handful of the cheese. Once that cheese is melted, add another handful and repeat until all the cheese is melted. Meanwhile, in a small bowl, make a slurry by whisking the cornstarch with 2 tablespoons water. Stir in the slurry to thicken the fondue slightly. Add the oregano and stir to combine. Taste the queso fundido and, if desired, season with salt and pepper.

Cook the soy chorizo in a large sauté pan over medium heat until crumbly. Drain off the fat into a heatproof container. Garnish the queso fundido in the pot with the soy chorizo and cilantro leaves. Serve in the pot on top of a metal stand or hot pad with the tortilla chips for dipping.

For the Queso Fundido

2 cloves garlic, peeled

1⅔ cups passata, such as Colavita or Cento brand (or use pureed tomatoes)

½ cup white wine, such as Monte Xanic Chenin Colombard

2¼ cups grated Ramonetti Real del Castillo cheese (raclette, Oaxaca, and Monterey Jack cheese are adequate substitutes)

1 tablespoon cornstarch

1 teaspoon dried Mexican oregano

Kosher salt and freshly ground black pepper (optional)

For Serving

9 ounces loose soy chorizo

10 attractive cilantro leaves

1 pound tortilla chips (freshly fried, baked, or store-bought)

ROASTED BRUSSELS SPROUTS AND CARROTS with Almond Mole

North of the border, we tend to think of mole as a sauce for poultry, and not without reason. Perhaps the most famous mole dish is turkey with mole poblano. But that is only one dish, and mole poblano is just one of hundreds of moles. Mole almendrado would certainly work well with poultry but perhaps pairs even more successfully with roasted vegetables.

While this recipe is written for the oven, there is no reason the carrots and Brussels sprouts could not be grilled or even smoked to intensify the Baja character of the dish. Doing so would only pair them better with the sweetness of the mole.

Preheat the oven to 425°F. Line a baking sheet with parchment paper.

Remove all but the last ¼ inch of the stems of the carrots. Toss the carrots in the olive oil and season with the cumin and salt. Put the carrots on the prepared baking sheet.

Trim off the brown part of the base of the Brussels sprouts and pull off any yellowed outer leaves. Slice the Brussels sprouts in half from the center of the top down through their base. Place the Brussels sprout halves a bowl, toss with the olive oil, and season with salt and pepper. Place them on the baking sheet with the carrots.

Place the baking sheet in the oven and roast until the Brussels sprouts are crisp on the outside and tender on the inside, 35 to 40 minutes. The carrots are done when you can pierce them with a knife and the blade slides easily into the middle. Check the vegetables for seasoning.

While the vegetables are roasting, put the almond mole and stock in a small saucepan, break up the paste with a wooden spoon, and bring to a boil over medium-high heat. Reduce the heat to maintain a simmer; simmer until it reaches a thick sauce-like consistency, about 20 minutes.

Arrange the vegetables on a plate and drizzle with the mole.

For the Roasted Carrots

12 medium carrots

2 tablespoons extra-virgin olive oil

1 teaspoon ground cumin

Kosher salt

For the Roasted Brussels Sprouts

12 Brussels sprouts

2 tablespoons extra-virgin olive oil

Kosher salt and freshly ground black pepper

For the Mole

1 cup Almond Mole (page 250)

½ cup Chicken Stock (page 232), Roasted Vegetable Stock (page 236), or Vegetable Stock (page 235)

HUITLACOCHE AND PEA RISOTTO

Serves 4 / GF / VEG

Making risotto is a culinary meditation. The secret to making good risotto is time. Time, patience, and the right kind of rice, along with a few basic concepts, yield a dish that's creamy, rich, and simultaneously soft and toothsome.

While risotto may hardly be the first dish that comes to mind when one thinks of Mexican cuisine, the strong influence of Italian immigrants on the Baja restaurant scene mean it is certainly not out of place. Add a classic Mexican ingredient, huitlacoche (corn truffle—more on page 153), and one can only wonder why it's not on the menu of every higher-end restaurant in Tijuana.

To make the tomato confit (if using), combine the tomatoes, garlic, and oil in a small saucepan and bring to a boil. Immediately reduce the heat to maintain a simmer and cook for 40 minutes. Remove from the heat and let the tomatoes cool in the oil.

Bring the stock to a boil in a medium saucepan, then immediately reduce the heat to maintain a simmer. In a heavy medium pot, heat the olive oil over medium-high heat. Add the shallots and cook until translucent, 2 to 3 minutes. Add the fennel and cook for 1 minute. Add the rice and stir well, just coating it in the oil.

Add ½ cup of the wine to the pan with the rice and cook, stirring, until most of the liquid has been absorbed. Do the same with ½ cup stock, then ½ cup wine, then another ½ cup stock, and repeat until all the wine has been absorbed and there is about ½ cup stock remaining, stirring constantly all the while. Turn the heat down to low and add the thyme. Cook, stirring, until fragrant, about 30 seconds. Taste and season with salt.

Test the doneness on the rice; it should be fully cooked but not mushy. The goal is al dente with each grain distinct but the whole dish creamy. If it is not done, continue cooking and adding stock. When it is nearly finished, add the huitlacoche and peas and cook for 2 to 3 minutes. Add the cheese and mix to combine. When the cheese is melted, fold to mix thoroughly. Season with salt and let rest for a minute or two to cool and thicken.

For each serving, spoon the risotto into a ring mold set on a plate. Using the bottom of a wineglass, spoon, or spatula, compress the risotto gently, just barely enough to make it stay in place. Spoon 1 confit tomato over the risotto and arrange some of the fennel fronds on top.

For the Tomato Confit (optional)

10 cherry tomatoes, cut in half (or quartered, if they are particularly large)

1 clove garlic, minced

¼ cup grapeseed oil

For the Risotto

4 cups Vegetable Stock (page 235) or Roasted Vegetable Stock (page 236)

2 tablespoons extra-virgin olive oil

2 large shallots, minced

1 tablespoon finely minced fennel (fronds reserved for garnish)

2 cups Arborio rice

2 cups very dry unoaked white wine, such as sauvignon blanc

1 ounce dried porcini mushrooms, soaked in 2 to 3 cups hot water until soft (about 20 minutes)

1 tablespoon fresh thyme leaves

Kosher salt

1 (7-ounce) can huitlacoche, such as Goya brand

1 cup frozen peas

½ cup grated Cotija cheese

SALT-BAKED SHEEPSHEAD
with Veracruzana Sauce

Salt-baking is a classic cookery technique that results in stunningly moist and flavorful proteins. Nearly every European country on the Mediterranean claims the technique of cooking in a salt crust as their own: the Spanish, French, and Italians in particular. Of course, the Chinese have been salt-baking chicken since the Qing Dynasty (1644–1911) and the North Africans cooked shad in salt back in medieval times. Salt-baked fish may even date back to the Phoenicians.

Salt-baking results in moist, flaky fish with its juices sealed in by the salt crust. Pairing it with warm corn tortillas and a classic Veracruz-style sauce completes the picture.

To make the fish, preheat the oven to 400°F. Line a baking sheet with aluminum foil.

Either by hand or using a stand mixer, whisk the egg whites to soft peaks and fold in the salt. Place the onion, cilantro, and limes in the fish's cavity and set aside. Place ¼ cup of the salt–egg white mixture on the prepared baking sheet and place the fish on top of the mixture. Spoon the remaining mixture over the top and mold it around the fish. Place the fish in the oven and bake for 30 minutes.

To make the Veracruz-style sauce, heat the olive oil in a medium saucepan over medium heat. Add the garlic and cook briefly to release its flavor, then add the tomatoes, onion, pickled chiles, olives, oregano, capers, and ¼ cup water. Bring to a boil, then reduce the heat to low and cook until the tomatoes soften, about 20 minutes. Taste the sauce and add salt if necessary.

While the sauce is simmering, remove the fish from the oven. Using a large knife, rap the salt crust sharply to crack it. Carefully remove the salt from the fish, brushing it away rather than ripping it off.

Serve the whole fish on a platter, top with the sauce, and garnish with cilantro. Serve with tortillas alongside.

Note: While this recipe is wonderful with sheepshead, you can use whatever firm-fleshed fish you can find at your local fishmonger. (You do have one of those, don't you? Supermarket fresh fish is rarely exceptional unless you have a truly superb supermarket.)

For the Salt-Baked Fish

1 (3- to 4-pound) whole sheepshead or other whole fish, such as red snapper, sea bream, or sea bass, cleaned and gutted

6 large egg whites

6 cups (about 1 box) kosher salt

1 medium white onion, cut into quarter-moons

1 bunch cilantro

3 limes, cut into thick slices

For the Veracruz-Style Sauce

¼ cup extra-virgin olive oil

5 cloves garlic, minced

2 cups diced seeded tomatoes

1 medium white onion, sliced

4 Pickled Jalapeño Chiles (page 260), chopped

5 green olives, pitted and roughly chopped

1 tablespoon dried Mexican oregano

1 tablespoon capers

Kosher salt

For Serving

Attractive cilantro leaves

Corn Tortillas (page 228), warmed

OPAH ABDUCTOR MEATBALLS IN CHILMOLE

Serves 4

Opah is a common bycatch in tuna fisheries. It was a rarely marketable catch in the Cali-Baja region until Tommy Gomes, then of San Diego's Catalina Offshore Products, worked hard to help restaurants see it as such. Among the amazing qualities of this fish is that its abductor muscle remarkably mimics the textures—and, to a large degree, the flavors—of red meat. If you cannot find opah abductor or special order it from your fishmonger, you can substitute ground flank steak.

It was with that in mind that I chose to use the opah abductor muscles for *albóndigas*—meatballs—and pair them as a starter with a chilmole sauce. The latter is a precursor to the grand moles of Mexican cuisine. The chilmole's charred flavors round out the flavors of the albóndigas, resulting in a rich, satisfying dish.

To make the opah balls, mince the opah abductor, either with a very sharp knife or in a meat grinder. Combine the opah, breadcrumbs, egg whites, sugar, and salt in a large bowl. Mix them thoroughly but gently. Fry up a teaspoon of the mixture to test the seasoning and add more salt as needed.

Form the opah mixture into 12 even, perfectly spherical balls. Heat the oil in a large wok or sauté pan over medium heat. When the oil is hot, add the balls to the wok in a single layer, working in batches if necessary. Let the opah balls sizzle in the pan for 2 to 3 minutes, until browned on the bottom, then flip and cook until browned on the second side (they don't have to be cooked through). Remove from the pan with a slotted spoon and set aside.

Line the bottom of a large pot with the bok choy leaves. Place the opah balls on top and turn the heat to medium-low. Cover and steam for 30 to 40 minutes, until the opah balls are cooked through, and the bok choy leaves have wilted and their stems are tender. Check periodically to see if the pot is dry and, if so, add a tablespoon or two of water. Transfer the balls to a side plate.

While the opah balls are steaming, make the chilmole sauce. Heat a dry pan over high heat. Spread out the garlic, onion, and both chiles on the hot pan and roast until all elements are well colored and begin to develop significant char (nearly black and generally after you've asked

For the Opah Balls

1 pound opah abductor muscle (not the loin)

¼ cup breadcrumbs

2 large egg whites

1 tablespoon sugar

1 tablespoon kosher salt, plus more if needed

2 tablespoons grapeseed, canola, or other neutral oil

2 large bok choy leaves

For the Chilmole

10 cloves garlic, peeled

1 medium white onion, roughly chopped

10 dried ancho chiles, stemmed and seeded

2 dried chiles de árbol, stemmed and seeded

1 cup boiling water

3 tablespoons dried Mexican or Greek oregano

1½ teaspoons ground Mexican cinnamon (canela)

1 teaspoon freshly ground black pepper

½ teaspoon ground allspice

¼ teaspoon ground cloves

2 teaspoons achiote paste

yourself whether you've burnt them). Depending on the size of your pan, you may need to do this in batches. It will take 5 to 10 minutes, depending on the heat of your stove. As each item achieves the necessary char, remove it from the pan and set aside. Remove the stems and seeds from the roasted chiles, roughly chop the chiles, put them in a medium bowl, and add the boiling water. Cover and soak while you prepare the toasted spices.

In a small nonstick pan, combine the oregano, cinnamon, black pepper, allspice, and cloves and toast over medium heat until fragrant, about 1 minute. Watch for smoke and remove the pan from the heat if the spices begin to burn.

Combine the achiote paste with the charred garlic, onion, and chiles and the toasted spices in a high-speed blender or food processor. Add the salt and tortillas and blend until the mixture comes together into a smooth paste. Add the stock and blend to a sauce consistency.

To plate the dish, spoon ¼ cup of the sauce in a circle in the middle of a plate. Top with 3 opah balls and garnish each with a cilantro leaf and some pickled pink onions.

2 teaspoons kosher salt

3 small Corn Tortillas (page 228), ripped into pieces

2 cups Chicken Stock (page 232)

For the Garnish

12 attractive cilantro leaves

Pink Pickled Onions (page 259), brunoised

MEXICALI AND LA CHINESCA

The Imperial Valley floods of the 1970s did more than drown crops and ruin the town of Ocotillo. Across the border in Mexicali those floods hit an area in the neighborhood of La Chinesca. The Chinese residents of Mexicali—who'd once outnumbered their Mexican hosts—were forced, once and for all, to abandon their underground city. Today the nearly three hundred Chinese restaurants in Mexicali may be the clearest evidence of the five thousand remaining Mexicali Chinese.

At one level, Mexicali Chinese cuisine is Chinese food made for Mexicans. Indeed, on multiple visits to Mexicali Chinese restaurants, I cannot recall seeing a single set of chopsticks. At another level, it is Chinese food made with Mexican ingredients: a truly organic form of fusion cuisine. At its base, the food of La Chinesca features the foodstuffs of the immediate vicinity. Asparagus is one of the highest-value crops farmed in the Mexicali Valley. Not surprisingly, it features heavily on Mexicali Chinese menus. Callo de hacha (a scallop-like mollusk; see page 82) is another high-value Baja ingredient that is common on La Chinesca menus.

Foodies and purists toss around terms like *authenticity* as some sort of culinary gold standard. Those so inclined tend to sneer at American-style Chinese food and would, quite probably, view Mexicali Chinese similarly. And yet just as there's a resurgence of Shaanxi, after being passed over as one of "China's eight great cuisines," perhaps Mexicali Chinese should be treated as a regional style of Chinese food in its own right, one worth serious consideration.

MEXICALI-STYLE CHORIZO, SHRIMP, AND ASPARAGUS FRIED RICE

Serves 4 / GF

This is a classic Cantonese-style dish seen through the lens of Mexicali's La Chinesca. It features Mexican chorizo and shrimp coming up the Gulf of California from Sinaloa, along with the asparagus that is one of Mexicali's main cash crops. The key to this dish, like all fried rice dishes, is to use day-old rice.

In a large wok or sauté pan, heat the grapeseed and sesame oils over high heat until they just ripple. Add the chorizo and cook, stirring occasionally, until golden brown, 4 to 5 minutes. Leave about 2 tablespoons of the chorizo oil in the wok and discard the remainder. Return the chorizo to the wok and add the shrimp, onion, garlic, bell peppers, and asparagus. Cook for about 1 minute, just until the shrimp are no longer translucent and the vegetables are cooked through.

Add the cooked rice and soy sauce and season with salt and pepper and the paprika. Toss to combine, keeping the wok moving all the time. Add the parsley. Garnish with lemon wedges, if desired, and serve.

1 tablespoon grapeseed, canola, or other neutral oil

1 teaspoon toasted sesame oil

8 ounces loose Mexican chorizo

1 pound shrimp, peeled and deveined

1 small white onion, chopped

3 cloves garlic, minced

2 medium red bell peppers, diced

8 ounces asparagus, trimmed and cut into ½-inch segments

3 cups day-old cooked jasmine or other long-grain rice

1 tablespoon soy sauce or tamari

Kosher salt and freshly ground black pepper

1 teaspoon sweet paprika

¼ cup chopped fresh parsley

Lemon wedges for serving (optional)

BACON-POACHED BLACK COD
with Fennel-Oregano Salt and Lime Vinaigrette

Serves 4 / GF

Black cod is neither black in color nor actually cod. Rather, it is sablefish! While it bears a passing resemblance to true cod, sablefish, when cooked, has flaky, oily flesh with a mild flavor, a soft buttery texture, and a pearly white color. It is, perhaps, my favorite of the fish on the Northern Mexico and Southern California coast. Like much seafood, black cod pairs wonderfully with the flavor of bacon, which finds its way onto the plate in multiple ways: the fat of the bacon is rendered and used to cook the fish and make the lime vinaigrette, and the meat of the bacon serves as a critical garnishing ingredient. The recipe makes more seasoned salt than will be used in this dish. Whatever's left can be used for just about any roasted meat or fish dish or even for the vegetables in the previous recipe.

2 to 3 pounds sliced bacon (depending on the fat content of the bacon)

2 tablespoons fennel seeds or aniseed

1 tablespoon fresh Mexican oregano leaves

2 tablespoons kosher salt

4 (4- to 6-ounce) skinless black cod fillets (have your fishmonger clean the fillets and remove any pin bones)

2 tablespoons fresh lime juice

1 tablespoon Dijon mustard

Pink Pickled Onions (page 259)

Heat a large skillet over medium-low heat. Working in batches, add the bacon to the pan and cook until the fat renders and the bacon is crispy and golden, 8 to 10 minutes per batch. After each batch, drain off the rendered fat, pouring it through a fine-mesh strainer into a saucepan just large enough to hold 2 of the cod fillets. Put the bacon in a food processor and pulse to chop it into bits. Reserve one-third of the bacon bits for garnish and the rest for another use.

Heat a small skillet over medium heat and add the fennel seeds. Cook for 1 minute, then add the oregano and cook until the aroma of the oregano becomes evident. Put the fennel, oregano, and salt in a spice grinder and grind to a fine powder.

While the bacon fat is still warm (or reheat 1 to 2 cups of the reserved bacon fat to 160° to 170°F), place 2 pieces of the fish in the fat. Lower the heat and poach the fish in the fat until just cooked through, 8 to 10 minutes, depending on the size of the fillets. Remove the pan from the heat and set aside for 10 minutes.

Put ½ cup of the bacon fat, the lime juice, and the mustard in a high-speed blender or food processor and blend to thoroughly combine.

Spoon a half-circle of the vinaigrette onto each plate. Place a black cod fillet at the apex of the half-circle. Sprinkle each fillet with some of the fennel-oregano salt and garnish with the bacon bits and pink pickled onions.

SHRIMP ZARANDEADO

For the first few years we had our place in Baja, going to Popotla—a small fishing village sitting in the shadow of a movie studio where *Pirates of the Caribbean* and *Titanic* were filmed—to buy the star of the night's dinner was something of a ritual. Most times we would take the opportunity to eat brunch with sand between our toes. That usually meant one thing: zarandeado. It was butterflied red snapper slathered in a mayonnaise, garlic, achiote, chile, and lime marinade and cooked over an open fire in a metal cage the cook would periodically flip. It was dramatic and it was delicious.

It was also something that a home cook is unlikely to replicate literally. This shrimp zarandeado, though, is a tasty version of the original that you can easily do on a backyard grill. The sand between the toes, on the other hand, you'll have to figure out yourself.

Soak wooden skewers in hot water for at least 30 minutes prior to use (or use metal skewers).

Cut the chiles into 4 or 5 pieces. Toast the chile pieces on a dry sauté pan or cast-iron skillet over medium heat for about 20 seconds, until fragrant. Do not overtoast the chiles. It is better to go too short than too long. Place the chile pieces in a bowl with enough hot water to fully cover them. Soak them for 10 minutes, or until they are pliable.

Put the soaked chile pieces, achiote, orange juice, lime juice, tomato paste, mayonnaise, garlic, olive oil, Maggi seasoning, soy sauce, Worcestershire, salt, cumin, and ginger in a high-speed blender or food processor. Beginning on low speed and gradually increasing the speed, blend until very smooth, about 3 minutes.

Transfer the sauce to a large bowl, add the shrimp, and marinate in the refrigerator for 45 minutes.

Prepare a grill for medium heat or put charcoal over the medium heat area of a grill. Place about 4 pieces of shrimp on each skewer. Cook the shrimp for 6 to 8 minutes, flipping them once, until opaque. Remove from the grill and place the skewers on a foil-lined plate or tray. Season with salt and pepper, squeeze plenty of lime juice over the shrimp, and garnish with the cucumbers and red onion.

Special Equipment

4 large wooden or metal skewers

8 dried guajillo chiles, stemmed and seeded

3½ tablespoons achiote paste

2 tablespoons fresh orange juice

¾ cup fresh lime juice

2 tablespoons tomato paste

¼ cup Mayonnaise (page 255)

6 cloves garlic, crushed

2 tablespoons extra-virgin olive oil

2 tablespoons Maggi seasoning

¼ cup soy sauce

¼ cup Worcestershire sauce

1 tablespoon kosher salt, plus more as needed

1 tablespoon ground cumin

1 tablespoon minced fresh ginger

2 pounds fresh U15 shrimp, peeled (tails left on) and deveined

Freshly ground black pepper

Lime wedges for squeezing

2 cups diced (¼-inch) Persian cucumbers

½ medium red onion, thinly sliced

SOUS-VIDE GRILLED OCTOPUS AND MEXICAN SQUASH with
Ginger-Chipotle Sauce, Avocado Puree, and Cilantro Jus

Serves 2 or 3 / GF

If Cali-Baja cuisine had a single signature ingredient, there is a very good chance it would be octopus. From high-end restaurants like Javier Plascencia's Animalón to Baja's ubiquitous mariscos stands, octopus appears on Baja—and Alta—California menus regularly. And it appears on those menus in a spectacularly ingenious variety of preparations.

This version takes the beautiful bounty of Baja's seas and shore and applies both classic and modern techniques as well as Baja's rich and surprising culinary and ethnic heritages to the ingredients, combining them in a new way. It is a dynamic dish, evolving on the palate as the ginger-chipotle sauce gives way to the octopus, then the fresh, crisp Mexican squash—think slightly squat and lighter in color than zucchini (though zucchini is a good substitute)—then the avocado, and finally the cilantro jus.

Cooking octopus may seem intimidating, but it should not be. If you can boil water, you can cook octopus. There is no reason you couldn't cook the octopus for this dish just that way, in fact: bring a large saucepan of salted water to a boil, add the octopus, reduce the heat to maintain a simmer, and cook until the center of a tentacle is tender when pierced by a knife, 45 to 60 minutes. But if you have sous vide equipment at your disposal, the method in this recipe is even easier.

To cook the octopus, set up a water bath with an immersion circulator and heat the water to 178°F. Bring a large pot of salted water to a boil and fill a large bowl with ice and water.

Cut the head off the octopus, slicing just under the eyes. Discard the head. Using kitchen shears or a very sharp paring knife, separate the tentacles by cutting through the flesh from the point where they join each other to the very center of the mass. Put the tentacles in the boiling water and blanch for 10 seconds. Remove the tentacles from the water and plunge them into the ice bath. Using clean hands, rub the tentacles to remove the slimy skin.

For the Octopus

Kosher salt

1 octopus (about 3 pounds), defrosted and cleaned

Extra-virgin olive oil

6 bay leaves

For the Avocado Puree

1 medium shallot, chopped

1 clove garlic, minced

½ medium tomato, peeled and chopped

2 tablespoons sherry vinegar, balsamic vinegar, or red wine vinegar

1 teaspoon soy sauce or tamari

1 tablespoon extra-virgin olive oil

4 medium Hass avocados

For the Ginger-Chipotle Sauce

1 medium white onion, diced

1 large carrot, diced

1 bulb fennel, sliced (fronds reserved for garnish or another purpose)

1 tablespoon extra-virgin olive oil

RECIPE AND INGREDIENTS CONTINUE

Divide the blanched tentacles among 4 food-grade vacuum sealer bags, adding 1 teaspoon olive oil and a bay leaf to each bag. Vacuum seal the bags, place them in the water bath, and cook the octopus for 5 hours.

To make the avocado puree, combine the shallot and garlic in a food processor and process for 10 to 15 seconds, until finely chopped. Add the tomato, vinegar, soy sauce, and olive oil and process for 30 seconds, or until combined. Scoop the avocado flesh into the food processor and process until as smooth as possible.

To make the ginger-chipotle sauce, sweat the onion, carrot, and fennel in the olive oil in a medium saucepan over low to medium heat for 3 minutes. Add the ginger and chipotles and bring to a boil. Reduce the heat to maintain a simmer and cook for 30 minutes. Transfer the sauce to a high-speed blender and blend to a very smooth puree with a sauce-like texture. Refrigerate the sauce, allowing it to cool completely. Transfer the sauce to a squeeze bottle.

To make the cilantro jus, bring the stock to a boil in a medium pot. Meanwhile, place the cilantro in a high-speed blender. Add the hot stock and puree. Refrigerate the sauce, allowing it to cool completely. Transfer the sauce to a squeeze bottle.

To cook the squash, heat a grill pan until nearly smoking hot (alternatively, prepare an outdoor grill for high-heat cooking). Meanwhile, cut the squash lengthwise into ¼-inch-thick slices and brush them with the oil. When the pan is hot, sear the squash, turning once, until just barely tender, about 3 minutes.

To finish the octopus, remove the tentacles from the bags and season with salt. Heat the oil in a large sauté pan over very high heat. Working in batches, add the tentacles to the pan and sear for 1 to 1½ minutes per side, until they are lightly colored.

To assemble the dish, pour a round pool of the ginger-chipotle sauce in the center of each plate. Swipe the avocado puree around the top, going from 9 o'clock to 12 o'clock. Place a segment of the squash at the center of the plate. Place an octopus tentacle on top of the squash extending downward toward the tip. Garnish with the cilantro leaves, fennel fronds (if using), and droplets of the cilantro jus.

Note: The recipe makes far more sauce than will be used for this dish. The sauces are both excellent on chicken or fish and tacos of nearly every type.

1 (2-inch) knob ginger, trimmed and sliced

4 chipotle chiles (from a can of chipotle chiles in adobo)

4 cups Chicken Stock (page 232)

For the Cilantro Jus

2 cups Chicken Stock (page 232)

2 bunches cilantro, leaves and tender stems, roughly chopped

For the Mexican Squash

3 medium Mexican squash (or zucchini)

1 tablespoon grapeseed, canola, or other neutral oil

Kosher salt

To Finish

2 tablespoons grapeseed, canola, or other neutral oil

4 to 6 attractive cilantro leaves

CHICKEN POZOLE VERDE

Serves 4 / GF

Pozole is a traditional class of soup or stew dishes in Mexico with a shared base of hominy cooked in broth. Pozole can be red (when the broth and flavor profile are based on dried chiles), green (based on fresh chiles), or white (without either green or red sauce). The proteins for pozole are usually pork (for red pozole), chicken (for green pozole), or beans or other vegetables for just about any pozole. This classic green pozole is built on chicken and fresh chiles along with pepitas.

Heat a sauté pan over medium heat. Add the pepitas and toast, stirring constantly, until the seeds start to pop and smell nutty, about 4 minutes. Transfer the pepitas to a bowl and set aside.

Pour the stock and 1 cup water into a Dutch oven large enough to accommodate both the chicken and the hominy with plenty of room to spare and place over medium-high heat. Put the chicken, tomatillos, onion, jalapeño and poblano chiles, oregano, and a large pinch of salt in the Dutch oven. Bring to a boil over high heat, then reduce the heat to maintain a bare simmer. Cook, stirring occasionally, until the chicken and vegetables are completely tender, about 40 minutes.

Using tongs, transfer the chicken to a large plate or bowl and set aside. Strain the broth through a large fine-mesh strainer set over a large bowl. Transfer the solids in the strainer to a high-speed blender or food processor and add the pepitas and cilantro. Blend on high speed until smooth. Set aside.

Using a ladle, skim off a few tablespoons of fat from the broth and add to the Dutch oven. Cook over high heat, stirring constantly, until the liquid completely evaporates and starts to form a browned layer on the bottom of the pan. When the fat starts to smoke (and knowing a lot of spattering is about to occur), pour in the contents of the blender and cook, stirring, for about 15 seconds. Immediately pour in the broth and any fat that has risen to the surface and stir to combine. Bring to a bare simmer, stir in the hominy, season with salt, and keep warm.

When the chicken is cool enough to handle, pull the meat from the skin and bones and shred it (discard the skin and bones). You could use two forks, but your hands are a vastly superior tool for the job. The goal is bite-size pieces and strips. Return the shredded chicken to the pot and stir to combine. Bring the soup back up to a simmer over medium heat. Ladle the pozole into soup bowls and serve with the garnishes alongside.

For the Pozole

½ cup pepitas (pumpkin seeds)

6 cups Chicken Stock (page 232)

1 (2½-pound) whole chicken

1 pound tomatillos, husked and rinsed

1 large white onion, roughly chopped

2 jalapeño chiles, stemmed, seeded, and roughly chopped

1 poblano chile, stemmed, seeded, and roughly chopped

2 tablespoons dried Mexican oregano

Kosher salt

Handful fresh cilantro, leaves and tender stems

1 (28-ounce) can white hominy, drained and rinsed

For the Garnish

Diced avocado

Shredded green cabbage

Thinly sliced red radishes

1 medium white onion, diced

Fresh cilantro leaves

Dried Mexican oregano

Chiles de árbol

Lime wedges

BAJA ROAST CHICKEN

Serves 2 to 4 / GF

Roast chicken might not strike one as a typically Baja (or Mexican) dish. But there is hardly a town in Baja large enough to have a gas station that does not have one or more roast or rotisserie chicken chains on the main drag. In our little town it's El Pollo Asil. In others it is El Rey del Pollo or any of a number of similar iterations. What they sell, what they all have in common, is the same homey, comforting hug that roast chicken has always represented, but with the added flair of the region's flavors, like citrus, chiles, and both sweet and savory spices. The classic accompaniments—corn tortillas, refried beans, and Mexican rice—complete the picture and the meal. The recipe will yield more spice blend than is needed for this recipe. It is excellent with just about any chicken or pork dish.

In a small bowl, whisk together the coriander, 1 tablespoon of the cumin, 1 tablespoon of the annatto, the garlic powder, 1 tablespoon of the salt, 2 teaspoons of the oregano, and 1 teaspoon of the pepper to combine. Transfer 2 tablespoons of this spice blend to a separate medium bowl and reserve the rest for another use.

Add the remaining 1 teaspoon cumin, 1 teaspoon annatto, 1 teaspoon salt, 1 teaspoon pepper, 1 tablespoon oregano, the ancho chile powder, olive oil, orange juice, lime juice, vinegar, and garlic to the bowl with the spice blend and whisk to thoroughly combine.

Rinse the chicken and pat dry. Put the chicken in a large resealable bag and pour the marinade over the chicken. Marinate in the refrigerator for at least 1 hour or preferably 3 to 5 hours.

Preheat the oven to 400°F. Line a baking sheet with parchment paper.

Place the chicken on the prepared baking sheet and roast for 30 minutes, or until the skin browns. Reduce the oven temperature to 350°F and roast for 30 to 45 minutes more, checking occasionally and basting the chicken with its juices, until a meat thermometer inserted into the thickest part of the thigh registers 175°F. Rest the chicken for 10 minutes before carving.

Serve the chicken with corn tortillas, Mexican rice, and refried beans along with shredded cabbage and your choice of salsas.

1 tablespoon ground coriander

1 tablespoon plus 1 teaspoon ground cumin

1 tablespoon plus 1 teaspoon ground annatto seeds (achiote) or turmeric

1 tablespoon garlic powder

1 tablespoon plus 1 teaspoon kosher salt

1 tablespoon plus 2 teaspoons dried Mexican oregano

2 teaspoons freshly ground black pepper

1 tablespoon ancho chile powder

½ cup extra-virgin olive oil

Juice of 1 large orange

Juice of 1 lime

2 tablespoons apple cider vinegar

6 cloves garlic, minced

1 (3- to 4-pound) whole chicken

For Serving

Corn Tortillas (page 228), warmed

Mexican Rice (page 237)

Refried Beans (page 239)

Shredded green cabbage

Salsas of your choice

ENRIQUE OLVERA'S CHICKEN TINGA

Serves 4 / GF

When I read *Tu Casa Mi Casa*, the home cookbook of Enrique Olvera—the superstar chef of Mexico City restaurant Pujol—I was struck by his description of chicken tinga as "the first recipe any Mexican will cook as soon as they move out of their parents' home and live on their own." When I cooked it, I could see why he wrote that. For one, as simple as the recipe is, it teaches so much about the basics of building flavor in Mexican cuisine. And, perhaps most important, it exemplifies the warm embrace that is the Mexican kitchen.

Olvera suggests using the dish for two meals: the first night served over rice with tortillas, and the next day cooked down and used as a tostada topping. *Iron Chef* and borderlands chef Claudette Zepeda-Wilkins used chicken tinga as the star of a taco at El Jardin in San Diego.

1 pound boneless, skinless chicken breast

2 large white onions: 1 halved, 1 sliced

6 cloves garlic: 3 peeled and kept whole, 3 sliced

Kosher salt

3 tablespoons grapeseed, canola, or other neutral oil

4 chipotle chiles (from a can of chipotle chiles in adobo), chopped to a paste

9 medium plum tomatoes, roughly chopped

In a medium pot, combine the chicken, onion halves, whole garlic cloves, and 1 tablespoon salt. Add water to cover and bring to a boil over medium-high heat. Reduce the heat to low and simmer, uncovered, until the chicken is cooked through, about 10 minutes, skimming the top occasionally to remove impurities.

Remove the chicken from the broth and let it rest until it is cool enough to handle. Using your hands, shred the chicken and reserve. Strain and reserve the broth.

In a medium to large pot, heat the grapeseed oil over medium heat. Add the sliced onion and garlic and cook until translucent, about 5 minutes. Add the shredded chicken, the chiles, tomatoes, and 1 cup of the chicken broth.

Cook until the tomato breaks down and changes to a brick color, 5 to 10 minutes. Season with salt. Add some more of the broth if needed; it should be a bit soupy (any remaining broth can be reserved for other uses).

PAN-ROASTED DUCK BREAST
"AL PASTOR" with Green Garbanzo Beans

Serves 4 / GF

Just about any dish made with pork can work with duck. And al pastor is no exception. Duck is one of my favorite proteins and duck breast is one of my favorite ingredients. When duck breasts are done right—seared with the skin all crispy, fat rendered, and lusciously rare in the middle—they are glorious.

But home cooks are often intimidated by duck breast. How do you get the skin crisp but not burnt and the fat rendered without cooking the meat to death? The answer lies in a trick from Gordon Ramsay: start the cooking skin-side down in a cold pan that you gradually bring up to heat, letting the fat render out from underneath the skin.

To make the adobada spice blend, put all the ingredients in a bowl and whisk to combine. Season the duck breasts with the spice blend.

To make the adobada sauce, toast the chile segments in a dry sauté pan over medium heat until just beginning to develop dark spots. Place them in a bowl with warm water to cover and soak for 10 minutes to rehydrate them. Drain the water. Combine the rehydrated chile segments, the shallot, garlic, achiote paste, orange juice, and lime juice in a medium saucepan and bring to a boil, stirring to dissolve the achiote paste. Turn the heat down to maintain a simmer and cook, stirring occasionally, until reduced by half, 15 to 20 minutes. Add the stock and bring back to a boil, then turn the heat down to low and cook the sauce until it just coats the back of a spoon, 20 to 30 minutes. Pass the sauce through a fine-mesh strainer.

While the sauce is reducing, bring a medium pot of water to a boil and add a pinch of salt. Add the garbanzo beans and cook until they are tender, 2 to 3 minutes. Strain the beans, transfer to a bowl, and toss with the olive oil. Taste and add salt as needed.

While the sauce is cooking, preheat the oven to 400°F.

Carefully score the skin of the duck breasts (be certain not to cut all the way through into the flesh), creating a diagonal checkerboard pattern. Season the duck breasts liberally with salt and pepper on both sides. Place the duck breasts skin-side down on a dry ovenproof sauté pan. Cook, starting over medium-low heat and gradually turning the heat up to medium over the course of 5 minutes or so, until nearly all

For the Adobada Spice Blend

2 tablespoons kosher salt

1 tablespoon smoked paprika

1 tablespoon ancho chile powder

1 teaspoon freshly ground black pepper

1½ teaspoons onion powder

1 teaspoon garlic powder

1 teaspoon dried Mexican oregano

½ teaspoon ground allspice

1 teaspoon ground coriander

½ teaspoon ground cinnamon

½ teaspoon ground cardamom

For the Duck Breasts

2 duck breasts (8 to 10 ounces each)

Kosher salt and freshly ground black pepper

For the Adobada Sauce

2 dried guajillo chiles, stemmed, seeded, and cut into 1-inch segments

2 dried ancho chiles, stemmed, seeded, and cut into 1-inch segments

RECIPE AND INGREDIENTS CONTINUE

MAIN COURSES 187

the fat from the skin renders, running out into the pan. Turn the heat up to high and continue to sear until the skin turns golden brown, about another minute. Flip the breasts back to the flesh side and cook for 1 minute, then flip skin-side down once more and transfer the pan to the oven. Roast for 6 to 8 minutes, until medium-rare, when the flesh gives a little resistance but still gives to the finger when poked. Remove the duck breasts from the pan and rest them for 5 minutes before slicing.

To serve, slice the duck breasts crosswise, starting at the meat end. Pour a line of the sauce horizontally across each plate, then arrange a few slices of duck over the sauce on each, some skin-side up, others with the cut surface up, leaving a few gaps here and there. Fill the gaps with the green garbanzo beans and garnish with edible flowers. Alternatively, slice the duck breast in half lengthwise, place the halved duck breasts over a line of sauce with the garbanzo beans arranged alongside the breast, and garnish with flowers.

Note: Green garbanzo beans—essentially the raw version of the beans you generally buy cooked and in cans—are a glorious ingredient widely available in Baja, though less readily available north of the border. In season they can be found at better Mexican and Middle Eastern markets. Unfortunately, their season is short. The good news is that you can readily substitute fresh or frozen fava beans or even peas for the garbanzo beans in this dish and the result will be both delicious and nearly as good as the original.

1 medium shallot, finely chopped

2 cloves garlic, minced

½ (3.5-ounce) bar achiote paste

½ cup fresh orange juice

¼ cup fresh lime juice

1 cup Chicken Stock (page 232)

Kosher salt and freshly ground black pepper

For the Green Garbanzo Beans

1 cup shelled green garbanzo beans

Kosher salt

1 tablespoon extra-virgin olive oil

For the Garnish

Edible flowers, such as nasturtiums

GRILLED QUAIL
with Chorizo Powder and Cauliflower Escabeche

Serves 4 / GF

8 quail, spatchcocked

¼ cup fresh lime juice

¼ cup extra-virgin olive oil

2 tablespoons Chorizo Powder (page 261)

Cauliflower Escabeche (page 258)

In Northern Mexico, grilled quail are found everywhere from casual roadside stands like Las Güeritas in the Valle de Guadalupe to outdoor near-fine-dining restaurants a few miles away like Deckman's en el Mogor. At Las Güeritas, Lucia Villasenor Padilla—assisted by her husband and two daughters, for whom the place is named—grills fresh *codorniz* (quail), *conejo* (rabbit), and sometimes *cochinita* (pork) to order over a wood fire. The setting is idyllic—abutting the family's nursery in the center of the Guadalupe Valley—with a bit of roadside grit tossed into the mix. The quail are the star of the show.

A few miles away at Deckman's, the restaurant's eponymous chef also grills quail over an open fire. But while there is much in common between the two spots, Drew Deckman pairs the quail with a chorizo powder that teaches us new things about the bird. As I sank my knife into the quail, he walked up behind me and said, "For God's sake, Michael, pick up the damn bird with your hands and have at it!"

Instead of using the chorizo powder as the base for a sauce, this recipe uses it as a marinade. The cauliflower escabeche completes the picture, its acidity pairing naturally with the richness of the quail.

Prepare a wood or charcoal fire or heat a gas grill to about 350°F.

Meanwhile, combine the lime juice, olive oil, and half the chorizo powder in a large bowl and whisk to combine.

Place the quail on the grill breast-side up and grill the birds for 5 minutes. As they cook, brush the breast side with the lime juice dressing. Turn the quail over, breast-side down, and paint the cooked side with dressing as well. Grill for 2 minutes, then turn breast-side up again and brush with the dressing one more time. Cover the grill and cook until the birds are at least medium-rare, 2 to 4 minutes. Sprinkle with the remaining chorizo powder and serve with cauliflower escabeche.

THE VALLE DE GUADALUPE AND DREW DECKMAN

It is fair to say that there is nowhere in Mexico with a greater per capita concentration of great chefs than Baja's Valle de Guadalupe. It is also fair to say that in the Valle there is no greater chef than Drew Deckman. Deckman, unlike any other chef currently working in Mexico, has run a Michelin-starred restaurant.

After earning a Michelin star running Restaurant Vitus in Reinstorf, Germany, and opening Deckman's at Havana in San José del Cabo, Deckman's arrival in the Valle de Guadalupe in 2011 raised eyebrows and focused eyeballs on the Valle and Baja. It is not an overstatement to suggest it conferred a perception of legitimacy on the Valle de Guadalupe that perhaps had been missing.

Deckman and his restaurant do not do things the easy way. For one thing, they do not cook over gas- or electricity-fueled fire. They cook over firewood. Always. Every minute and every day, every dish at Deckman's en el Mogor is cooked over a wood-burning fire. Sustainability is the essence of what Deckman's cooks. The product is local. Their salt is from San Felipe, the cheese is from Ojos Negros, the beef is Mexican, the lamb is estate-grown, and the quail and pork come from nearby in Baja. The wine, beer, and kombucha are local. The restaurant's wastewater is used for irrigation and organics are composted. Even Deckman's cutting board is recycled from the floorboards of an old gymnasium.

SMOKED PULLED LAMB SHOULDER with Seared Tomatillos and Microwave "Fried" Cilantro

Serves 8 to 10 / GF

3 or 4 medium chunks
mesquite wood
for smoking

For the Rub

2 tablespoons
kosher salt

1 tablespoon ancho
chile powder

1 tablespoon guajillo
chile powder

1 tablespoon
ground cumin

2 teaspoons dried
Mexican oregano

2 teaspoons
onion powder

2 teaspoons
garlic powder

1 teaspoon chipotle
chile powder

¼ teaspoon
ground cloves

For the Lamb

1 (5-pound) boneless
lamb shoulder roast,
tied

1 tablespoon
extra-virgin olive oil

1 medium white onion,
finely chopped

1 medium bulb fennel,
finely chopped

1 medium carrot,
finely chopped

4 cups Chicken Stock
(page 232)

2 bay leaves

2 sprigs rosemary

6 cloves garlic, peeled

When you walk into Chef Miguel Angel Guerrero's Valle de Guadalupe restaurant, La Esperanza, it doesn't take long to notice that meat, particularly red meat, plays a significant role in the restaurant's culinary affairs. You can see haunches dry-aging through a window and meat going into the wood-fired oven or onto the grill. Guerrero is well-known as a hunter and many of the fruits of those adventures end up on his menus.

One of my favorite dishes at La Esperanza is the cordero primal al horno. It is Guerrero's take on barbacoa, a classic Mexican dish in which primal cuts are slow-steamed in an earthen pit over maguey leaf–covered coals. Guerrero twists this, roasting a side of lamb in a wood-fired oven for the better part of a day, with a bowl below collecting the meat's juices. Guerrero presents a mound of the meat, flamed in Spanish brandy, in a pool of those juices. It's a simple dish with astonishing depth of flavor: Mexican ingredients and flavors presented with a touch of European technique and a nod to classic American barbecue based on the Caribbean origins of both the Mexican and American dishes.

Few of us have the setup for the original or even La Esperanza's variation. This recipe is a way to get much of the same feeling using equipment many of us have readily available.

Prepare a smoker with the mesquite chunks for very low heat, about 250°F, or set up a grill for indirect cooking.

To make the rub, mix together all the rub ingredients in a small bowl. Rub the mix liberally all over the lamb. Place the lamb in the smoker and smoke for 1½ hours.

Preheat the oven to 250°F.

About 10 minutes before the lamb comes out of the smoker, heat the olive oil in a soup pot or Dutch oven (large enough to comfortably fit the lamb) over low heat. Add the onion, fennel, and carrot and sweat the vegetables until the onion gives up its water, about 5 minutes. Add the stock, bay leaves, rosemary, and garlic, increase the heat to high, and bring to a boil. Add the lamb to the pot, cover the pot with the lid slightly ajar, and transfer the pot to the oven. Cook until a metal skewer can be inserted into the lamb with little to no resistance, 2 to 3 hours. Remove the lamb from the pot, reserving the broth, and let it rest.

Untie the lamb roast and pull the meat into shreds using 2 forks.

To cook the tomatillos, heat the oil in a large sauté pan over high heat. When the oil ripples, add the tomatillos and sear until nicely browned on the bottom, about 1 minute. Immediately remove the tomatillos from the pan.

To serve, divide the meat into 8 to 10 separate bowls and pour some of the broth around each. Garnish each pile of meat with a "fried" cilantro leaf and arrange the seared tomatillo quarters in the bowls. Pass warm corn tortillas at the table.

For the Tomatillos

1 tablespoon grapeseed, canola, or other neutral oil

8 to 10 large tomatillos, husked, rinsed, and quartered

For Serving

8 to 10 Microwave "Fried" Cilantro leaves (page 60)

Corn Tortillas (page 228), warmed

THE SACRAMENTAL HISTORY OF POZOLE

Pozole—whether green or white and regardless of whether the featured protein is pork, chicken, or something else—is one of the great treasures of Mexican cuisine. The real star of the dish is always the hominy itself. Indeed, the word *pozole* is derived from the Náhuatl (Aztec language) word *pozolli*, meaning "foamy," a reference to the foam produced when the hominy is boiled.

It is also a very old dish dating back to before the arrival of the Spaniards. The origins of the dish lie in religion and privilege. Pozole was reserved for the Aztec elite. As documented by sixteenth-century Spanish Franciscan missionary Bernardino de Sahagún in his *Florentine Codex: General History of the Things of New Spain*, the precursor to today's pozole was a dish called tlacatlaolli, which was associated with human sacrifice:

> *...a maize stew fed to the captor and his family at the time when they would also be eating a piece of the flesh of the captive after his heart was removed for offering to the deities.*

The dish was an essential part of Aztec religious rituals, with the remains of the sacrificed—the heart of whom was reserved for the gods—shared among the privileged along with the maize in the pozole as an act of religious communion.

Today, of course, pozoles use different proteins. Perhaps the most common is pork. The reason for that is simple and goes back to the dish's origins. Pork, Sahagún reported, tastes most similar to human flesh.

PORK POZOLE ROJO

Serves 4 to 6 / GF

Perhaps the most traditional of pozole recipes, the one that goes back to the legendary origins of the dish, is this one: savory pork and earthy hominy in a broth infused with guajillo and ancho chiles and served with the classic garnishes of shredded cabbage, diced onion, sliced radish, Mexican oregano, chiles de árbol, and lime to bring it all together.

Heat a large sauté pan over medium heat. Toast the chiles in the pan until they just begin to develop dark marks, about 30 seconds. Flip the chiles and toast the other side. Transfer the chiles to a bowl with hot water to cover and set aside to soak for 30 minutes, or until they are tender and pliable. Drain the chiles and transfer to a high-speed blender or food processor along with ¼ cup of the stock. Blend to a smooth paste, about 30 seconds.

While the chiles are soaking, heat the oil in a Dutch oven or other pot (large enough to comfortably fit the pork butt with room to spare) over medium heat. Add the onion, carrot, celery, and garlic and cook until the aroma of the garlic just begins to fill the room. Add the salt and cumin. Push the vegetables to one side and sear the pork on the other side, turning until lightly browned on all sides, about 5 minutes. Add the hominy, bay leaves, the chile-infused stock from the blender, and the remaining stock and bring to a boil over high heat. Reduce the heat to maintain a simmer and cook for at least 45 minutes or up to 1 hour, until the stock takes on a rich porky flavor and the pork is cooked through. Strain the stock into a soup pot, removing the pork with tongs and setting it aside to cool.

Once the pork butt is cool enough to handle, shred the meat into bite-size pieces. Return the shredded meat to the pot with the broth and bring to a boil. Reduce the heat to maintain a simmer and cook for 10 minutes to marry the flavors. Taste the pozole for seasoning and adjust accordingly (if it needs more acidity, add some lime juice).

Ladle the pozole into soup bowls and serve with the garnishes alongside.

5 dried guajillo chiles, stemmed and seeded

2 dried ancho chiles, stemmed and seeded

6 cups Chicken Stock (page 232)

2 tablespoons grapeseed

1 medium white onion, roughly chopped

1 medium carrot, roughly chopped

1 large or 2 small ribs celery, chopped

3 cloves garlic, crushed

1 teaspoon kosher salt, plus more if needed

2 teaspoons ground cumin

3 pounds boneless pork butt

1 (30-ounce) can hominy, drained and rinsed

2 bay leaves

Fresh lime juice (optional)

For the Garnish

Diced avocado

Shredded green cabbage

Thinly sliced red radishes

1 medium white onion, diced

Fresh cilantro leaves

Dried Mexican oregano

Chiles de árbol

Lime wedges

PORK CARNITAS
with Preserved Lemon Salsa Verde

Serves 5 or 6 / GF

One of culinary Baja's regional pastimes appears to be spotting the influence of non-Mexican cuisines on the food of Baja California. The influence of Italy is most apparent in some of the Plascencia family restaurants, and France is felt in the food of chefs Martín San Román and Jair Téllez. These were some of the chefs that made the notion of Baja Med seem plausible.

But one of the most exotic takes on the theme was Chef Bo Bendana Sein's now-closed Mi Casa Supper Club, which squarely placed the Med of Baja Med in her original home country: Morocco. Similarities in climate, ingredients, and even some cooking techniques made an interesting and plausible case for the proposition. And that is the inspiration in this recipe, with Moroccan preserved lemon providing the acidity for an Italian-style salsa verde. If you do not want to make your own preserved lemon, bottled versions are available at most Middle Eastern markets.

To make the carnitas, combine the pork, lard, garlic, and salt in a large Dutch oven and add 6 to 8 cups water, enough to cover the meat. Cover and bring to a boil over medium heat. Reduce the heat to low and simmer until the pork is nearly tender, about 45 minutes.

While the pork is simmering, make the preserved lemon salsa verde. Combine the shallot, lemon juice, and vinegar in a small bowl and allow to sit to slightly pickle the shallots, about 10 minutes. In a separate bowl, combine the parsley and cilantro with the olive oil and stir to thoroughly coat the herbs in the oil. Add the preserved lemon and chile to the bowl with the shallot mixture. Stir to combine and season with salt.

Uncover the Dutch oven, turn the heat to medium-high and cook to reduce the liquid until the meat starts frying in its own fat and the lard. Reduce the heat to medium-low and cook, stirring frequently, until the pork is evenly browned, 15 to 20 minutes. Do not over cook at this point or the meat will get very dry.

Serve the carnitas with warmed corn tortillas and the preserved lemon salsa verde.

For the Carnitas

2 pounds boneless pork butt, cut into 2-inch cubes

¼ cup lard (but, if you must, a neutral oil is acceptable instead)

3 cloves garlic, peeled

1 tablespoon kosher salt

For the Preserved Lemon Salsa Verde

2 tablespoons minced shallot

2 tablespoons fresh lemon juice

2 teaspoons apple cider vinegar

1 cup packed fresh parsley leaves, minced

1 cup packed fresh cilantro leaves, minced

½ cup good-quality extra-virgin olive oil

1 tablespoon minced Quick Preserved Lemon rind (page 259)

2 tablespoons minced jalapeño chile

Kosher salt

For Serving

Corn Tortillas (page 228), warmed

CHICHARRONES
with Salsa Verde and Pickled Red Cabbage

Makes 6 servings / GF

As Mexican culinary culture expands its influence in the US, classic Mexican snack foods have come along for the ride. Prime among those are chicharrones, a popular Mexican snack made from fried pork skin, rinds, and cracklins and sold bagged in massive, long sheets of piggy goodness. While so-called chicharrones can also be made from wheat, that product is vastly inferior.

Paired with an acidic salsa verde and the sweetness and color of pickled red cabbage, chicharrones are great as a stew or as the filling for a taco. Perhaps best of all, you can almost convince yourself that they're good for you.

Put one-third of the chicharrones in a resealable medium freezer bag and seal the bag, pushing out the air (or you can wrap them in a clean kitchen towel). Using a heavy skillet or rolling pin, crush the chicharrones into pea-size pieces; set aside for serving.

Heat a large, heavy skillet, preferably cast-iron, over medium-high heat. Toast the remaining two-thirds of the chicharrones in the skillet, tossing occasionally, until lightly charred on several sides, about 5 minutes. Transfer to a medium bowl.

Combine the lard, chiles, garlic, and onion in the same skillet over medium-high heat; season with the salt and pepper. Cook, stirring occasionally, until the vegetables soften and turn slightly golden, 6 to 8 minutes. Add the tomatillos, season with salt again, and cook, stirring occasionally, until the tomatillos are softened and start to lose their shape, about 5 minutes. Add the toasted chicharrones and 3 cups water and bring to a boil. Reduce the heat to medium-low and simmer, uncovered, stirring occasionally, until the sauce notably thickens, 15 to 18 minutes. Taste the sauce and chicharrones for seasoning and adjust if needed.

Turn the chicharrones out into a serving bowl, spoon the refried beans around them, and garnish with cilantro and pickled red cabbage. Pass corn tortillas at the table.

8 ounces chicharrones, broken into 1-inch pieces (about 6 cups)

2 tablespoons lard or bacon fat (or grapeseed, canola, or other neutral oil)

3 jalapeño chiles, stemmed, seeded, and finely chopped

5 cloves garlic, minced

1 cup finely chopped white onion

1½ teaspoons kosher salt, plus more as needed

½ teaspoon freshly ground black pepper

1 pound tomatillos, husked, rinsed, and chopped

For Serving

Refried Beans (page 239)

Attractive cilantro leaves and minced tender cilantro stems

Pickled Red Cabbage (page 258)

Corn Tortillas (page 228), warmed

PORK BELLY ADOBADA with Refried Bean, Sweet Corn, and Pickled Red Cabbage Sopes and Avocado, Pineapple, and Jalapeño Sauce

Serves 4 / GF

Adobada—Baja California's version of al pastor—is both ubiquitous in the cities of Northern Baja and one of those great dishes that is very difficult to make at home. Few of us have a vertical spit (called a *trompo*) sitting around in our kitchen or enough mouths to feed at home to justify the amount of meat.

Part of what makes adobada so good is the incredibly flavorful marinade. There are, however, some ways to go about getting some of what makes adobada (and al pastor) such a delightful treat and do so at home. Another part is the meat itself and, in particular, its fat content. Pork belly lends itself well to that treatment, and this pork belly adobada is a variation on a dish we cooked at La Justina when I staged there. It can be sliced and served with the sauce in tacos for a simpler meal. Indeed, the sauce can be added to pretty much any pork taco.

To make the pork belly adobada, slice the pork belly into 3-inch by 1-inch blocks. Toast the dried chiles in a dry sauté pan or cast-iron skillet over medium heat for about 20 seconds, until fragrant. Do not overtoast the chiles. It is better to go too short than too long. Place the chiles in a bowl with enough hot water to fully cover them. Soak them for 10 minutes, or until they are pliable. Drain the water.

Put the rehydrated chile segments in a high-speed blender or food processor, add the achiote paste, cinnamon, cardamom, cumin, pineapple juice, vinegar, and salt and pepper to taste, and blend on high speed until the marinade is thoroughly blended. Set aside ¼ cup of the marinade for use later in the recipe. Season the pork belly blocks with salt and pepper, place in a container, and pour in the remaining marinade to fully submerge them. Cover and refrigerate for at least 30 minutes or up to overnight.

Preheat the oven to 300°F and line 2 baking sheets with parchment paper.

Place a sauté pan large enough to comfortably accommodate the pork belly blocks over medium heat. Thoroughly dry the skin of the

For the Pork Belly Adobada

2 pounds skin-on pork belly

3 dried guajillo chiles, stemmed, seeded, and cut into 1-inch segments

3 dried ancho chiles, stemmed and seeded

5 ounces achiote paste (about ½ cup)

1 teaspoon ground cinnamon

½ teaspoon ground cardamom

½ teaspoon ground cumin

½ cup pineapple juice

½ cup apple cider vinegar

1 cup kosher salt, plus more as needed

Freshly ground black pepper

For the Avocado, Pineapple, and Jalapeño Sauce

3 medium Hass avocados

2 tablespoons fresh lime juice

2 tablespoons finely minced red onion

2 to 3 jalapeño chiles, stemmed and seeded

RECIPE AND INGREDIENTS CONTINUE

pork belly. When the pan is hot, add the pork belly and sear for 4 to 5 minutes per side, until the tip of a knife slides into the side of a pork belly segment with ease.

Arrange the pork belly on the prepared baking sheet and spread the 1 cup salt over the pork belly. Bake for 1½ hours.

Remove the pork belly from the oven and increase the oven temperature to 450°F.

Wipe the salt off the pork belly segments, brushing the tops to get any last bits of salt cleaned off. Brush the reserved marinade over all the surfaces of the pork belly segments, arrange them on the second prepared baking sheet, return them to the oven, and roast until the skin is golden and crispy, 15 to 20 minutes.

While the pork belly is cooking, to make the sauce, scoop the flesh of the avocados into a high-speed blender or food processor, then add the lime juice, onion, chiles, garlic, cilantro, pineapple, and 1 teaspoon salt. Blend, using a tamper and adding additional water, if needed, to achieve a smooth puree.

To make the Ash de Mar: Preheat the oven to broil, at least 500°F. While the oven is heating, line a baking sheet with aluminum foil (not parchment paper). Spread the sliced onions and leeks in a single layer on the foil and place under the broiler. Cook, turning once or twice, until the alliums are fully charred and crisp, about an hour. Remove from the oven and cool fully. Reduce the heat of the oven to 350ºF. Working in batches, add the alliums to a high-speed blender or food processor and pulverize the charred vegetables to a powdered ash. Weigh the ash and then combine it with an equal (by weight) amount of sea salt. Pulverize the combined salt ash then store indefinitely in a tightly sealed container.

To serve, swipe 2 tablespoons of the sauce across each plate from lower left to upper right. Place a block of the pork belly at the lower end and a sope at the upper end. Top each piece of pork belly with microgreens and dust the plate with ash de mar.

2 cloves garlic, crushed and minced

¼ cup fresh cilantro leaves and tender stems

½ cup finely diced fresh pineapple

Kosher salt

For the Ash de Mar:

3 large onions, sliced

3 large leeks (white parts only), sliced

Sea salt (or Kosher salt)

For Serving

4 Refried Bean, Sweet Corn, and Pickled Red Cabbage Sopes (page 138)

Microgreens

CARNE ASADA

Serves 6 / GF

My Sunday ritual used to be: wake up early to play thirty-and-over Huff-n-Puff soccer—a gringo on a mostly Mexican team—then slowly sidle into the afternoon eating carne asada, drinking Tecates, and telling exaggerated accounts of in-game exploits. While the tales should have revolved around age and treachery prevailing over youth and skill, they never did. But the carne asada was really good.

The term *carne asada* means different things in different contexts. At one level it means backyard barbecue—a social event. At the most basic level it means roasted meat, and not necessarily beef. When it refers to a dish, however, carne asada is beef—usually a tough, flavorful cut such as skirt, flank, or flap steak—marinated in a lime-based concoction, sliced thin, and grilled over mesquite wood or charcoal.

In a high-speed blender or food processor, combine the lime juice, garlic, orange juice, cilantro, salt, pepper, oil, chile, and vinegar. Starting on low speed and gradually increasing to high, blend the marinade until smooth. Put the steak and marinade in a large bowl and get in there with your hands to fully coat the steak with the marinade. Marinate the steak in the refrigerator for at least 2 hours or up to overnight. Remove the steak from the refrigerator and drain off the marinade about 30 minutes before cooking.

Set up an outdoor kettle-style grill with two zones (one direct, one indirect). When the grill comes to temperature, cook the steak over direct heat for 5 minutes per side. Move the steak to the cooler side of the grill and cook for another 5 to 6 minutes, until it reaches your desired temperature: 130°F for rare, 140°F for medium-rare, 155°F for medium, and 165°F well-done (aka sacrilege). Remove the beef from the grill and let it rest for 5 to 6 minutes, then slice (always against the grain for tenderness).

Serve with guacamole, grilled onions, salsa, and tortillas.

Ingredients

Juice of 2 limes

4 cloves garlic, crushed

½ cup fresh orange juice

1 cup chopped fresh cilantro

½ teaspoon kosher salt

¼ teaspoon freshly ground black pepper

¼ cup grapeseed, canola, or other neutral oil

1 jalapeño chile, stemmed and seeded

2 tablespoons apple cider vinegar

2 pounds skirt steak (arrachera)

For Serving

Guacamole (page 252)

Grilled onions

Salsa Bandera (page 242), Salsa Macha (page 241), or Carlos Salgado's Salsa Negra (page 243)

Corn Tortillas (page 228) or Flour Tortillas (page 229), warmed

BEEF BRISKET BIRRIA
with Marrow Bones

Serves 4

At Tuétano Taquería in San Diego, Priscilla Curiel takes birria, a dish originally from Jalisco, and shows why it now may be owned by the Cali-Baja region. In the right hands, birria—red meat slow-cooked in broth with chiles, cinnamon, cloves, and vinegar—is a glorious stew. Even average cooks can put out a half-decent bowl, because it's an inherently forgiving dish. And that's the problem. There's a birria joint on just about every corner in much of Mexico, and in Southern California too. It's ubiquitous and mostly less than extraordinary.

And that's what makes Tuétano Taquería's version remarkable. It's comfort food, yes, but also deceptively complex: savory, sweet and sour, with bitter and umami flavors. All of it is rendered with precision, definition, and balance. It hits nearly all the marks.

That's where the *tuétano* (roasted bone marrow) comes in. Beef marrow is one of the most flavorful fats on the rock. Curiel offers her tuétano as a side with the idea of adding a bit of the marrow to her tacos. It's a minor stroke of brilliance that takes the birria tacos to another level. The birria already had balance, but with the tuétano, it has soul too. This recipe is my take on her dish, adapted for the home kitchen.

To make the birria, heat a large sauté pan over medium heat. Toast the chiles in the pan until they just begin to develop dark marks, about 30 seconds. Flip the chiles and toast the other side. Transfer the chiles to a bowl with hot water to cover and set aside to soak for 30 minutes, or until they are tender and pliable.

Drain the chiles and transfer to a high-speed blender or food processor along with the garlic, cloves, oregano, cinnamon, and star anise. Beginning on low speed and gradually increasing to high, blend to a smooth paste, 30 to 45 seconds.

Coat the beef brisket with the paste and place in a zip-top bag or plastic container with a cover. Marinate in the refrigerator overnight.

The next day, preheat the oven to 350°F.

For the Birria

1 (1½- to 2-pound) beef brisket

5 dried guajillo chiles, stemmed and seeded

3 dried ancho chiles, stemmed and seeded

6 cloves garlic, crushed

1 teaspoon ground cloves

1 tablespoon dried Mexican oregano

1 teaspoon ground cinnamon

3 star anise pods

4 bay leaves

1 bottle Mexican-style beer, such as Tecate (this is not the place for craft beer)

For the Marrow Bones

4 marrow bone segments

Kosher salt

For Serving

At least 8 Corn Tortillas (page 228), warmed

½ small head green cabbage, cored and shredded

Leaves from 1 bunch cilantro

4 to 8 chiles de árbol

Place the beef in a Dutch oven along with the bay leaves, beer, and enough water to just cover the meat. Place the pot with the beef in the oven and cook until you can pull the meat apart with a fork, 4 to 5 hours, depending on the cut you use.

Remove the birria from the oven and set aside while you make the marrow bones. Increase the oven temperature to 450°F. Line a baking sheet with parchment paper.

Put the marrow bones on the prepared baking sheet, season with salt, and roast until the marrow begins to bubble, 15 to 20 minutes, depending on the size of the bones.

Transfer the birria to serving bowls and place 1 marrow bone in each bowl of birria. Pass the tortillas, cabbage, cilantro, and chiles at the table.

RIB EYE STEAK with Pasilla Salsa, Chiles Toreados, and Avocado Mousse

Serves 4

Andrew Bent is a gringo who cooks with the passion of a Mexican grandmother. With a résumé that includes stints at Enrique Olvera's Criollo, Noma's Tulum pop-up, and many others, Bent created a menu at San Diego's Lola 55 that garnered Michelin recognition. More important, perhaps, he did the nearly impossible: he created upscale tacos that managed to retain the soul of a taco. This dish is one of Bent's best tacos, taken the other way: back to its fine-dining origin.

To marinate the steak, combine the guajillo and pasilla chiles, chipotles, garlic, fish sauce, soy sauce, and stock in a blender. Blend on high speed to a smooth puree. Put the steaks in a bowl and coat with the marinade. Cover and marinate the steaks in the refrigerator for 8 to 12 hours. Remove the steaks from the fridge and let stand at room temperature for 30 minutes before cooking.

Meanwhile, to make the jalapeño toreados, hold the jalapeño chiles with tongs or suspend them over a gas burner set to medium heat. Toast the chiles until their exteriors are slightly blackened and blistered. Remove the stems and slice the chiles into strips. Put the chile strips, lime juice, and soy sauce in a bowl and marinate for about 1 hour.

To make the crispy onions, hold the pasilla chile with tongs or suspend it over a gas burner set to medium heat (make sure you have your fan going). Toast the chile lightly, just until it begins to puff and you see wafts of smoke and charred flecks. Remove the stem, then blend the chile in a blender or spice grinder to a fine powder. Transfer to a shallow bowl and whisk in the flour and salt. Cut the top and bottom off the onion and remove the skin. Cut the onion into thin strips. Dredge the onion strips in the flour mixture, gently tapping away excess flour.

In a shallow skillet, heat the oil over medium heat to 375°F. Working in batches, add the coated onion strips, gently stir, and fry for 2 to 3 minutes, then flip the strips and cook for another 2 to 3 minutes, until browned all over. Using a spider, transfer the fried onions to a baking sheet lined with a wire rack, arranging them in a single layer (to prevent the strips from getting soggy and allow any excess oil to drip off).

For the Rib Eye Steak

4 dried guajillo chiles, stemmed and seeded

4 dried pasilla chiles, stemmed and seeded

2 chipotle chiles (from a can of chipotles in adobo)

2 cloves garlic, peeled

2 teaspoons fish sauce

2 teaspoons soy sauce

½ cup Beef Stock (page 234)

4 rib eye steaks (about 10 ounces each)

Kosher salt

For the Jalapeño Toreados

2 medium jalapeño chiles (not stemmed and seeded)

¼ cup fresh lime juice

¼ cup soy sauce

For the Crispy Onions

1 dried pasilla chile

1 cup all-purpose flour

1 teaspoon kosher salt

1 medium white onion

3 cups grapeseed, canola, or other neutral oil

To make the tomatillo-pasilla salsa, start by heating a sauté pan over medium-high heat and add the tomatillos, onion, and garlic. Cook until the tomatillos char lightly, blister, slightly blacken, and soften and the edges of the onion and garlic are slightly charred, removing each as they are done and putting them in a high-speed blender. Hold the pasilla chile with tongs or suspend it over a gas burner set to medium heat. Toast the chile lightly until it begins to puff and you see wafts of smoke and charred flecks. Remove the stem. Add the pasilla chile to the blender, then add the chipotle chiles and blend on medium speed or pulse to create a chunky salsa. Taste the salsa and adjust the seasoning with salt and sugar as needed.

To cook the steak, season it generously with salt, place on the grill, and close the lid. Grill on the first side for 6 minutes, rotating the meat 90 degrees halfway through. Flip and grill until you reach your desired internal temperature: 105°F for rare, 115°F for medium-rare, or 125°F for medium. Beyond that, you're on your own. Keep in mind that the temperature will continue to rise after you take the steak off the grill. Let the steak rest for 10 to 15 minutes before slicing.

To plate the dish, start by first slicing the steak into thin lengthwise strips. Put 3 to 5 strips of steak down the middle of each plate. On one side of the steaks, spoon 1 to 2 tablespoons of the avocado mousse. On the other side, spoon 1 to 2 tablespoons of the pasilla salsa. Top the steak with about 1 teaspoon of the jalapeño toreados and the crispy onions and a squeeze of lime juice.

For the Tomatillo-Pasilla Salsa

5 medium tomatillos, husked and rinsed

¼ small red onion

2 cloves garlic, peeled

3 dried pasilla chiles

2 ounces chipotle chiles (from a can of chipotles in adobo)

Kosher salt

Sugar

For Finishing

Avocado Mousse (page 252)

Lime wedges

SANTA MARIA–STYLE BARBECUE

Serves 4

The first thing to know about Santa Maria barbecue is that it is not actually barbecue at all. The second thing to know about Santa Maria barbecue is that it truly highlights the Mexican heritage of California. Santa Maria barbecue is a century-and-a-half-old tradition of grilling large cuts of beef (in particular tri-tip) over red oak, classically on a grilling rig that can be raised and lowered for temperature control.

As important as the beef is, so too are the traditional accompaniments: pinquito beans and a unique salsa that features Worcestershire sauce, celery, and green onions and yet has an unmistakable family resemblance to salsa bandera. Santa Maria barbecue stands as a testimony to the fact that every inch of the state of California was once Mexico.

Pick through the beans to remove any small stones. Put the beans in a large pot, cover with water by a few inches, and let soak overnight.

The next day, drain the beans (reserving the soaking liquid) and put them in a saucepan large enough to accommodate the beans with ample room to spare. Cover the beans with fresh water and bring to a boil over high heat. Reduce the heat to low and simmer until the beans are tender, about 2 hours.

Meanwhile, put the salt, pepper, garlic powder in a small bowl and whisk to combine. Rub the spice mixture all over the meat, place on a plate, and let sit for 1 to 2 hours in the refrigerator.

Put all the salsa ingredients in a medium bowl and mix to combine. Cover the bowl and let stand for at least 1 hour to allow the flavors to meld. (This will make about 3½ cups salsa.)

In a large sauté pan, cook the bacon and ham over medium heat until lightly browned. Add the garlic and cook for 1 to 2 minutes longer. Add the tomato puree, red chile sauce, sugar, mustard, and salt and stir to combine. Reduce the heat to low and simmer for 30 minutes, adding some of the reserved bean soaking liquid if it starts getting dry.

Preheat the oven (or a grill) to 350°F.

Heat a large cast-iron skillet over medium-high heat. Add the tri-tip and sear for 4 minutes, then turn and cook on the other side for another 4 minutes. Transfer the tri-tip to the oven or grill and cook until an instant-read thermometer registers 130°F.

For the Santa Maria–Style Beans

1 pound pinquito (or peruano or pinto) beans

1 slice bacon, diced

½ cup diced cooked ham

1 clove garlic, peeled

¾ cup tomato puree

¼ cup red chile sauce, such as Las Palmas brand, or enchilada sauce

1 tablespoon granulated sugar

1 teaspoon dry mustard

1 teaspoon kosher salt

For the Beef

2 tablespoons kosher salt

1 teaspoon freshly ground black pepper

1 teaspoon garlic powder

1 tri-tip roast (about 2½ pounds)

For the Santa Maria Salsa

3 medium plum tomatoes, chopped

½ cup finely chopped celery

½ cup finely chopped green onions

½ cup finely chopped seeded jalapeño chiles

2 tablespoons finely chopped fresh cilantro

Remove the meat from the oven or grill and allow it to rest for 5 minutes. Slice and plate the tri-tip with the salsa and beans. Serve with warm corn tortillas.

Note: Almost as important as how you cook a tri-tip is how you cut it. The primary challenge lies in the fact that a tri-tip consists of two different muscles and the grains of those muscles run in different directions. As a result, the first step to cutting a tri-tip is to identify the two muscles. From there it's easy: slice each muscle thinly and *against* (perpendicular to) the grain.

1 tablespoon apple cider vinegar

1 teaspoon Worcestershire sauce

½ teaspoon garlic salt

½ teaspoon dried Mexican oregano, crushed

1 tablespoon Chiltepin Hot Sauce (page 247) or hot sauce of choice

For Serving

Corn Tortillas (page 228), warmed

CHILE-DUSTED SWEETBREADS OVER MASA "POLENTA"
with Salsa Macha and Cilantro Gremolata

Serves 4

At first blush it might seem that Italian cuisine and Baja cuisine have little in common. In addition to the profound influence of Italian cuisine on the restaurant scene in Tijuana (and larger Baja), there is one ingredient that highlights my point: cornmeal.

Cornmeal—masa harina—may well be the signature ingredient in Mexican cookery. Cornmeal—polenta—may not be quite as important to Italian cuisine, but it is important. And it did not exist in Italy until it was brought back from Mexico. Sadly, though, when European traders brought maize to Europe, they did not bring with them the secrets of nixtamalization, a process of soaking and cooking the corn kernels in an alkaline solution to increase the cornmeal's nutritional value and improve its taste. That process is critical to allowing the human body to extract important nutrients from cornmeal. The result was massive malnutrition and disease. This dish is intended to bring Mexican and Italian cornmeal back into happy harmony.

To make the masa "polenta," in a large saucepan, whisk together the stock, masa harina, and salt. Bring to a simmer over medium-high heat while whisking, then reduce the heat to low. The polenta should not be bubbling but should have some steam coming up off its surface. Cook, stirring every 5 to 10 minutes, until the polenta is tender and thick, 45 to 50 minutes. If it gets too thick before it gets tender, add a little more stock or water to the pan. Stir in the butter. Taste the polenta and add the more salt if needed.

Meanwhile, to make the sweetbreads, fill a large bowl with ice and water. Place the sweetbreads in a small pot, cover with water, and add a generous pinch of salt (about 1 teaspoon) and the lemon juice. Bring the water to a boil over high heat, then reduce the heat to low and simmer until the skin of the sweetbreads looks firm and has changed color from pink to pale beige, about 5 minutes. Remove the sweetbreads from the pot and plunge them into the ice bath.

When the sweetbreads are cool enough to handle, remove the membrane and other tissues and tubes using your fingers and a thin knife by pulling and tugging the thin layer away from the sweetbreads. Keep the sweetbreads in large clumps (about 1 inch by 1 inch). Combine

For the Masa "Polenta"

2 cups Chicken Stock (page 232) or water

1 cup masa harina (the coarser the better)

1 teaspoon kosher salt (2 teaspoons if using water instead of stock), plus more as needed

2 tablespoons unsalted butter

For the Sweetbreads

1 pound veal sweetbreads

Kosher salt

Juice of ½ lemon

¼ cup all-purpose flour

1 tablespoon guajillo or ancho chile powder

1 tablespoon unsalted butter

For Serving

½ cup Salsa Macha (page 241)

⅓ cup Cilantro Gremolata (page 253)

12 attractive cilantro leaves

the flour, chile powder, and 1 teaspoon salt in a large bowl. Coat the sweetbread pieces in the flour mixture, and set aside.

Melt the butter in a large sauté pan over medium heat. Add the sweetbreads and cook, without moving them, for 2 to 3 minutes, until the bottom is browned. Turn and cook to brown the other side. Taste a sweetbread and add more salt if needed.

To serve, ladle ¼ cup of the polenta in the bottom of each bowl. Spoon a circle of salsa macha around the bowl and arrange 3 sweetbread nuggets around the circle. Spoon small piles of the cilantro gremolata in between the sweetbreads and top each nugget with an attractive cilantro leaf.

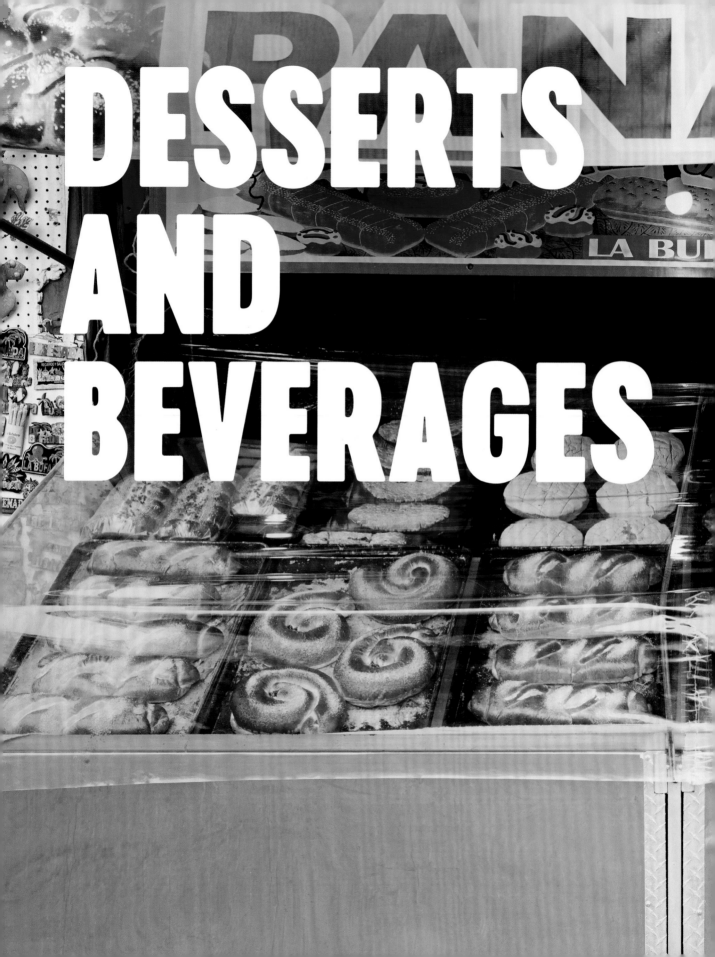

DESSERTS
AND
BEVERAGES

GRILLED PAPAYA
with Coconut Milk Vanilla Ice Cream

Fresh fruit needs absolutely nothing to be delicious. Papaya is no exception. But grilling fresh papaya caramelizes the surface and lends the fruit a smoky allure. Pairing that grilled papaya with coconut milk vanilla ice cream creates a dish with textural, flavor, and temperature contrasts.

To make the ice cream, combine the coconut milk and sugar in a high-speed blender or food processor and blend until the sugar has fully dissolved. Split the vanilla bean lengthwise and scrape the seeds into the coconut mixture. Add the vanilla and salt and blend to combine. Churn the mixture in an ice cream maker according to the manufacturer's directions. Pack the soft ice cream into a freezer-safe container and freeze until solid, about 4 hours.

To make the grilled papaya, put the honey, lime juice, ginger, salt, and chile powder in a small bowl and whisk to combine. Brush both sides of the papaya rings with the glaze.

Heat a grill to medium-high or heat a grill pan over medium-high heat. Grill the papaya for 30 seconds on each side. The goal is to warm the papaya and get light grill marks on it while keeping the fruit firm.

Remove the papaya rings from the grill or grill pan and put 2 on each plate. Top each ring with ¼ cup of the ice cream and garnish each with a mint leaf.

For the Coconut Milk Vanilla Ice Cream

4 cups canned full-fat coconut milk

¾ cup sugar

½ vanilla bean

1 tablespoon vanilla extract

Pinch of fine sea salt

For the Grilled Papaya

¼ cup honey

1 tablespoon fresh lime juice

1 tablespoon grated fresh ginger

¾ teaspoon kosher salt

¾ teaspoon ancho chile powder

2 large ripe papayas, peeled, sliced into 4½-inch-thick rings, and seeded

4 fresh mint leaves

FLOURLESS MEXICAN CHOCOLATE CAKE with Cajeta

Serves 6 to 8
GF / VEG

Cajeta is a classic Mexican caramel sauce traditionally made with goat's milk. While it can be drizzled over ice cream, spread on thin cookies, or used to make tres leches cake, some argue its highest and best use is as the object of a late-night refrigerator raid, armed only with a spoon. I'll take the fifth on that one, but I will acknowledge that cajeta pairs perfectly with this flourless Mexican chocolate cake.

To make the cajeta, put the baking soda and 1 tablespoon water in a small bowl and whisk to combine. In a large pot, combine the goat's milk, granulated sugar, and cinnamon stick and bring to a boil over high heat. Immediately remove the pot from the stove. Stir in the dissolved baking soda. When the contents of the pot begin to foam, place the pot over medium heat and cook, stirring constantly, for 30 to 40 minutes, until it thickens and turns an attractive caramel brown color. Remove from the heat and remove the cinnamon stick. Add the vanilla and salt. The cajeta will thicken more as it cools, so do not let it thicken too much in the pot.

While you're making the cajeta, preheat the oven to 350°F. Line the bottom of a 9½-inch springform pan with a circle of parchment paper cut to fit. Butter the sides of the pan and the parchment.

Combine the chocolate and butter in a microwave-safe bowl and microwave on high for 1 minute, then whisk. Continue microwaving and stirring in 30-second increments and whisking until all the chocolate has melted and the mixture is well combined.

In a large bowl, whisk together the eggs, granulated sugar, and vanilla. Working slowly, a little at a time, whisk the melted chocolate mixture into the egg mixture. Add the cinnamon, chile powder, and salt. Pour the chocolate mixture into the prepared pan and bake until a toothpick inserted into the center comes out mostly clean, 22 to 26 minutes. Let the cake cool completely in the pan on a wire rack. Release the springform ring and remove it before serving.

Dust the cake with powdered sugar and drizzle with the cajeta.

For the Cajeta

½ teaspoon baking soda

4 cups goat's milk

1 cup granulated sugar

1 cinnamon stick

½ teaspoon vanilla extract

½ teaspoon kosher salt

For the Chocolate Cake

7 tablespoons unsalted butter, cut into pieces, plus more for greasing

10 ounces semisweet (60% cacao) chocolate, roughly chopped

5 large eggs, at room temperature

1 cup granulated sugar

½ teaspoon vanilla extract

½ teaspoon ground cinnamon

¾ teaspoon chipotle chile powder

¼ teaspoon kosher salt

Powdered sugar for dusting

CAPIROTADA BLANCA

Serves 4 to 6 / VEG

Capirotada blanca is essentially Mexico's take on bread pudding. It's a classic Lenten and Easter dish. The recipe below is a family heirloom of this book's photographer, Cintia Soto. If you cannot find picón bread, substitute the same number of conchas, which can be found at pretty much any Mexican bakery.

Preheat the oven to 325°F.

Put the coconut milk, condensed milk, vanilla, egg yolks, wine, and orange zest in a food processor and process to combine.

Spread the butter over the bottom of a 9 by 13-inch Pyrex baking dish and put a layer of the picónes rings on top. Arrange the plantain slices in a layer over the picónes. Repeat with an additional layer of picónes and top that with the raisins, almonds, and walnuts. Pour the milk mixture over the entire contents of the baking dish.

Place the dish in the oven and bake until the top is lightly browned, about 45 minutes.

Notes: Picónes are a traditional pastry originally from Guadalajara that are similar to large conchas. Just about every region of Mexico has its own classic pastry.

Brandy infused with a vanilla bean overnight would be a good substitute for the port.

2½ cups unsweetened full-fat coconut milk

1½ cups sweetened condensed milk, such as La Lechera brand

1 tablespoon vanilla extract

4 large egg yolks

1 tablespoon port wine

1 tablespoon grated orange zest

1 tablespoon unsalted butter, softened

1 large or 2 small picónes (6 to 7 inches total), sliced into ½-inch-thick rings

1 ripe plantain, sliced

⅓ cup raisins

¼ cup almonds

¼ cup walnuts

MANGO LIME TART

Serves 6 to 8 / VEG

The combination of mango and lime is a natural one. The inherent sweetness of the mango is enhanced by the acidity of the lime. Add some chile to the party, and you have a classic Tijuana street food: mango with Tajín (a prototypical Mexican salt-chile-lime seasoning blend). This simple tart echoes the classic Mexican mango-lime pairing.

12 graham crackers

½ cup (1 stick) unsalted butter, melted and cooled

½ cup sugar

½ teaspoon kosher salt

1 large ripe mango, peeled, pitted, and cut into chunks (about 1½ cups)

⅓ cup fresh lime juice

3 large egg yolks

1 (14-ounce) can sweetened condensed milk

Lightly sweetened whipped cream for serving

Preheat the oven to 350°F.

Break the graham crackers into pieces, place them in a food processor, and grind to a fine crumb. Add the melted butter, ¼ cup of the sugar, and the salt and process until completely combined. Transfer the mixture to a 9-inch tart pan with a removable bottom and press the mixture over the bottom and up the sides of the pan. Place the pan on a baking sheet and transfer to the oven. Bake until the crust is fragrant and slightly darkened, 10 to 12 minutes. Transfer to a wire rack and let cool completely; keep the oven on.

Clean the food processor bowl. Combine the mango chunks and lime juice in the food processor and process to a smooth puree. Add the egg yolks and the remaining ¼ cup sugar and pulse a few times to combine. With the food processor running, steadily stream in the condensed milk through the hole in the top until combined. Pour the mixture into the cooled tart shell and bake until the center is set, 20 to 25 minutes. Remove the tart from the oven, place on a wire rack, and cool to room temperature. Cover with plastic wrap and transfer to the refrigerator to chill for at least 1 hour before serving.

When ready to serve, remove the tart from the pan and top with lightly sweetened whipped cream. Slice and serve.

HIBISCUS TEA
AGUA DE JAMAICA

Makes 2 quarts
GF / VEGAN

Agua de jamaica is ubiquitous in Mexican kitchens. There has been a water cooler–size vessel of it in just about every Mexican kitchen I've cooked in. It is delicious, cooling, and refreshing, and it's good for you too.

2 quarts water

¾ cup sugar

½ cinnamon stick

1 (¼-inch) knob fresh ginger, thinly sliced

4 allspice berries

1 cup dried hibiscus flowers

¼ cup fresh lime juice

Orange slices for garnish

Put 1 quart of the water and the sugar in a medium saucepan and add the cinnamon, ginger, and allspice berries. Bring to a boil, whisking periodically until the sugar dissolves. Remove the pan from the heat and stir in the hibiscus flowers. Cover and let sit for 20 minutes.

Strain the liquid into a pitcher and discard the hibiscus flowers, ginger, cinnamon, and allspice berries. The resulting hibiscus concentrate can be chilled and held in the refrigerator for up to 4 days until you are ready to make the drink.

Add the remaining 1 quart water and the lime juice to the concentrate and chill until ready to serve. Serve in glasses over ice and garnish with orange slices.

TAMARIND WATER
AGUA DE TAMARINDO

Makes about 1 gallon
GF / VEGAN

Much like agua de jamaica, agua de tamarindo has a long list of claimed health benefits: lowering blood pressure, boosting immunity, promoting weight loss, aiding digestion, and improving nerve and muscle function. And also like agua de jamaica, it tastes good!

1 pound tamarind pulp, with seeds

1 gallon water

1 cup sugar

Combine the tamarind pulp, water, and sugar in a large pot and bring to a boil over high heat. Reduce the heat to medium and cook for about 30 minutes, until the tamarind flesh is very soft, occasionally stirring and mashing with a whisk to break up the flesh and separate the seeds.

Strain the liquid and discard the solids. Cool to room temperature and chill before serving. Serve in tall glasses with plenty of ice.

CUCUMBER AGUA FRESCA

Serves 6
GF / VEGAN

Cucumber may seem like a counterintuitive choice for an agua fresca. But the combination of cucumber, lime, and mint is deeply, surprisingly refreshing. Those latter two ingredients are the low-key stars of the drink.

4 medium Persian cucumbers

3 medium limes, halved

⅓ cup fresh mint leaves

⅓ cup sugar, plus more if needed

5 cups water

Slice each cucumber in half lengthwise, then cut each half in the middle, resulting in 4 segments. Combine the cucumbers, limes (with their skin intact), mint, and sugar in a high-speed blender. Add 4 cups of the water and blend, starting on low speed and gradually increasing to high, until the liquid is smooth. Pass the liquid through a fine-mesh strainer into a pitcher, pressing on the pulp to get as much juice out as possible. Add the remaining 1 cup water. Taste and add more sugar if needed. Pour into glasses over ice.

HORCHATA

Serves 4 / GF / VEG

Perhaps the best known agua fresca north of the border is horchata, typically a rice and almond–based concoction that traces its roots back to Moorish Spain. A quick comparison of the main ingredients of horchata and ajo blanco (white gazpacho) shows the shared bloodlines of the drink and the soup.

1¼ cups uncooked long-grain white rice

½ cup sliced almonds

2 cinnamon sticks (about 2½ inches long each)

4 cups cold water

½ cup granulated sugar, or more as needed

1 teaspoon vanilla extract

2 cups whole milk

Ground cinnamon or cinnamon sticks for garnish

Combine the rice, almonds, and cinnamon sticks in a high-speed blender and blend, starting on low and gradually increasing the speed to high, until finely pulverized, 45 to 60 seconds, stopping occasionally and shaking the blender if the mixture sticks at the bottom. Pour in 2 cups of the water along with the sugar and vanilla and blend for an additional 30 seconds. If your blender can fit the additional liquid, pour in the remaining 2 cups water and the milk. If not, transfer the liquid from the blender into a vessel large enough to contain it along with water and milk. Cover and refrigerate for 8 to 12 hours.

Strain the mixture through a fine-mesh strainer into a pitcher. Serve in glasses over ice, if desired, and garnish each glass with ground cinnamon or cinnamon sticks.

MARGARITAS AND RELATED COCKTAILS

There is, perhaps, no single cocktail more closely associated with Baja California than the margarita. There is also likely none with a more disputed origin. Perhaps the most common, if not most likely, origin story is that Carlos "Danny" Herrera of Tijuana's Rancho La Gloria restaurant invented it for Ziegfeld showgirl Marjorie King because she said tequila was the only hard liquor she could abide. He mixed her tequila with lime juice and named the cocktail after her. Another version of the story is set not in Tijuana but in Ensenada's Bar Andaluz (with King cast as the owner). The star of another popular story is Hollywood actress Rita Hayworth (whose real name was Margarita Cansino), for whom the first margarita was both mixed and named during a Tijuana gig at the Agua Caliente racetrack in the 1940s. Perhaps the most likely story is that the margarita was created as a variation of a pre-existing cocktail—the brandy daisy—with tequila replacing the brandy in the original. The English word *daisy* translates in Spanish to *margarita*, and other than the liquor, the two recipes are nearly identical.

ORIGINAL HUSSONG'S CANTINA MARGARITA

Makes 1 cocktail
GF / VEGAN

Among the many claimants to the title of inventor of the margarita is the famed bar Hussong's Cantina in Ensenada. One of the owners, and current manager, says that it was in 1941 that Hussong's bartender Don Carlos Orozco mixed the first version of the cocktail for Margarita Henkel, daughter of the German ambassador to Mexico, and named it for her. He may be right.

Kosher salt

¼ key lime

1 ounce good-quality white tequila

1 ounce Damiana liqueur (or, if you must, Controy, Cointreau, or other orange liqueur)

1 ounce fresh key lime juice

Ice cubes

Lime peel for garnish

Pour some salt onto a small plate. Moisten the rim of a large margarita glass with the lime quarter and dip the rim into the salt to coat. Pour the tequila, Damiana, and lime juice into a shaker, fill the shaker with ice cubes, and shake until the liquid is ice-cold, about 30 seconds. Pour the margarita into the rimmed glass. Garnish the rim of the glass with a lime peel.

MEZCAL AND MANGO MARGARITA

Makes 1 cocktail
GF / VEGAN

The margarita is the face that launched a thousand variations (even if we don't know whose face inspired the drink). Modern mixologists use different liquors (like smoky mezcal in place of tequila), sweeteners (like agave syrup, fruit juices, or even grilled fruit), rimming salts (perhaps including chiles), or even some more exotic variations. While these modern versions may not be authentic, they are no less so than the ubiquitous frozen margarita.

¾ cup Oaxacan mezcal

¾ cup mango juice

¼ cup fresh lime juice (squeezed limes reserved)

¼ cup Cointreau

Ice cubes

Kosher salt

1 mango slice

Julienned lime rind for garnish

Combine the mezcal, mango juice, lime juice, and Cointreau in a shaker. Fill the shaker with ice cubes and shake until the liquid is ice-cold, about 30 seconds. Pour some salt onto a small plate. Moisten the rim of a margarita glass with one of the squeezed limes and dip the rim into the salt to coat. Pour the margarita into the rimmed glass. Garnish with a slice of mango and 1 or more strips of lime rind.

THE PURPLE GECKO

Makes 2 cocktails
GF / VEGAN

It began as a joke and became a real thing! After a nice dinner out with friends in La Jolla, we walked over to an upscale cocktail bar and, for no apparent reason, I asked for a purple gecko. The bartender looked puzzled, cocked her head, and sheepishly admitted she did not know how to make one. "You don't?" I replied. "They're all the rage in Paris and Milan!" By way of explanation, my friend piped up and told her that we were the Mobile Bartending Consulting Service.

Then she asked: "So how do you make one?" After a moment or three of being stumped, I rattled off the following ingredients. By some miracle, it worked!

Kosher salt

2 lime quarters

1½ ounces tequila

½ ounce blue Curaçao

½ ounce grenadine

½ ounce fresh lime juice

1 ounce cranberry juice

1 ounce sweet and sour mix

1 dash bitters

Pour some salt onto a small plate. Moisten the rim of a large margarita glass with a lime quarter and dip the rim into the salt to coat. Pour the tequila, Curaçao, grenadine, lime juice, cranberry juice, sweet and sour mix, and bitters into a shaker, fill the shaker with ice cubes, and shake until the liquid is ice-cold, about 30 seconds. Pour into the rimmed glass and garnish the rim with the remaining lime quarter.

PONCHE

For Mexicans, as for those of some other nationalities in Christendom (I'm looking at you, Polish Wigilia celebrants), Christmas Eve is a bigger thing than Christmas Day. In Mexico it could, at least in part, have to do with the ponche that's passed at Christmas Eve parties.

Place all the ingredients except the brandy in a large stockpot. Bring to a boil over high heat, then lower the heat to maintain a simmer, cover, and cook for 30 minutes, occasionally stirring gently and checking to ensure the piloncillo has completely dissolved.

Pour 1 ounce of the brandy into each mug. Fill the mugs by ladling in the ponche, taking care to give each some chunks of the fruit.

4 quarts water

6 guavas, peeled and quartered

2 large red apples, cored and roughly chopped

1 large green apple, cored and roughly chopped

2 pears, roughly chopped

1 orange, sliced

1 small cone piloncillo, or 1 cup dark brown sugar

6 whole cloves

4 cinnamon sticks

2 tablespoons dried hibiscus flowers

1 dried tamarind pod, husked and seeded

1 (750 ml) bottle Mexican brandy (or rum or tequila)

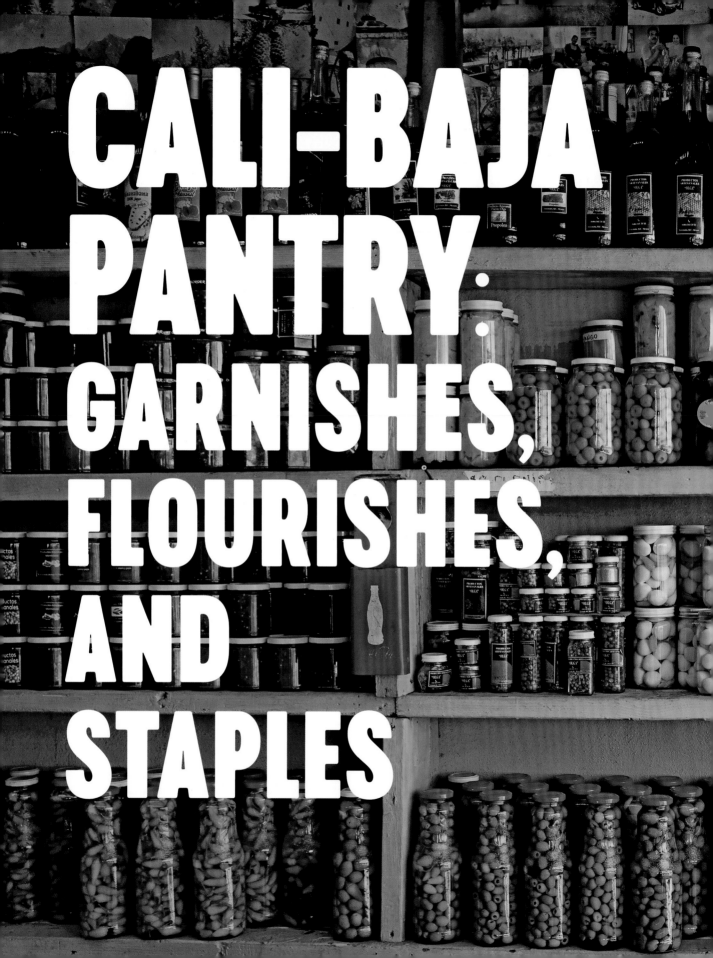

CALI-BAJA PANTRY: GARNISHES, FLOURISHES, AND STAPLES

CORN TORTILLAS

Makes about
10 tortillas / GF

2 cups masa harina

**½ teaspoon
kosher salt**

**1¾ cups plus
1 tablespoon warm
water**

**1 teaspoon fish sauce
(optional)**

The counterintuitive secret ingredient in this recipe is the fish sauce. Its purpose is to add back some of the umami—the depth (perhaps the life)—lost by the maize in the industrial mass-drying process. In addition to a tortilla press, you will need two 8-inch squares cut from a zip-top-style bag or even a trash bag. These are necessary to keep the masa from sticking to the plates of the tortilla press. While this recipe calls for the masa to be mixed by hand (the old-school way), you can, of course, use a stand mixer.

Heat a comal or large sauté pan to about 450°F over medium heat. Combine the masa harina and salt in a large metal bowl. Mix with your hands to ensure even distribution of the salt throughout the masa.

Add 1 cup of the warm water and the fish sauce (if using) to the dry masa mixture. Shape your hand like a claw and begin stirring in a clockwise motion to mix. The dough will be crumbly (similar to pie dough) at this point. Begin massaging the masa using both hands, ensuring even distribution of water to flour, to form a dough ball. Continue adding the water ¼ cup at a time (reserving the final tablespoon until the end) and then mixing until the masa is wet to the touch but doesn't stick to your hands (it should have the texture of Play-Doh from a freshly opened can).

Portion the masa into walnut-size balls, about 40 grams each. Keep the portioned balls beneath a damp towel to avoid moisture loss. Take a ball of masa and slightly flatten it (to about ¼ inch thick). Place the ball on an 8-inch square piece of plastic wrap on the bottom disc of a tortilla press. Place another square of plastic wrap on top. Gently press down on the tortilla press to create a thin, even-surfaced tortilla.

Using a smooth, quick backhand gesture, lay the tortilla on the hot comal or pan, ensuring that you leave no air bubbles between tortilla and the cooking surface (this would negatively impact the final product). Cook on the first side until you just begin to see the tortilla curl at the edges, about 15 seconds. Flip and cook on the second side for 30 to 45 seconds. At 30 seconds, begin feeling the bottom of the tortilla—it should be dry to the touch. Flip the tortilla and cook for, about 15 seconds, after which a properly cooked tortilla will begin to visibly puff (the top surface rising as steam is created inside).

Remove the tortilla and repeat with the remaining masa balls.

FLOUR TORTILLAS

Makes 10 tortillas
VEGAN

⅔ cup very warm water

1 teaspoon fine sea salt

2 cups (260 grams) all-purpose flour, plus more for dusting

5 tablespoons grapeseed, canola, or other neutral oil, melted lard, or melted butter

There is a perception held by many people north of the border that flour tortillas are pretty much only for burritos in Mexico. In reality, burritos are far less prominent in Mexico than some Americans believe, but flour tortillas are quite popular in Northern Mexico, particularly in Sonora but also in Baja. The best I've ever tasted are at Tortillas de Harina Caseras, an open-air shop just west of the Mercado Globos in Ensenada. While they do sell burritos, the tortillas are so good there is no need to fill them with anything: you can eat them straight up.

Pour the warm water into a small bowl, add the salt, and stir until the salt dissolves.

Put the flour in a large bowl. Using a fork, combine the flour with the oil (or other fat) until it looks crumbly. Pour in almost all the salty water and stir until a shaggy dough forms. If the mixture seems dry, add a bit more of the water.

When the dough comes together, transfer it to a floured work surface and knead until smooth, 2 to 3 minutes. Cover with a clean dish towel and let stand for at least 15 minutes or up to 2 hours. Resting the dough makes rolling it out easier.

Divide the dough into 10 equal-size balls. Press each ball into a roughly 8-inch round (the thinner the better) using a tortilla press or rolling pin. Stack the rolled tortillas with a piece of parchment paper between them.

To cook the tortillas, heat a wide, heavy-bottomed comal, skillet, or sauté pan over medium-high heat. When it's hot, add the first tortilla. Within 20 to 30 seconds, you should start to see it puffing up and forming bubbles. When the bottom of the tortilla has some brown spots, flip it and cook until the second side is browned in spots and the tortilla looks dry around the edges. Each tortilla will take 1 to 2 minutes to cook. If it is taking longer, increase the heat. Conversely, if the pan starts to smoke and the tortillas are cooking too quickly, turn down the heat.

Transfer each cooked tortilla to a dish towel and cover it, then continue with the remaining tortillas.

SOPES

Makes 10 sopes
GF / VEGAN

1½ cups masa harina

1¼ cups warm water

¼ cup grapeseed, canola, or other neutral oil

Sopes, like tacos, are a wonderful delivery vehicle for many different toppings. If it can go inside a corn tortilla, it can probably go on top of a sope with relatively little adaptation. And any salsa that works on a taco probably will work on a sope. In fact, sopes could—and probably should—be seen as a form of tortilla.

One of the most common topping ingredients for sopes is refried beans. They sit inside the lips of the sope and are topped by cheese and/or vegetables such as shredded lettuce or cabbage, sautéed onions or a medley of sautéed vegetables, pickles, tomatoes, and many more. Meats work well too. The sope-specific recipes in this book are Refried Bean, Sweet Corn and Pickled Red Cabbage Sopes (page 138), Chorizo, Black Bean, and Queso Fresco Sopes (page 139), and Oyster Sopes (page 139). For other topping ingredients, try carnitas (see page 198), chorizo, braised oxtail (see page 96), grilled chicken livers (see page 123), or duck confit (see page 108).

Combine the masa harina and warm water in a large bowl and knead with your hands until you achieve a uniform texture. If the resulting masa feels dry, add more water in small increments until the dough is soft and manageable and feels a bit like Play-Doh.

Divide the dough into 10 equal-size pieces. Roll each piece of masa into a sphere 1½ to 2 inches in diameter. Cover the masa balls with a wet kitchen towel to keep the dough moist.

Heat a griddle, comal, or large cast-iron pan over medium-high heat. To form the sopes, cut a plastic bag into 2 squares of about 6 inches each. Place one piece of the plastic on a tortilla press, then put down one of the masa balls and cover with the other piece of plastic, close the press, and press down gently with the handle to form a medium-thick tortilla of about 4½ inches.

Lift the handle and remove the top plastic. Pick up the tortilla, and holding it with the plastic at the bottom, gently flip the tortilla into the palm of your hand. A large part of the tortilla will cover your hand.

Place the tortilla on the hot surface in a fast but gentle motion. Cook for up to 1 minute, but no longer or the masa will begin to dry and crack. Using a spatula, turn the tortilla and cook for another 20 to 30 seconds. Remove the tortilla, cover it with a dry, clean towel, and allow to cool for 30 to 45 seconds. Using your fingers, raise a border around the top surface of the tortilla by pinching around its edges. Cover again with the kitchen towel as you make more sopes.

To serve the sopes, heat the grapeseed oil in a large sauté pan or griddle over medium heat. Place the sopes on the skillet and lightly fry them on both sides until they take on a bit of golden color, about 30 seconds per side. Remove from the heat to a plate and cover with paper towels to absorb excess fat.

TORTILLA CRUMBS

Makes about ¼ cup
GF / VEGAN

4 Corn Tortillas (page 228)

½ teaspoon kosher salt

Whether you make your own tortillas or buy tortillas at your closest Mexican (or non-Mexican) market, chances are that after a Mexican meal, you'll have a bunch of leftover less-than-fresh tortillas. This recipe is a great way of using those old tortillas. You can use these tortilla crumbs in many recipes that call for breadcrumbs, and get a bit more texture and flavor in the process.

Preheat the oven to 325°F with a rack in the center. Line a baking sheet with parchment paper.

Arrange the tortillas on the prepared baking sheet and place in the oven. Toast until the tortillas are dry and hard, 10 to 15 minutes (depending on the moisture content of the tortillas).

Break the dried tortillas into little pieces and add them to a high-speed blender or food processor. Add the salt and blend on low speed until the tortillas are broken down to the texture of breadcrumbs, 3 to 5 minutes.

STOCKS

Stocks are the basis of the classic sauces, soups, and stews of many cuisines and provide a solid base for just about any dish. Matching proteins—chicken stock for a chicken dish, for example—makes sense but is ultimately a matter of taste. If a recipe calls for vegetable stock, you can feel free to use roasted vegetable stock. Mix and match for different effects.

Follow the recipes as desired for the described result. But use what you have. You can also make a great stock by employing a frugal use of vegetable trimmings. That's exactly what's done in many professional kitchens. Perhaps the single most important feature in stock-making is the temperature: it should be low—very low. The idea is to simmer the stock, not boil it. While it is not exactly like making tea—you should get some reduction—it is not terribly far off.

CHICKEN STOCK

Makes about 3 quarts
GF

Preheat the oven to 400°F with a rack in the center. Bring a small saucepan of water to a boil.

Drizzle olive oil over all the chicken parts and arrange them in an even layer in a roasting pan. Transfer to the oven and roast, turning once or twice, until the bones turn golden brown, about 30 minutes. Transfer the roasted chicken bones to a stockpot.

Pour off and discard (or save) any accumulated fat from the roasting pan. Pour a little boiling water into the roasting pan and scrape up any browned bits from the bottom with a wooden spoon or spatula. Add the browned bits and juices to the stockpot.

Add the onion, carrot, celery, garlic, thyme, parsley, tomato paste, water, and salt to the stockpot and bring to a boil over high heat. Reduce the heat to maintain a very gentle simmer and cook, uncovered, for about 1 hour 30 minutes, until the stock takes on a pronounced chicken flavor, skimming off the foam periodically. Pour the stock through a fine-mesh strainer and discard the solids. Let the stock cool to room temperature, then transfer to containers and refrigerate until completely chilled, about 6 hours. Skim off and remove any fat and scum from the surface before using. Refrigerate for up to 5 days or freeze for up to 6 months.

Extra-virgin olive oil

5 pounds chicken bones, such as backs, wings, and legs (pretty much whatever you can get from the butcher)

1 medium onion, roughly chopped

1 medium carrot, roughly chopped

1 large or 2 small ribs celery, roughly chopped

2 medium cloves garlic, crushed

2 sprigs thyme

1 bunch parsley

2 tablespoons tomato paste

4 quarts water

2 tablespoons kosher salt

BEEF STOCK

Makes about 2 quarts

GF

Preheat the oven to 400°F with a rack in center. Bring a small saucepan of water to a boil.

Drizzle olive oil over the beef bones and arrange them in an even layer in a roasting pan. Transfer to the oven and roast, turning once or twice, until the bones begin to brown, about 15 minutes.

Lightly toss the onion, carrot, and celery with olive oil. Scatter the vegetables around and over the bones and roast until the bones and vegetables are nicely browned, about 30 minutes longer. Be careful not to let anything burn. Monitor the bones and rotate them if the bones on one side of the pan are browning too fast. Transfer the roasted bones, onion, carrot, and celery to a stockpot.

Pour off and discard (or save) any accumulated fat from the roasting pan. Pour a little boiling water into the roasting pan and scrape up any browned bits from the bottom with a wooden spoon or spatula. Add the browned bits and juices to the stockpot.

Add the garlic, thyme, parsley, tomato paste, water, and salt to the stockpot and bring to a boil over high heat. Reduce the heat to maintain a very gentle simmer and cook, uncovered, for at least 3 hours or up to 6 hours, until it takes on a distinct beef flavor, skimming off the foam periodically. Pour the stock through a fine-mesh strainer into a heatproof bowl, discarding the solids. Let the stock cool to room temperature, then transfer to containers and refrigerate until completely chilled, about 6 hours. Skim off and remove any fat and scum from the surface before using. Refrigerate for up to 5 days or freeze for up to 6 months.

Extra-virgin olive oil

5 pounds beef bones (pretty much whatever you can get from the butcher)

1 medium white onion, roughly chopped

1 medium carrot, roughly chopped

1 large or 2 small ribs celery, roughly chopped

2 medium cloves garlic, crushed

2 sprigs thyme

1 sprig parsley

2 tablespoons tomato paste

4 quarts water

2 tablespoons kosher salt

VEGETABLE STOCK

Makes about 3 quarts
GF / VEGAN

Combine all the ingredients in a large stockpot and add water to cover (about 4 quarts). Bring to a boil over high heat, then reduce the heat to maintain a simmer and cook, uncovered, until the vegetables lose their texture and the stock takes on a soft but distinctly vegetal flavor, about 1 hour. Strain the stock into a heatproof bowl and discard the solids. Taste the stock and add more salt if needed. Cool the stock to room temperature, then cover and transfer to the refrigerator until completely chilled. Refrigerate for up to 5 days or freeze for up to 6 months.

Note: Vegetable stocks are common in many cuisines. This is a straightforward version one key addition: kombu. Including this dried kelp in the stock provides a huge dose of umami. Kombu can be found in most Asian (and all Japanese) markets.

1 ounce dried mushrooms, such as shiitake, oyster, porcini, morel

1 medium onion, roughly chopped

1 large carrot, roughly chopped

2 large or 4 small ribs celery, roughly chopped

3 leeks, green parts only (reserve the whites for another use), washed and roughly chopped

4 cloves garlic, crushed

2 large russet potatoes, peeled and roughly chopped

1 (4-inch) piece kombu

3 bay leaves

6 sprigs thyme

6 sprigs parsley

1 tablespoon whole black peppercorns

1 tablespoon whole white peppercorns

1 teaspoon fennel seeds

1 teaspoon coriander seeds

1 tablespoon kosher salt, plus more as needed

ROASTED VEGETABLE STOCK

Makes about 2 quarts
VEGAN

Preheat the oven to 400°F with a rack in the center. Bring a medium saucepan of water to a boil.

In a heavy-bottomed roasting pan, toss the onions, leek, carrots, celery, tomatoes, parsnip, potatoes, garlic, and mushrooms with the tomato paste and olive oil to coat. Transfer to the oven and roast, shaking the pan occasionally and turning the ingredients once or twice, until everything is nicely browned, about 45 minutes. Transfer the vegetables to a large stockpot.

Set the empty roasting pan across 2 burners and turn both to high. Pour in 2 cups of the boiling water and stir, scraping up all the browned bits from the bottom of the pan. Pour the water and browned bits into the stockpot.

Add the soy sauce, parsley, thyme, peppercorns, white wine, salt, and 6 cups water to the stockpot. Bring to a boil, then reduce the heat to low. Cover with the lid ajar and simmer until the vegetables begin to lose their texture, 30 to 45 minutes. Taste and adjust the seasoning. Strain the stock through a fine-mesh strainer, pressing on the vegetables to force out as much stock as possible, then discard the solids. Let cool to room temperature, then transfer the stock to containers and refrigerate until completely chilled, about 6 hours. Refrigerate for up to 5 days or freeze for up to 6 months.

2 large onions, roughly chopped

1 leek, washed and roughly chopped

4 large carrots, cut into chunks

2 large or 4 small ribs celery, roughly chopped

4 large tomatoes, roughly chopped

1 medium parsnip, peeled and roughly chopped

2 medium potatoes, peeled and quartered

6 cloves garlic, crushed

20 medium white mushrooms (about 12 ounces), trimmed and halved

2 tablespoons tomato paste

1/3 cup extra-virgin olive oil

1/4 cup soy sauce or tamari

10 sprigs parsley

2 or 3 sprigs thyme

10 whole black peppercorns

1/2 cup white wine

1 tablespoon kosher salt, plus more as needed

STAPLES

MEXICAN RICE

Serves 4 / GF

Heat the oil in a large saucepan over medium heat and add the rice, garlic salt, and cumin. Cook, stirring constantly, until the rice is puffed and golden, about 5 minutes. Add the onion and cook until the onion is translucent and tender, 3 to 5 minutes. Add the tomato sauce and stock and bring to a boil. Reduce the heat to low, cover, and simmer for 20 to 25 minutes, until the stock has been absorbed. Fluff with a fork.

3 tablespoons grapeseed, canola, or other neutral oil

1 cup uncooked long-grain rice

1 teaspoon garlic salt

½ teaspoon ground cumin

¼ cup chopped white onion

¼ cup tomato sauce

2 cups Chicken Stock (page 232)

SMOKED TOFU

Makes 1 block
GF / VEGAN

Smoked tofu is wonderfully versatile. It stars in vegetarian recipes such as Cotija and Smoked Tofu Stuffed Artichokes (page 164) and can be swapped in for meat in many dishes. The keys to the dish are ① using extra-firm tofu and ② the combination of smoking, soy sauce, and salsa negra.

14 to 16 ounces extra-firm tofu

½ cup soy sauce or tamari

¼ cup fresh lime juice

2 tablespoons Carlos Salgado's Salsa Negra (page)

2 tablespoons extra-virgin olive oil

¼ teaspoon kosher salt

Place a cutting board on a baking sheet. Place the tofu on the cutting board, top with another cutting board, and weight the board with a couple of heavy cans or a cast-iron pan. Press the tofu for 1 to 2 hours, periodically tipping the liquid from the baking sheet into the sink.

Put soy sauce, lime juice, salsa negra, olive oil, and salt in a large bowl and whisk to combine. Slice the pressed tofu into 2-inch by ½-inch blocks. Put the tofu blocks in the marinade and gently toss to coat. Cover and refrigerate for at least 1 hour or up to overnight, periodically spooning the marinade over the tofu.

Prepare a smoker for low heat—optimally 165°F—and maximum smoke and preheat it with the lid closed for 15 minutes. When the smoker is ready, put the marinated tofu blocks in a grill pan (or directly on the smoker grates), close the lid, and smoke for 1 hour.

Remove the tofu from the smoker and let it cool on the counter for 1 hour. Use immediately or cover and refrigerate for up to 1 week.

PINTO BEANS

Serves 8 to 12
GF / VEGAN

While this recipe is for pinto beans, it can serve as a base recipe for just about any bean, including black beans, peruano beans, and pinquito beans.

Put the beans in a large bowl and add water to cover by a few inches. Set aside to soak overnight. Drain. (Alternatively, to quick soak the beans, put them in a colander and rinse with cold water for 1 to 2 minutes. Transfer the rinsed beans to a large saucepan, add 1½ tablespoons salt and 8 cups water, and stir to dissolve the salt. Bring the water to a boil and boil for 2 minutes. Turn off the heat, cover, and let soak for 1 hour, then drain.)

In a large pot, heat the olive oil over medium heat. Add the onion and garlic and cook until tender and fragrant, 4 to 5 minutes. Add the guajillo chile, cinnamon stick (if using), cumin, coriander, guajillo chile powder, oregano, and bay leaves and cook for 1 minute to toast the spices. Add 2 quarts water, the tomato paste, and the drained beans. Stir in the salt and bring to a rapid boil. Reduce the heat to low and simmer, uncovered, for 45 to 60 minutes, until the beans are tender.

Drain the beans and tip them into a bowl. Stir in the adobo sauce and vinegar. Taste the beans and adjust the seasoning, if needed, with salt and/or vinegar.

Store the cooked beans, covered, in the refrigerator for up to 4 days.

Ingredients:

1 pound dried pinto beans

1 tablespoon extra-virgin olive oil

1 medium white or yellow onion, diced

4 cloves garlic, crushed

1 dried guajillo chile, stemmed, seeded, and torn into small pieces

1 cinnamon stick (optional)

1 tablespoon ground cumin

1 tablespoon ground coriander

1 tablespoon guajillo chile powder

2 teaspoons dried Mexican oregano

2 bay leaves

1 tablespoon tomato paste

2 teaspoons kosher salt, plus more if needed

1 tablespoon adobo sauce (from a can of chipotles in adobo)

½ teaspoon distilled white vinegar, plus more if needed

REFRIED BEANS

Makes about 6 cups
GF

Refried beans are a Mexican staple. They're essential for sopes and useful for many tortas, tacos, burritos, and more.

Put the beans in a large bowl and add water to cover by a few inches. Set aside to soak overnight. Drain. (Alternatively, to quick soak the beans, put them in a colander and rinse with cold water for 1 to 2 minutes. Transfer the rinsed beans to a large saucepan or pot, add 1½ tablespoons salt and 8 cups water, and stir to dissolve the salt. Bring the water to a boil and boil for 2 minutes. Turn off the heat, cover, and let soak for 1 hour, then drain.)

Combine the drained beans, onion, garlic, and bay leaves in a medium pot and add water to cover. Bring to a boil over medium heat, then lower the heat to maintain a simmer and cook for 1 hour, stirring occasionally and adding more water if needed. Check the beans—they are done when they break apart when you press them with the back of a spoon. If they don't, let them simmer a bit longer, checking every 5 minutes. Remove from the heat and season with salt. Let them sit for at least 15 minutes or up to 1 hour. Remove the bay leaves, onion, and garlic from the pot.

Melt the lard in a large sauté pan over medium heat. Using a large slotted spoon, transfer the beans to the pan, reserving their cooking liquid. Using the back of the spoon or a potato masher, crush the beans into the lard, adding some of the reserved bean cooking liquid to thin them a bit. Continue cooking and smashing the beans until you achieve a texture similar to hummus, then remove from the heat.

Store in an airtight container in the refrigerator for up to 4 days.

1 cup dried pinto beans, rinsed and picked over for stones

1 medium white onion, quartered

1 head garlic, cut in half widthwise

2 bay leaves

Kosher salt

2 tablespoons lard (or neutral oil to make them vegetarian/ vegan)

SALSAS AND SAUCES

Though I call for specific salsas and sauces for specific dishes, the reality is that there are very few rules and even fewer wrong choices about which salsa to use with which taco. If I call for salsa taquera and you prefer a Baja-style salsa roja, I have one thing to say to you: go for it!

SALSA MACHA

Makes about 2 cups
GF / VEGAN

Set a large heavy skillet over medium heat and add the olive oil. When the oil is hot but not smoking, add the garlic and cook, stirring frequently, for about 1 minute, until it starts to gain color. Add the guajillo, chipotle, morita, and árbol chiles and the cashews and cook until the guajillo chile just starts to blacken, about another 2 minutes. Add the sesame seeds and cook for 1 to 2 minutes, until they just begin to pop. Remove from the heat. Carefully transfer the contents of the skillet a high-speed blender or food processor. Let cool for about 10 minutes.

Add the salt, brown sugar, and vinegar and blend until smooth, starting on low speed and building up to high speed. Pour into a container and set on the counter to cool. Store in an airtight container in the refrigerator for up to 1 month.

1 cup extra-virgin olive oil

4 cloves garlic, peeled

1 dried guajillo chile, stemmed, seeded, and torn into pieces

4 dried chipotle chiles, stemmed and torn into pieces

1 dried morita chile, stemmed and torn into pieces (if unavailable, add an extra chipotle)

3 dried chiles de árbol , stemmed and seeded

⅓ cup raw unsalted cashews (or other nuts such as peanuts, pecans, or pine nuts, or a combination)

2 tablespoons sesame seeds

1 teaspoon kosher salt or sea salt, plus more as needed

2 tablespoons brown sugar

3 tablespoons distilled white vinegar

ROASTED TOMATILLO SALSA VERDE

Makes about 2½ cups

GF / **VEGAN**

Preheat the oven to 450°F with a rack about 4 inches from the heat source. Line a baking sheet with parchment paper or aluminum foil.

Place the tomatillos, chiles, onion, and garlic on the prepared pan and drizzle the onion segments with 1 tablespoon of the olive oil. Roast until the tomatillos and chiles are blackened in spots, about 5 minutes. Remove the pan from the oven and turn the vegetables over. Return to the oven and roast for 4 to 6 more minutes, until the tomatillos are splotchy-black and blistered.

Peel the garlic and add it along with the other vegetables to a food processor or blender. Pulse until the vegetables are combined but still slightly chunky. Add the cilantro, lime juice, and salt and pulse until incorporated. With the food processor running, drizzle in the remaining 3 tablespoons olive oil until the salsa is slightly runny but not completely smooth.

Taste the salsa and adjust the seasoning with additional lime juice or salt if needed. Store in an airtight container in the refrigerator for up to 1 week.

12 medium tomatillos (about 1½ pounds), husked and rinsed

2 medium jalapeño chiles, stemmed and seeded

1 medium white onion, quartered

4 cloves garlic, unpeeled

4 tablespoons olive oil

½ cup packed fresh cilantro leaves

¼ cup fresh lime juice, plus more if needed

½ teaspoon kosher salt, plus more if needed

SALSA BANDERA (PICO DE GALLO)

Makes about 1½ cups

GF / **VEGAN**

While this sauce is often called *pico de gallo* north of the border, it's rarely referred to as such in Baja. And while it appears on the table with a bowl of tortilla chips in many Mexican restaurants in America, that is rarely the case in Baja (or most of Mexico), where you are more likely to find Baja-style salsa roja.

Combine the onion, tomatoes, chiles, cilantro, lime juice, and salt in a large bowl and mix thoroughly. Taste the salsa and adjust the seasoning with more salt and/or lime juice if needed. Store in an airtight container in the refrigerator for up to 3 days.

½ medium white onion, finely diced

1 pound plum tomatoes, diced

2 jalapeño chiles, stemmed, seeded, and minced

3 tablespoons finely chopped fresh cilantro

2 tablespoons fresh lime juice, plus more if needed

½ teaspoon kosher salt, plus more if needed

ÁRBOL CHILE SALSA

Makes about 1½ cups
GF / VEGAN

1 ounce dried chiles
de árbol (about 25),
stemmed

2 medium plum
tomatoes

4 cloves garlic, peeled

½ teaspoon
kosher salt

This is one of the spicier salsas frequently available at taquerias and stands in Baja. It is, to be frank, just this side of a hot sauce. But there is no better way to add a little nuclear to the deliciousness of a taco.

Bring 4 cups water to a boil in a medium saucepan over high heat. Add the chiles to the water and stir with a wooden spoon to make sure they are all saturated. Remove from the heat, cover the pan, and let the chiles soak until softened, about 15 minutes.

Drain the softened chiles and put them in a high-speed blender or food processor. Add the tomatoes, garlic, salt, and ¾ cup water and blend until completely smooth.

Store in an airtight container in the refrigerator for up to 5 days.

CARLOS SALGADO'S SALSA NEGRA

Makes about 1 cup
GF / VEGAN

¾ cup plus
2 tablespoons
grapeseed, canola,
or other neutral oil

¾ ounce dried chiles
de árbol, stemmed

3 dried guajillo chiles,
stemmed, seeded, and
cut into 1-inch pieces

10 cloves black garlic,
minced

10 cloves regular
garlic, minced

1 tablespoon white
wine vinegar

1 tablespoon light
brown sugar

¾ teaspoon cumin
seeds

1 teaspoon kosher salt

Chef Carlos Salgado of the Michelin-starred Orange County restaurant Taco María makes this smoky, spicy, and rich salsa negra with black garlic—garlic that has been aged until the cloves literally turn black from the Maillard reaction—and two types of dried chiles. It's an earthy, sweet, and intriguingly spicy sauce that hints at Asian influences. The black garlic in particular makes this take on salsa negra unique; look for it at any gourmet store and many Southeast Asian markets.

In a large saucepan, combine the oil whole chiles and guajillo chile de árbol, segments and toast until the chiles are just beginning to develop dark spots. Remove from the heat and stir in both types of garlic, the vinegar, brown sugar, cumin, and salt. Cover and let cool.

Transfer the chile mixture to a high-speed blender or food processor and blend to a smooth puree. Store in an airtight container in the refrigerator for up to 5 days.

BAJA-STYLE SALSA ROJA

This salsa, not pico de gallo, is the one that is most likely to be found on tables at Baja taquerias. The reason why is clear to me: it is both delicious and very versatile.

Heat a grill to high or heat a grill pan over high heat.

Add the tomatoes and grill for 10 minutes, or until they are very charred and blackened. Add the onions and serrano and jalapeño chiles to the grill, turn the tomatoes over, and grill until all the vegetables are charred and blackened, another 6 to 8 minutes. Turn the chiles periodically to make sure all sides get charred. Take the tomatoes, onions, and chiles off the grill and place in a resealable plastic bag to steam for about 10 minutes.

Transfer the tomatoes, chiles, and any liquid in the bag to a high-speed blender or food processor, add the garlic, salt, and cilantro, and blend on high speed until pureed. Add 1½ cups water and the lime juice and blend to combine, then let cool.

Store in an airtight container in the refrigerator for at least 1 week.

Makes about 6 cups
GF / VEGAN

7 medium
plum tomatoes
(about 2 pounds)

2 medium white
onions, quartered

1 serrano chile,
stemmed and seeded

2 jalapeño chiles,
stemmed and seeded

2 cloves garlic, peeled

1 teaspoon kosher salt

12 whole sprigs
cilantro, trimmed

Juice of 1 lime

ANCHO CHILE SALSA

Heat a large sauté pan over medium heat. Toast the chiles in the pan until they just begin to develop charring, about 30 seconds. Flip the chiles and toast the other side. Transfer the chiles to a bowl with hot water to cover and set aside to soak for 30 minutes, or until they are tender and pliable. Drain the chiles, reserving their soaking liquid, and transfer to a high-speed blender or food processor.

Add the onion, tomatoes, sugar, garlic, vinegar, and salt to taste to the blender and blend until completely smooth, about 5 minutes. Thin the salsa with the reserved chile soaking liquid until you reach your desired consistency. Strain the salsa through a fine-mesh strainer if needed and season with salt. Store in an airtight container in the refrigerator for up to 3 weeks.

Makes about 2 cups
GF / VEGAN

8 dried ancho chiles,
stemmed and seeded

½ large red onion,
roughly chopped

4 medium plum
tomatoes, blanched
and peeled

1 teaspoon sugar

3 cloves garlic,
crushed

1 teaspoon white wine
vinegar

Kosher salt

ROASTED TOMATO, ÁRBOL CHILE, AND GARLIC SALSA

Makes about 2 cups
GF / VEGAN

Slice the tomatoes in half lengthwise, then slice the halves widthwise. Heat a dry sauté pan over high heat and place the tomatoes on the pan. Toast until they blacken on the bottom, 2 to 3 minutes, then flip and repeat until all the cut surfaces are blackened. Transfer the tomatoes to a high-speed blender or food processor.

Toast the chiles in a large dry sauté pan over medium heat, shaking the pan occasionally, until they darken and start to brown in spots, about 2 minutes, then transfer to a small heatproof bowl. Pour the boiling water over the chiles and let soak for 15 minutes. Drain.

In the same sauté pan, toast the garlic over medium heat, turning it regularly, until it is soft and starts to brown in spots, about 5 minutes. Remove from the heat, cool, then peel and chop the garlic. Add the onion to the pan and cook until the onion is lightly caramelized, 2 to 3 minutes.

Add the soaked chiles, garlic, onion, cilantro, and salt to the blender or food processor with the tomatoes. Pulse to combine, then blend, starting on low speed and gradually increasing, to evenly chop and combine the ingredients but not puree them, about 1 minute. Taste the sauce for seasoning and add more salt or some lime juice, if needed. Store in an airtight container in the refrigerator for up to 1 week.

2 medium plum tomatoes

8 dried chiles de árbol, stemmed and seeded

½ cup boiling water

4 cloves garlic, unpeeled

½ medium white onion, chopped

½ cup chopped fresh cilantro

1 teaspoon kosher salt, plus more as needed

Fresh lime juice (optional)

SALSA TAQUERA

Makes 2 cups
GF / VEGAN

Go to a good taco stand in Baja and there will often be a selection of salsas on offer, gratis. This will generally be one of them.

Heat the oil in a medium sauté pan over medium-high heat. Add the onion and garlic and cook until they start to brown, 2 to 3 minutes. Remove the onion and garlic and put them in a high-speed blender or food processor.

Add the chiles to the same oil and cook until they start to darken in color, about 1 minute. Transfer them to the blender.

Add the quartered tomatoes to the pan and cook, turning as each side blisters, until they are blistered on all sides, 2 to 3 minutes in total. Transfer the tomatoes to the blender and add the salt, pepper, oregano, and lime juice. Blend to a perfectly smooth puree. Store in an airtight container in the refrigerator for up to 1 week.

2 tablespoons grapeseed, canola, or other neutral oil

¼ medium white onion, chopped

3 cloves garlic, crushed

3 to 8 dried chiles de árbol, stemmed and seeded

5 medium plum tomatoes, quartered

1 teaspoon kosher salt

½ teaspoon freshly ground black pepper

¼ teaspoon dried Mexican oregano

Juice of 2 limes

CHIPOTLE-AVOCADO SAUCE

Makes about ½ cup
GF / VEGAN

Scoop the flesh from the avocado into a small bowl and mash it. Transfer the mashed avocado to a food processor, add the remaining ingredients, and process to a smooth puree. Taste and adjust the seasoning with salt and/or additional lime juice as needed.

1 medium Hass avocado

1 chipotle chile (from a can of chipotles in adobo), minced, plus 2 tablespoons adobo sauce from the can

1½ tablespoons extra-virgin olive oil

Juice of ½ key lime, plus more as needed

Kosher salt

CHILTEPIN HOT SAUCE

Makes 2 cups

GF / VEGAN

Small, bright red, and slightly larger than peppercorns, chiltepin chiles bring big heat in a tiny package. They are also called tepin chiles and can be found at specialty grocers.

Combine the garlic, chiles, salt, paprika, vinegar, and ½ cup water in a high-speed blender and blend for 1 to 2 minutes, until thoroughly combined. In a small bowl, whisk the xanthan gum with 2 tablespoons water until dissolved, then add to the blender and blend for an additional 30 seconds. Transfer the sauce to a glass jar and let it settle. Store in the refrigerator for up to 9 months.

6 cloves garlic, roughly chopped

½ cup dried chiltepin chiles

1 teaspoon kosher salt

2 tablespoons smoked paprika

1 cup apple cider vinegar

¼ teaspoon xanthan gum

AVOCADO, PINEAPPLE, AND JALAPEÑO SAUCE

Makes about 2 cups

GF / VEGAN

Scoop the flesh of the avocados into a high-speed blender or food processor. Add the remaining ingredients and blend, using a tamper (for the blender) and adding water, if needed, until a smooth puree is achieved.

3 ripe Hass avocados

2 tablespoons fresh lime juice

2 tablespoons minced red onion

1 jalapeño chile, stemmed and seeded

¼ cup fresh cilantro leaves and tender stems

2 teaspoons kosher salt

½ cup finely diced fresh pineapple

MOLES AND MORE SAUCES

ALMOND MOLE

Makes 2 quarts

Remove the seeds and veins of the ancho and pasilla chiles. In a large sauté pan, melt ¼ cup of the lard over medium heat. Add the ancho, pasilla, and chipotle chiles and fry until they take on a darker color, 1 to 2 minutes. Using a slotted spoon, transfer the chiles to a high-speed blender or food processor.

Add the almonds, walnuts, sesame seeds, peanuts, and raisins to the sauté pan and cook until they take on some color, 1 to 2 minutes, then transfer to the blender. Add the tortilla and bolillo to the sauté pan and cook until they, too, take on color, about 40 seconds. Transfer them to the blender.

Melt the remaining ¼ cup lard in the sauté pan over medium heat and add the plantain, tomatoes, onion, garlic, cloves, anise, cumin, coriander, and peppercorns and cook, stirring regularly, until the onion is soft. Transfer the contents of the pan to the blender and add 3 cups of the stock. Blend on high speed to fully combine the ingredients.

Combine the chocolate tablet, remaining 5 cups stock, and the salt in a Dutch oven and bring to a boil over high heat, stirring regularly. Reduce the heat to low and simmer, stirring regularly, until the chocolate has fully melted and the mixture is incorporated, about 5 minutes.

Add the contents of the blender to the Dutch oven and raise the heat to return the mixture to a boil. Reduce the heat to low and simmer, stirring periodically, until the mole thickens and acquires a more intense color, 20 to 30 minutes. Use the immediately or cool and store in an airtight container in the refrigerator for up to 1 week.

5 dried ancho chiles

5 dried pasilla chiles

½ cup lard

5 dried chipotle chiles

1½ cups almonds

1 cup walnuts

½ cup sesame seeds

½ cup unsalted roasted peanuts

5 tablespoons raisins

1 Corn Tortilla (page 228)

½ bolillo (Mexican roll), or ¼ small baguette

½ unripe plantain, sliced

2 medium plum tomatoes, cored

½ medium white onion, chopped

2 cloves garlic, crushed

3 whole cloves

½ teaspoon aniseed

½ teaspoon cumin seeds

½ teaspoon coriander seeds

5 whole black peppercorns

8 cups Chicken Stock (page 232)

1 (3.2-ounce) tablet Mexican chocolate

1½ teaspoons kosher salt

MOLE VERDE/PIPIÁN SAUCE

Makes 5 cups / GF

Toast the pepitas in a heavy medium skillet or sauté pan over medium heat until they start to pop and turn light golden brown, about 5 minutes. Transfer to a high-speed blender or food processor and blend until they are finely ground. Add the tomatillos, 1 cup of the stock, the onion, jalapeño and serrano chiles, cilantro, oregano, lettuce, and garlic and blend until smooth.

Heat the olive oil in a medium saucepan over medium-high heat until it is just shimmering. Add the puree and cook, stirring constantly, until thickened almost to the consistency of tomato paste, about 10 minutes. Stir in the remaining 2 cups stock and bring to a boil. Reduce the heat to maintain a simmer and cook until all the flavors come together, about 10 minutes. Season to taste with salt.

Use the mole immediately or cool, transfer to an airtight container, and store in the refrigerator for up to 3 days.

1 cup pepitas (pumpkin seeds)

4 large tomatillos, husked, rinsed, and halved

3 cups Chicken Stock (page 232)

1 cup roughly chopped white onion (about 1 medium onion)

1 medium jalapeño chile, stemmed, seeded, and roughly chopped

1 serrano chile, stemmed, seeded, and roughly chopped

1½ cups packed roughly chopped fresh cilantro leaves and tender stems

1 tablespoon dried Mexican oregano

½ cup packed roughly chopped romaine lettuce leaves

1 tablespoon minced garlic (about 3 cloves)

1 tablespoon extra-virgin olive oil

Kosher salt

GUACAMOLE

Serves 6
GF / VEGAN

Combine the shallot and tomato in a food processor and process for 10 to 15 seconds, until finely chopped. Scoop the avocado flesh into the food processor and pulse to combine. Add the lime juice, salt, and olive oil and pulse to fully combine but not puree. Add the cilantro and pulse several more times. The idea here is to retain some texture, not to end up with a smooth puree.

1 medium shallot, roughly chopped

½ medium plum tomato, roughly chopped

3 medium Hass avocados

Juice of 1 lime

1 teaspoon kosher salt

1 tablespoon extra-virgin olive oil

Leaves from several sprigs cilantro

AVOCADO MOUSSE

Makes about 2 cups
GF / VEGAN

Scoop the avocado flesh into a high-speed blender or food processor. Add the lime juice, cilantro, chile, salt, and 2 tablespoons water and blend on high speed to a smooth puree. Taste the mousse and adjust the seasoning with more salt and the consistency with more water as needed. Store in an airtight container in the refrigerator for 3 to 5 days.

1 large Hass avocado

1 tablespoon fresh lime juice

2 tablespoons chopped fresh cilantro

1 medium serrano chile, stemmed

1 teaspoon kosher salt, plus more as needed

MEXICAN AMBA SAUCE

Makes about 1½ cups
GF / VEGAN

Amba sauce is a beguiling, delicious concoction of Indian origin that found its way out of South Asia on the backs of Iraqi Jews. It began its life as an Indian mango chutney, then took on a new form in Israel and the Middle East. While it is not exactly common in Mexico, it got to the New World with the Jews who settled in Mexico City and, before that, crypto-Jews who came to the north. Its key ingredient (mango), is of course, common in Mexico, and the spice factor works perfectly.

2 ripe mangoes (about 1½ pounds), pitted and peeled

Juice of 4 limes

1½ tablespoons extra-virgin olive oil

4 cloves garlic, crushed

1 teaspoon fenugreek seeds

1 serrano chile, stemmed and seeded

1 habanero chile, stemmed and seeded

2 teaspoons Spanish smoked paprika (pimentón)

1 tablespoon ground cumin

Put the mangoes and lime juice in a high-speed blender or food processor. Pulse several times to combine, then increase the speed and puree, about 20 seconds.

Heat the olive oil in a small sauté pan over medium heat. When the oil is hot, add the garlic, fenugreek seeds, and serrano and habanero chiles and cook, shaking the pan occasionally, until the garlic is light golden, 2 to 3 minutes. Add the contents of the sauté pan, along with the paprika and cumin, to the food processor and, starting on low and gradually increasing the speed, process to a smooth, sauce-like puree, about 20 seconds. Let the sauce cool, then transfer to an airtight container and store in the refrigerator for up to 1 week.

CILANTRO GREMOLATA

Makes about ⅓ cup
GF / VEGAN

2 limes

1 bunch cilantro, leaves and tender stems, finely minced

1 clove garlic, finely minced

Kosher salt and freshly ground black pepper

Using a zester, remove about 1 teaspoon of the zest from the limes and finely mince it. Reserve the limes for another use. (Keep in mind that the zest is the outer skin of the lime, not the inner white pith. Be careful not to include any of the pith, because it will be bitter.) Place the minced zest in a small bowl, add the cilantro and garlic, and season with salt and pepper. Store any unused gremolata in an airtight container in the refrigerator for up to 1 day.

AVOCADO CREMA

Makes about 2½ cups

GF / VEG

Scoop the flesh of the avocados into a high-speed blender or food processor. Add the remaining ingredients and blend until smooth. Store in an airtight container in the refrigerator for up to 5 days.

2 large Hass avocados

¼ cup sour cream

¼ cup Mayonnaise (opposite)

2 tablespoons fresh lime juice

½ teaspoon kosher salt

½ teaspoon ground cumin

½ teaspoon garlic powder

AVOCADO MAYONNAISE

Makes about 1½ cups

GF / VEGAN

Scoop the flesh of the avocado into a food processor. Add the vinegar, lime juice, mustard, garlic, and 2 tablespoons of the olive oil and pulse to combine the ingredients, then process on high until completely smooth and creamy, adding the remaining 1 tablespoon oil if necessary. Season with salt. Use immediately or transfer to an airtight container and store in the refrigerator for up to 3 days.

1 medium Hass avocado

1 teaspoon apple cider vinegar

2 teaspoons fresh lime juice

1 teaspoon Dijon mustard

1 teaspoon minced garlic

2 to 3 tablespoons avocado oil or extra-virgin olive oil

Kosher salt

MAYONNAISE

Makes about 1½ cups

GF / **VEG**

1 clove garlic, crushed

1 teaspoon kosher salt

1 large egg

1 large egg yolk

1 tablespoon Dijon mustard

Juice of 1 lemon

1½ cups grapeseed, canola, or other neutral oil

There are many decent mayonnaise products sold in nearly every grocery store in America. None, however, match what can be easily made at home by anyone competent at the use of a food processor or blender. Start with good-quality fresh ingredients and be sure to use a neutral oil. If you want to take the finished product further in the direction of an aioli, double or even triple the garlic.

Place the garlic and salt in a food processor. Pulse until the garlic is pulverized, 4 or 5 pulses. Add the egg and egg yolk and process until fully integrated, about 5 seconds. Add the mustard and lemon juice and process to fully combine, another 5 to 10 seconds. With the machine running, slowly, almost drop by drop, drizzle in the oil through the hole in the lid, until it is fully incorporated and the sauce is emulsified and smooth. Store in an airtight container in the refrigerator for up to 1 week.

MEXICAN CREMA

Makes about 1 cup

GF / **VEG**

1 cup heavy cream

1 tablespoon buttermilk

Juice of ½ lime

Kosher salt

Pour the heavy cream into a small saucepan and warm over medium heat to room temperature. Add the buttermilk and mix well. Pour the cream mixture into a canning jar and lightly cover. Set the jar on the counter (or in warm place) and let stand for the next 12 to 24 hours. How long you leave the jar on the counter is up to you, and is primarily based on the temperature in your house: the colder your house, the longer you should leave it.

Fasten the lid on the jar tightly and refrigerate for 2 to 3 hours, until the crema reaches your desired thickness. Add the lime juice and a pinch of salt to the jar and mix well. Taste and add more salt if needed, then serve immediately or store in the jar, in the refrigerator for up to 2 weeks.

PICKLES AND ESCABECHES

One of the best ways to add a new dimension to a dish is by tossing in a pickle. The recipes that follow are quick pickles. They're not the traditional time- and space-consuming dill or half-sour pickles. They're ready in under an hour, not in a matter of days. You could get home from work and have them done in time for dinner. Quick pickles are one of the cook's best tools—maybe even "cheats"—to elevate any dish quickly and easily. Pickled cabbage is an excellent addition to any taco or pita dish. Pickled onions do that same trick and work great on any slab of meat.

CARROT, JALAPEÑO, AND CAULIFLOWER IN ESCABECHE

Makes about 1 quart
GF / VEGAN

Combine the vinegar, water, sugar, salt, cloves, allspice, oregano, bay leaves, and garlic in a medium saucepan and bring to a boil over high heat. Meanwhile, place the cauliflower, carrots, onion, and chiles in a wide-mouthed 1-quart canning jar (or a heatproof glass or ceramic bowl).

When the vinegar mixture comes to a boil, remove it from the heat. Place the canning jar in the sink to catch any overflow and carefully pour the vinegar mixture over the vegetables. When the jar is cool enough to handle, set it aside for about 1 hour, until completely cooled. Screw the lid on the jar and let sit at room temperature for 24 hours before serving or storing. The pickle will keep in the refrigerator for 2 to 3 weeks.

1 cup apple cider vinegar

1 cup water

2 tablespoons sugar

2 tablespoons kosher salt

5 whole cloves

2 allspice berries

1 tablespoon dried Mexican oregano

3 bay leaves

4 large cloves garlic, lightly crushed

1 cup small cauliflower florets

1 cup sliced carrots (1/8-inch-thick coins)

1/2 cup sliced red onion (1/2-inch-thick slices)

1 1/2 cups sliced medium jalapeño chiles (1/4-inch-thick rounds)

CAULIFLOWER ESCABECHE

Makes about 1 quart
GF / VEGAN

Combine the cauliflower florets, habanero and jalapeño chiles, garlic, and lime juice in a 1-quart mason jar (or divide the ingredients equally between two smaller jars).

Combine the vinegars, sugar, and salt in a small saucepan and bring to a simmer over medium heat, stirring to fully dissolve the salt and sugar. Taste and adjust the flavor of the brining liquid as needed, adding more salt and/or sugar to taste. Pour the hot brine into the jar over the cauliflower and chiles until the jar is full. Make sure the cauliflower is fully submerged. If needed, add more vinegar or a little more water to cover.

Seal well and shake to combine, then refrigerate for at least 1 hour before serving or storing. The flavors will deepen and intensify the longer it marinates. Optimal flavor is achieved after 24 hours.

The escabeche will keep in the refrigerator for 2 to 3 weeks.

1 small head cauliflower, cut into small florets

1 habanero chile, stemmed, seeded, and minced

1 jalapeño chile, stemmed, seeded, and minced

3 cloves garlic, peeled

¼ cup fresh lime juice

1 cup apple cider vinegar

1 cup distilled white vinegar

2 tablespoons sugar, plus more as needed

1½ teaspoons kosher salt, plus more as needed

PICKLED RED CABBAGE

Makes about 1 quart
GF / VEGAN

Place the cabbage in a large heatproof bowl. Combine the garlic, chiles, allspice, coriander, vinegars, brown sugar, and 1 cup water in a medium pot and bring to a boil over high heat. Pour the mixture over the cabbage and stir. Let cool to room temperature, then cover and transfer to the refrigerator to chill for at least 1 hour before serving. The pickled cabbage will keep in an airtight container in the refrigerator for up to 1 week.

1½ pounds red cabbage (about ½ small head), cored and thinly sliced

2 cloves garlic, crushed

6 dried chiles de árbol, stemmed and seeded

6 allspice berries

12 coriander seeds

½ cup red wine vinegar

½ cup apple cider vinegar

2 tablespoons brown sugar

PINK PICKLED ONIONS

Makes about 1 quart
GF / VEGAN

Place the onions in a heatproof bowl and cover with boiling water. Let stand for 1 minute, then drain. Combine the vinegar, sugar, allspice, peppercorns, salt, and 1 cup water in a small saucepan and bring to a boil over high heat. Pour the vinegar mixture over the onions and let stand for 1 to 2 hours. Transfer to a 1-quart mason jar and cool. Cover and store in the refrigerator for up to 2 weeks.

2 medium red onions, halved and thinly sliced

1 cup red wine vinegar

½ cup sugar

6 allspice berries

20 whole black peppercorns

¼ cup kosher salt

HABANERO PICKLED WHITE ONIONS

Makes about 1 quart
GF / VEGAN

This is a condiment that is well-represented at many a taco stand and restaurant throughout Baja California.

Put the onion and chile in a 1-quart mason jar. Combine the salt, sugar, oregano, and vinegar in a medium saucepan and bring to a boil over high heat, mixing to fully combine the ingredients.

Pour the vinegar mixture into the jar over the onion and chile, being sure the vegetables are fully submerged, then set aside to cool; if the liquid doesn't cover the vegetables, add more vinegar as needed. Cover and refrigerate for at least 2 hours before serving. Store in the refrigerator for up to 2 weeks.

1 medium white onion, thinly sliced

½ habanero chile, stemmed and thinly sliced lengthwise

2 tablespoons kosher salt

2 tablespoons sugar

1 teaspoon fresh Mexican oregano leaves

About 2 cups distilled white vinegar

QUICK PRESERVED LEMONS

Makes about ¼ cup
GF / VEGAN

With a very sharp knife, slice the biggest and prettiest lemon crosswise into ¼-inch-thick rounds and gently remove the seeds. Juice the other lemons to yield ½ cup juice. Combine the lemon slices, juice, and salt in a medium saucepan. Bring to a boil over high heat, stirring to dissolve the salt. Cover, reduce the heat to low, and simmer until the lemon slices are almost tender and the peel looks translucent, about 10 minutes. Transfer the lemon slices and brine to a glass container and set aside to cool. Cover and store in the refrigerator for up to 1 week.

3 or 4 large lemons

1 tablespoon kosher salt

PICKLED SERRANO CHILES

Pack the chiles into a 1-quart mason jar. Combine the vinegar, garlic, peppercorns, sugar, coriander seeds, salt, and 1½ cups water in a medium saucepan and bring to a boil over high heat. Reduce the heat to medium and simmer for 5 minutes. Pour the hot brine over the chiles in the jar and set aside to cool. Seal the jar and transfer to the refrigerator. The pickles will keep for up to 1 month.

Makes about 2 cups
GF / VEGAN

2 cups whole serrano chiles, very thinly sliced into rings (about ⅛ inch thick)

1½ cups distilled white vinegar

3 cloves garlic, peeled

2 tablespoons whole black peppercorns

2 tablespoons sugar

2 tablespoons coriander seeds

2 tablespoons kosher salt

PICKLED JALAPEÑO CHILES

This recipe works equally well with Fresno chiles.

Put the chiles and garlic in a 1-quart mason jar. Combine the vinegar, water, brown sugar, and salt in a small saucepan. Place over low heat and heat, stirring occasionally, until the sugar has dissolved, about 5 minutes. Pour the brine over the chiles. Set the jar aside to cool to room temperature, then cover and refrigerate for at least 30 minutes before serving. Store in the refrigerator for up to 2 weeks.

Makes about 1 quart
GF / VEGAN

10 jalapeño chiles, stemmed and thinly sliced

3 cloves garlic, crushed

1 cup distilled white vinegar

1 cup water

⅓ cup packed brown sugar

1 tablespoon kosher salt

POWDERS, DUSTS, AND SALTS

CALI-BAJA SPICE BLEND

Makes about ½ cup
GF / VEGAN

2 tablespoons kosher salt

2 teaspoons freshly ground black pepper

1 tablespoon ancho chile powder

1 teaspoon guajillo chile powder

1 tablespoon paprika

2 teaspoons garlic powder

2 teaspoons onion powder

1 teaspoon dried Mexican oregano

1 teaspoon ground cumin

Stir together all the ingredients in a small bowl. Place in an airtight container and store in a cool, dry place for up to 6 months.

RED ADOBO SEASONING

Makes about ⅓ cup
GF / VEGAN

2 tablespoons kosher salt

1 tablespoon paprika

2 teaspoons freshly ground black pepper

1½ teaspoons onion powder

1½ teaspoons dried Mexican oregano

1½ teaspoons ground cumin

1 teaspoon garlic powder

1 teaspoon guajillo chile powder

Stir together all the ingredients in a small bowl. Place in an airtight container and store in a cool, dry place for up to 6 months.

CHORIZO POWDER

Makes about ¼ cup
GF / VEGAN

1 bay leaf, broken into small pieces

½ teaspoon dried Mexican oregano

½ teaspoon dried thyme

2 tablespoons ancho chile powder

1 tablespoon guajillo chile powder

2 teaspoons paprika

1 teaspoon kosher salt

1 tablespoon garlic powder

1 tablespoon onion powder

1 teaspoon ground cumin

½ teaspoon freshly ground black pepper

½ teaspoon ground coriander

⅛ teaspoon ground cinnamon

Combine all the ingredients in a high-speed blender and blend to combine. Store in an airtight container in a cool, dry place for up to 3 months.

CILANTRO POWDER

Makes about ¼ cup
GF / VEGAN

2 bunches cilantro,
tough parts of stems
trimmed

Think about this recipe, like the Scallion Salt (opposite), as a base recipe, without the salt. You can substitute any tender fresh herb—for example, basil, tarragon, parsley, or even celery leaves—for the cilantro.

Turn the oven to as low a temperature as it will go (preferably lower than 200°F). If you have a dehydrator, set it to 145°F.

Spread the cilantro on a wire rack set inside a rimmed baking sheet and dry in the oven or dehydrator until dry and brittle, 1 to 1½ hours. Working in batches, grind the cilantro in a spice grinder or high-speed blender to a fine powder.

Store in an airtight container at room temperature for up to 3 weeks.

FENNEL-OREGANO SALT

Makes about ¼ cup
GF / VEGAN

¼ cup fennel seeds

¼ cup dried Mexican
oregano

2 teaspoons whole
black peppercorns

1½ tablespoons
kosher salt

This blend pairs particularly well with fish or pork. It also works well with egg dishes.

Toast the fennel seeds in a small, dry skillet over medium heat, shaking often, until fragrant, 1 to 2 minutes. Transfer the fennel seeds to a plate to cool. Finely grind the fennel seeds, oregano, and peppercorns in a spice grinder or high-speed blender. Transfer to a small bowl, add the salt, and whisk to combine.

Store in an airtight container at room temperature for up to 1 month.

SCALLION SALT

Makes about ⅓ cup
GF / VEGAN

½ cup chopped
scallion greens
(or other soft herbs)

2 tablespoons
kosher salt

Herb salts can work wonders on a dish. Think of this as a base recipe that you can adapt to use any soft herb or combination of herbs. Add parsley and celery leaves along with the scallion greens, and you have a wonderful blend for steamed fish. Get creative and an herb salt can serve at least half the function of a sauce. A light dusting adds a whole new dimension to a dish. While the bright color of herb powders will fade within weeks, the flavor persists and they can be kept indefinitely.

Turn the oven to as low a temperature as it will go (preferably lower than 200°F). If you have a dehydrator, set it to 145°F. Line a baking sheet with parchment paper.

Arrange the scallion greens on the prepared baking sheet. Dry in the oven or dehydrator until they are completely dry, at least 45 minutes; depending on the water content of the scallions and the temperature of the oven, it could take up to twice as long.

Combine the dried scallion greens and salt in a high-speed blender (you could also use a spice grinder, working in small batches) and blend to a fine powder. Store in an airtight container at room temperature indefinitely.

ACKNOWLEDGMENTS

There is no way I could have written this book without my life partner and love of my life, Nancy Gardiner. She wears so many different hats in our life together; for this book and my food writing, she has served as recipe tester, reality tester, critic-in-chief, cheerleader, proofreader, first editor, sous chef, and so much more. She has been a support system to me in so many different ways that it is hard to name them all, and harder to imagine how this book would have happened without her.

I have to thank David Rolland, my original editor at *San Diego CityBeat*, for suggesting I go on a food and wine boondoggle of a press tour of Rosarito Beach. That tour confirmed for my wife and me that we wanted to buy a place in Baja, and that weekend we saw the house that we ultimately bought. It was also on that trip that I met a number of people in the Cali-Baja food world for the first time, including W. Scott Koenig (aka *A Gringo in Mexico*). That community of Baja food and wine writers and other professionals—including Fernando Gaxiola, Jackie Bryant, and Troy Johnson—has been critical in shaping and growing my love (and that of many others) of the Cali-Baja food world. It is impossible to say with certainty what might have come to pass had that event not occurred, but there is a very good chance this book would not have happened but for that press junket.

My editors over the years have each taught me things that I almost certainly could not have learned (or learned as quickly and easily) on my own. Among those are my current book editor, Martynka Wawrzyniak at Rizzoli; my previous book editor, for *Modern Kosher*, Jono Jarrett; my editor at the *San Diego Union-Tribune*, Martha Lynch; Maria Hesse at *Edible San Diego*; and Denise Landis of *The Cook's Cook*.

Thank you to the many chefs who have given me the opportunity to come into their kitchens to stage, cook, learn, and come to understand the standard of professionalism. Among those are William Bradley, Chad White, Iker Castillo, Bo Bendana, William Eick, Drew Bent, and Davin Waite. I owe special thanks to Ruth Henricks and Special Delivery for giving me the opportunity to do something along the lines of "run" something and create in a professional kitchen setting.

But no chefs are more critical to this book or deserve more of my thanks than those of the Cali-Baja movement: Javier Plascencia, Drew Deckman, Roberto Alcocer, Miguel Angel Guerrero, Claudette Zepeda-Wilkins, Benito Molina, Solange Muris, David Castro Hussong (who beat me to the punch), Flor Franco, Ryan Steyn, and Sabina Bandera. This book would not have happened without the insight and inspiration they provided.

Kris Magnussen of Lechuza Winery has been a friend and directly helped me see that the single best person to photograph this book was Cintia Soto. To say this book would look different without her is an understatement. Her input has gone beyond the photography, and she has become a sounding board who let a thickheaded author know when it was time to rethink something. I owe great thanks to both Kris and Cintia. I have no doubt that my love affair with Baja California was only enhanced by the wineries of the Valle de Guadalupe and their owners and winemakers. Among the many winemakers I need to thank are Hans Backhoff; Dr. Victor Torres Alegre and his son, Leonard; Tru Miller; Fernando Perez Castro; Alvaro Alvarez-Parrilla; Phil and Eileen Gregory; and Paolo Paoloni.

I also need to thank the many food friends who, over the years, have tried and commented on dishes in this book: Christina and Steve Wickman, Fred and Carla Sorilla, Rob Colosia, and Nicole Verdugo Preston. While just about anyone who writes a cookbook thinks they know how to write a clear recipe, there is sometimes that moment when a reader misunderstands something and the writer realizes that ambiguity, that bastard, snuck into the recipe somehow. Thanks to those who showed me.

Every writer wants to thank their agents, and I am no different. I owe Deborah Ritchken a lot. Those thanks are not owed just because she got me the deal, though she did, and put in a tremendous amount of work in doing so. Her role with this book was greater than that. The day we first met—about my first book, *Modern Kosher*—we discussed what the next project might be. I mentioned I was thinking about a book on the food of Baja California. Her eyes lit up, and she told me she had been working on a cross-border concept. It was a moment of brilliant synchronicity. In many ways, Deborah has been a collaborator.

INDEX

AUTHOR'S BIOGRAPHY

MICHAEL GARDINER is the author of *Modern Kosher: Global Flavors, New Traditions*, published by Rizzoli in 2020. Gardiner is a regular food feature writer for the *San Diego Union-Tribune*, San Diego's newspaper of record, as well as *Edible San Diego* magazine. Gardiner is also a contributing editor for *The Cook's Cook*, a weekly online publication with over eighteen thousand monthly unique website visitors. He was the longtime restaurant reviewer for the late lamented *San Diego CityBeat* (a pandemic casualty), an alternative weekly that had a weekly circulation of fifty thousand. Gardiner won 2018, 2019, 2020, and 2021 San Diego Press Club awards (most recently two Golds and a Bronze) for his contributions to these various publications, including for articles relating directly to the food of Baja on both sides of the border. Gardiner has freelanced for Thrillist and Fox News Latino, among other publications and outlets.

PHOTOGRAPHER'S BIOGRAPHY

CINTIA SOTO is an international photographer and food stylist. Most recently she did the photography and food styling for Pía Quintana's cookbook *El Arte de lo Sencillo*, and she photographed twenty-eight female chefs from Baja California for Sergio Núñez's *Mexicanas*. Soto's work has appeared in *Travel & Leisure*, the *New York Times Food and Travel*, *Vogue Mexico*, *Cosmopolitan Italy*, *Business Class Italy*, *Southwest Airlines Magazine*, *Condé Nast Traveler United Kingdom*, and the *Daily Mail UK*. In 2015 Soto was nominated as editor in chief of the Mexican recipes blog of the Milan International Expo in Italy (where she lived for a decade). She is passionate about traveling, gastronomy, and world culture. She turned her professional attention to photography in 2011 and won an award as Best Panoramic Photographer of the Year in 2012.

First published in the United States of America in 2023
by Rizzoli International Publications, Inc.
300 Park Avenue South
New York, NY 10010
www.rizzoliusa.com

Publisher: Charles Miers
Author: Michael A. Gardiner
Editorial Direction: Martynka Wawrzyniak
Designer: Jan Derevjanik
Copy Editor: Leda Scheintaub
Production Manager: Kaija Markoe
Managing Editor: Lynn Scrabis

2023 2024 2025 2026/ 10 9 8 7 6 5 4 3 2 1

Distributed in the U.S. trade by Random House, New York

Printed in China

ISBN: 9780847873555
Library of Congress Control Number: 2023934456
Visit us online:
Facebook.com/RizzoliNewYork
Twitter: @Rizzoli_Books
Instagram.com/RizzoliBooks
Pinterest.com/RizzoliBooks
Youtube.com/user/RizzoliNY
Issuu.com/Rizzoli